Keys to Effective Teaching
Instructor's Manual and Test Item File to accompany
Keys to Success, Brief Fifth Edition

Carol Carter
Joyce Bishop
Sarah Lyman Kravits

PEARSON
Prentice
Hall

Upper Saddle River, New Jersey
Columbus, Ohio

10 9 8 7 6 5 4 3 2
1

ISBN-13: 978-0-13-512847-3
ISBN-10:   0-13-512847-1

ACKNOWLEDGMENTS

Many hands do indeed make light work. We would especially like to thank instructor Martha Martin for her comprehensive work in generating material for this instructor's manual and accompanying PowerPoint slides and consulting us throughout the process. We also are deeply indebted to our developmental editor Charlotte Morrissey for her overseeing all aspects of the process and offering salient comment on the materials.

This manual is dynamic; please feel free to communicate with us regarding ideas that you might have to enhance the teaching-learning experience in this course.

CONTENTS

PART I: GETTING STARTED

PART II: CHAPTER GUIDES

PART I: GETTING STARTED

Welcome

Welcome to the instructor's manual to accompany *KEYS TO SUCCESS* Brief 5e. We believe this course can be one of your most rewarding teaching experiences. With the help of this text and manual, students can develop skills and habits needed to succeed in college and beyond.

Who We Are

Our collective experience and research brings you proven teaching methods to improve student learning and achievement. Author **Joyce Bishop** of Golden West College has been in the classroom as a professor of psychology for 26 years and of student success for 18 years. She has won numerous teaching awards for her in-class techniques and personal attention to individual student needs. In addition to teaching students, she is currently a staff development coordinator at Golden West. She is a pioneer in online learning and hosts the *Keys* faculty development training site where you can ask her questions, share ideas, or watch her teach a course. Author **Carol Carter** is the president of her own seminar and coaching company for high school and college students called LifeBound. Through her speaking and writing, she also reaches out to disadvantaged audiences around the United States. Carol has a track record of success in the business world, having served fifteen years in executive positions.

With the benefit of these two perspectives, students learn the powerful advantage of their education and what the real world expects of them.

Who Students Are Today

Fact: *Fewer students are prepared to manage their lives, achieve in school, and bring value to the workplace*. Many causes may be at work:

- Educators and researchers have witnessed a "sense of entitlement" in students that can inhibit their ability to succeed. Some researchers attribute this to parents who do too much for children or a K-12 educational system that allows many students to "get by."
- Due in some measure to high exposure to media, many students have an unrealistic image of the workplace; i.e., the types of careers they find attractive, the commitment and amount of work they will have to perform, and the amount of their compensation.
- Many students find that their ability to focus on school is compromised due to other responsibilities – primarily work, parenting, or other family demands.

From its first edition, *Keys to Success* has anticipated this serious issue with its focus on college realities and the linking of school success with work and life success. This brief fifth edition strengthens the tradition. We have designed this revision, instructor's manual, and supporting materials to support and educate students who will be able to achieve goals, manage themselves, and continue to learn – in college, in the workplace, and in their lives.

1

Your
Instructor's
Manual

This manual will help you plan a well-crafted, engaging course with a minimum of prep work. Our goal was to create an instructor's manual that gives practical, current information to improve your students' experience and enhance your teaching. We've revised the manual in the following ways:

- Provided **detailed chapter overviews**
- **Reorganized the chapter walk-through** and groupings of activities (see below)
- Included **all chapter-related activities in the chapter section**, so you don't have to search through appendices
- Included **handouts**, where applicable for exercises, **formatted so that you can photocopy them** directly from this manual

We trust you will enjoy this manual as much as we have enjoyed writing it. It is our hope that the suggestions in this manual enhance your teaching success from the first day of class to the last.

What You'll Find in Each Chapter of the IM

Brief Chapter Overview: A quick overview of the chapter, including thoughts on the chapter's particular topics and a grid highlighting the ways in which the chapter builds analytical, creative, and practical thinking.

Chapter Outline: A basic outline of the primary and secondary topics covered in the chapter.

Communicate Content: This section goes through chapter material, offering ways to present topics in a classroom setting. Each "Communicate Content" section begins with questions to help you start conversations related to that chapter's *Real Problems, Practical Answers* feature. PowerPoint references help you use the PowerPoint presentations to enhance your coverage of the content.

Create Community: Focused on group exercises and other classroom activities that help students forge connections with one another and with the material, this section is divided into seven subsections.

- <u>Discussion Starters</u> consists of chapter-related questions you can ask to get people talking.
- <u>Group Exercises</u> contains a selection of exercises for pair or group work.
- <u>Pop Culture Links</u> has ideas for how to use movies and music to connect to chapter topics.
- <u>Successful Intelligence Exercises</u> offers suggestions for how to use the in-text exercises inside and outside of class.
- <u>Homework</u> lists ideas for assignments after class time.

- Quotes for Reflection lists quotes, relevant to chapter material, which you can use to start conversations or inspire thought.
- Handouts offers an at-a-glance list of the chapter-specific handouts (sometimes including an exercise description), followed by each handout in ready-to-photocopy format.

Consider Comprehension: Here we focus on helping students understand and retain what they learn in the classroom:

- Review With Students lists important topics to go over before you begin the next chapter.
- Vocabulary Quiz is a matching quiz on important vocabulary words found in the chapter.
- Chapter Assessment is the test item file for this chapter, containing objective questions (multiple choice, true/false, fill-in-the-blank, short answer) as well as subjective questions (essay). The answer key directly follows the assessment.

There is an assortment of possible activities and strategies for every chapter. You can pick and choose what's best for that particular lesson, given your time constraints. Stress those activities that best suit your teaching style and your students' needs. There are more ideas than you will have time to use, especially if you add your own ideas for activities and projects.

Additional Resources
Both of these sections appear at the end of the introductory segment of this instructor's manual.

SUPPLEMENTAL RESOURCE GUIDE Here you will find an extensive list of the ancillaries that accompany this text.

PRE-COURSE AND POST-COURSE ASSESSMENTS This section contains a photocopy-ready version of the pre- and post-course assessments found in the text, as well as some ideas for how to use them.

Your Text ●

Over the last three years as we worked with instructors and students all over the country to improve this text, the message we consistently received was that people responded to the text's successful intelligence theme and wanted to see it more effectively integrated. We listened to the suggestions and have integrated them. This brief fifth edition of *Keys to Success* brings you a stronger, more functional focus on the theme of **successful intelligence** and its three key skills – analytical, creative, and practical thinking. Other important changes are detailed later in this section. First, more about successful intelligence and why it makes sense for this course and your students.

Why Successful Intelligence Works – and How to Use It

This is the first student success text to use a framework that has been <u>*proven* to improve student learning and achievement</u>—the theory of successful intelligence, developed by psychologist Robert Sternberg. This information offers you a more in-depth look at this theory, why we think it will help your students, and how to teach it with confidence.

Defining Successful Intelligence

Successful intelligence is the ability to succeed in life, given one's personal goals within one's personal environment. (Sternberg, 2003 at 7). This theory challenges the traditional notion that intelligence is a single construct--sometimes known as "general intelligence"--that can be measured by IQ or similar tests. It also disputes the idea that intelligence is static (i.e., an individual has a certain, quantifiable amount of intelligence that cannot grow). In contrast, Sternberg believes intelligence is dynamic; it can be developed. It is by building and balancing three types of intelligence processes (*analytical, creative,* and *practical*) that students can learn and achieve effectively, even students who do not do well in conventional lecture-and-learn courses. Sternberg ought to know, having received a C in his introductory psychology course and an even lower grade in his advanced mathematics course his freshman year. Currently, he is the Dean of Arts and Sciences at Tufts University. (Sternberg, 2003b at 7).

Analytical, Creative, and Practical Intelligence Processes

What are the analytical, creative, and practical processes that underlie intelligence? *Analytical intelligence* is the one instructors tend to value most in college. It's the ability to assess, analyze, compare, and evaluate information. *Creative intelligence* is the ability to innovate, shift perspective, or think out-of-the-box. *Practical intelligence* is more than innate street smarts or common sense. It's developed by learning from experience. It's often unspoken, tacit information that one gathers by observing others, actively seeking people with past experience, or by being sensitive to internal and environmental cues. (*See* Sternberg, 1997, and Sternberg and Grigenko, 2002).

To illustrate how these processes work, consider a freshman whose goal is to get into a prestigious law school. That person must obtain top grades, an appealing set of extra-curricular activities, and some honors or awards that will set her apart from the crowd. The student must use her analytical intelligence to master her course material. However, she must also be innovative in her choice of courses and extra curricular activities to develop a résumé that will enhance her chance of law school admission. She must also "learn the ropes" for each class by using practical intelligence: she surveys others to find out who the best professors are, takes the initiative to ask teaching assistants how the instructor grades tests and projects, complies with important class policies, adapts her study habits to match the demands of the course, and so on. She finds a mentor to improve her chances of gaining law school admission. In sum, she uses all three types of intelligence to reach her goals.

How Does the Successful Intelligence Theory Differ From Others?

Several recent learning theorists have expanded our views of intelligence, but their theories differ in important ways from the Successful Intelligence theory. This text, for instance, highlights Gardner's theory of multiple intelligences in chapter 3. Gardner, however, focuses on how people take in information to learn, whereas Sternberg focuses on how people process and *apply* information to reach personal goals. In addition, Gardner focuses on intelligence <u>domains</u> (musical, spatial, linguistic) and Sternberg focuses on <u>processes</u> (analytical, practical, creative). To illustrate, a student can use practical, creative, and analytical intelligences in the linguistic sphere to analyze a poem, create a short story, or write a practical letter to the university explaining why he should receive financial aid. Not everyone has all eight forms of multiple intelligences, nor do they need them to survive. Everyone uses all three successful intelligence processes. To survive in our environment, we have to have some modicum of analytical, creative, and practical intelligence.

Why Teach Student Success with Successful Intelligence?

Why use the successful intelligence framework in this course? We offer four reasons.

- **Proven Results**: Unlike other learning theories, this theory has been tested. The results prove that this theory works at all age and socioeconomic levels, and across cultures. Simply put, teaching all three types of intelligence processes improves student learning and achievement. [See Sternberg, Torff, and Grigorenko (1998), Sternberg (1999); Sternberg (2003a); Grigorenko, Jarving, & Sternberg (2002); Sternberg, Castejon, Prieto, Hautamaki, & Grigorenko (2001)].
- **More Students Meet Their Potential**: Students who are taught using teaching methods that match their pattern of intelligence abilities "outperform students who are mismatched." [Sternberg (2003a) at 149]. Thus, teaching aimed at *more* than memory and analytical abilities may help students who might not otherwise excel.
- **Increased Self-Awareness**: This framework helps students recognize (and appreciate) their innate abilities and identifies areas where they can continue to grow.
- **Transferable Skills**: The validity of the successful intelligence theory applies in life outside the classroom (Sternberg, 2003b). These skills prepare students for the work world--where practical and creative intelligence are often highly prized--and can help them reach personal goals at all stages of life.

How to Teach Using the Successful Intelligence Framework

Most college courses are heavily geared toward analytical thinking processes. To teach using successful intelligence as a framework, instructors should vary teaching methods to engage all three types of thinking processes. The class environment, then, should allow for creativity and practicality. Here are some ideas to try.

- **Assess All Three Areas**: One of the most helpful things a student success instructor can do is to help students assess their intelligence strengths and weaknesses and adapt accordingly. *Keys to Success* Brief gives students self-assessments in chapter 1 to help them gauge their analytical, creative, and practical intelligence abilities, and repeats the assessments in chapter 8 to help students look at how they perceive their growth.
- **Use Activities to Develop All Three Skills**: The instructor's manual and the text offer numerous activities that help students build each type of intelligence. Through the use of these simple exercises, students can begin building their intelligence within a few class sessions. The resulting positive experiences are likely to give them the confidence to take risks and see their abilities in a new light.
- **Use Integrated Activities**: Offer a variety of assignments and activities that allow students to use a combination of analytical, creative, and practical thinking skills. For instance, class discussion can focus on an analytical concept such as the listening process, and a teamwork exercise can focus on generating new ways to listen effectively in class (creativity and practicality combined).
- **Encourage Creativity**: Ensure the classroom environment encourages creativity. Does the class culture tolerate brainstorming, the use of metaphor, and unusual ideas?
- **Encourage Practicality**: Ensure the classroom environment encourages practical thinking. Do you link concepts to practical application? Do you allow students to shape the class environment? For instance, are you willing to let an art student create a CD on Art in 20th Century Germany instead of a research paper on a pre-selected topic? Do you actively help students learn from mistakes?

How the Text Helps You Teach Successful Intelligence

We provide you all you need to integrate successful intelligence into your classroom. Each chapter offers you multiple ways to teach it effectively.

- Each chapter opens with a Successful Intelligence Preview that uses a mind map to indicate analytical, creative, and practical concepts that appear in the chapter, and closes with a Successful Intelligence Wrap-Up that reminds students of analytical, creative, and practical actions that they took in the course of the chapter.
- Chapter 1 introduces the concept of successful intelligence by way of a story and clear explanation. Three in-chapter self-assessments give students the opportunity to gauge their analytical, practical, and creative thinking skills at the start of the course.
- From chapter 1 onward, three in-chapter exercises (*Get Analytical*, *Get Practical*, and *Get Creative*) build each intelligence process (see Table 1 on p. 8 for a list of these exercises).

- Each chapter has one <u>end-of-chapter exercise</u> that has students <u>apply their analytical, practical, and creative thinking processes in combination</u> (*Successful Intelligence: Think, Create, Apply*).
- Chapter 4 expands the discussion of successful intelligence with an exploration of critical, creative, and practical thinking.
- The life skills and study skills chapters (2 through 8) revisit the concept of successful intelligence as it applies to chapter topics, integrating the concepts of analytical, creative, and practical thinking throughout the text of each chapter.
- Each chapter has a link to a <u>podcast</u>, downloadable on the Companion Web site, that offers successful-intelligence-related tips on a chapter topic.

Finally, within each chapter, students have many ways to enhance creative and practical intelligence. For instance, each chapter's Teamwork exercise gives students the practical experience of working with others and each chapter's Personal Portfolio activity offers students creative and practical experience building a portfolio.

We believe your students will benefit from learning and applying successful intelligence. We're also confident that you'll enjoy reaching students in new ways.

****

References

Gigorenko, E. L., Jarvin, L., & Sternberg, R.J. (2002). School-based tests of the triarchic theory: Three settings, three samples, three syllabi. *Contemporary Educational Psychology*, 27, 167-208.

Sternberg, R. J. (2002). Beyond *g*: The theory of successful intelligence. In Sternberg, R. J., & Grigorenko, E. L. (Eds.), *The General Factor of Intelligence: How General Is It?* (447-479). Mahwah, NJ: Lawrence Earlbaum Associates.

Sternberg, R. J. (2003a). Implications of the Theory of Successful Intelligence for career choice and development. *Journal of Career Assessment*, 11(2), 136-152.

Sternberg, R. J. (1997). *Successful intelligence.* New York: Plume.

Sternberg, R. J. (2003b). Teaching for successful intelligence: Principles, practices, and outcomes. *Educational and Child Psychology*, 20(2), 6- 18.

Sternberg, R. J., Castejon, J. L., Prieto, M. D., Hautamaki, J., & Grigorenko, E. L. (2001). Confirmatory factor analysis of the Sternberg Triarchic Abilities Test in three international samples: An empirical test of the triarchic theory of intelligence. *European Journal of Psychological Assessment*, 17(1), 1-16.

Sternberg, R. J., Torff, B., & Grigorenko, E. L. (1998). Teaching triarchically improves school achievement. *Journal of Educational Psychology*, 90.

Table 1: Successful Intelligence Exercises

Chapter 1 Welcome to College	■ Get Analytical – *Assess Yourself as an Analytical Thinker* ■ Get Creative – *Assess Yourself as a Creative Thinker* ■ Get Practical – *Assess Yourself as a Practical Thinker* ■ *Successful Intelligence: Think, Create, Apply* —Activate Yourself
Chapter 2 Values, Time, and Goals	■ Get Analytical – *Explore Your Values* ■ Get Creative – *Map Out a Personal Goal* ■ Get Practical – *Make a To-Do List* ■ *Successful Intelligence: Think, Create, Apply* —Make Your First Term Count
Chapter 3 Learning, Diversity, Communication	■ Get Analytical, Creative, and Practical – *Maximize Your Classroom Experience* ■ *Successful Intelligence: Think, Create, Apply* —Learn from Joyce Bishop's Experience
Chapter 4 Critical, Creative, and Practical Thinking	■ Get Analytical – *Analyze a Statement* ■ Get Creative – *Activate Your Creative Powers* ■ Get Practical – *Take a Practical Approach to Building Successful Intelligence Skills* ■ *Successful Intelligence: Think, Create, Apply* —Make an Important Decision
Chapter 5 Reading and Studying	■ Get Analytical – *Survey a Text* ■ Get Creative – *See the Movie. Read the Book.* ■ Get Practical – *Mark Up a Page to Learn a Page* ■ *Successful Intelligence: Think, Create, Apply* —Studying a text page
Chapter 6 Listening, Note Taking, and Memory	■ Get Analytical – *Discover Yourself as a Listener* ■ Get Creative – *Craft Your Own Mnemonic* ■ Get Practical – *Face a Note-Taking Challenge* ■ *Successful Intelligence: Think, Create, Apply* —Learn from Victoria Gough's Experience
Chapter 7 Test Taking	■ Get Analytical – *Write to the Verb* ■ Get Creative – *Write Your Own Test* ■ Get Practical – *Learn from Your Mistakes* ■ *Successful Intelligence: Think, Create, Apply* —Prepare Effectively for Tests
Chapter 8 Wellness, Careers, and Money	■ Get Analytical – *Evaluate Your Self-Activators* ■ Get Creative – *Find More Fun* ■ Get Practical – *Take Steps Toward Better Health* ■ *Successful Intelligence: Think, Create, Apply* —Learn from Joe Martin's Experience

Changes to This Edition

You spoke, we listened. Through our extensive reviewing program and focus groups with both instructors and students all over the country, <u>we received detailed input on this revision from over 80 individuals</u>. Their comments resulted in important changes beyond the increased integration of successful intelligence, including enhanced practical topics (money and social intelligence are two examples), increased focus on academic integrity, more material on studying, a shorter, more to-the-point chapter 1, and updated material on how you learn. Here are the specifics:

Key Highlights

- ∞ The **extensive integration of successful intelligence** as discussed in the previous section
- ∞ **Reworked chapter 1** contains a more dynamic, comprehensive introduction to successful intelligence as well as a selection of topics you told us you most wanted to see right up front (academic integrity, group work, using a syllabus, responsibility, the value of college).
- ∞ **Material on how you learn in chapter 3 has been reworked** to update and expand the descriptions of the self-assessments, and to give more extensive information on how students can use what they discover with these assessments. The material on **diversity and communication** has also been integrated into this chapter, forming a comprehensive chapter on discovering and managing differences of all kinds.
- ∞ **Revised material on thinking in chapter 4** includes a new example throughout the section on analytical thinking, a reorganization of the strategies for creative thinking, and an expansion of the discussion of emotional and social intelligence in the context of practical thinking.
- ∞ Within both topics and exercises, focus on **practical application of ideas** is even more extensive throughout the text.
- ∞ The concepts of **emotional intelligence** and **social intelligence** are introduced in detail (chapter 1) and integrated within particular topic areas (chapter 4, chapter 8).
- ∞ Chapter 3 has **updated information on eating habits and drug use** as well as a revised, more **practical section on money management**.
- ∞ Throughout the text wherever applicable, **modern references** let readers know that we are paying attention to change and to their lives. This includes an enhanced connection of college success skills to succeeding in **the global workplace** and "knowledge economy," as well as periodical references to information literacy and the technology issues that arise when students use PDAs, cell phones, computers, and sites such as Facebook and MySpace.

Exercise and Feature Revisions

In addition to the successful-intelligence-oriented changes described previously, the following changes and improvements appear:

∞ **Reworked Multiple Intelligence grids** have a new **cross-disciplinary focus**. Each grid shows how to apply chapter-specific multiple-intelligence-linked strategies to questions or tasks in a specific discipline other than this course. Examples include criminal justice, environmental science, economics, and human development.

∞ Q & As that start each chapter renamed **"Real Problems, Practical Answers"** and made more concise. One-fourth of Q & A pairs have been replaced.

∞ **Personal Triumph Case Studies** at ends of chapters 3, 6, and 8 feature one new case study (a returning adult student) and now include student artwork. For those who want more case studies, each student artist's case study appears on the Companion Web site.

∞ Two new **end-of-part features** focus on **time management and test taking** to address what research indicates are two of the top challenges students face in college.

∞ **New foreign words** used to close each chapter

∞ End-of-chapter exercises reworked:
  ∞ *Successful Intelligence: Think, Create, Apply* more effectively **builds the three aspects of successful intelligence.**
  ∞ *Writing: Journal and Put Skills to Work* has been revised to include two questions: one ("Journal Entry") is a **journal prompt**, and the other ("Real-Life Writing") focuses on a **practical writing skill.**
  ∞ *Personal Portfolio: Prepare for Career Success* has a **stronger focus on practical actions** and useful products that help readers prepare for success in any career area.

Chapter-by-Chapter View of Changes in Coverage and Topic Location

Here's a look at the most significant updates, by chapter.

Chapter	Focus	Changes and Highlights
1	Getting adjusted to college	∞ More comprehensive successful intelligence introduction ∞ New section on working with others includes diversity intro, emotional/social intelligence, group work strategies ∞ In-chapter exercises now consist of successful intelligence self-assessments ∞ Academic integrity (formerly chapter 2) and group work material (formerly chapter 5) moved here ∞ Discussion of how to use a syllabus, with sample syllabus
2	Values, goals, and time	∞ Majors material moved here, in response to student feedback, and revised in the context of goal setting ∞ Material on stress shortened (some material moved to chapter 8) and put in context of time management
3	Learning, diversity, and communication	∞ New introductory section more effectively supports the value of knowing how you learn and how intelligence can grow ∞ Revised and updated explanations of both self-assessments

		∞ Information on Naturalist intelligence revised to reflect Gardner's latest definition
		∞ Skills lists associated with Multiple Intelligences and Personality Spectrum separated from study strategies lists, to allow better focus on one or the other
		∞ Topics of diversity and communication moved here
		∞ Updated material on cultural competence
		∞ New section on managing communication technology (cell phones, e-mail, instant messaging, personal web pages)
4	Critical thinking, creative thinking, problem solving, decision making	∞ More clear and concise explanations of successful intelligence elements and how they work within the problem-solving and decision-making processes
		∞ Expanded section on practical thinking includes more extensive discussion of social and emotional intelligence
5	Reading	∞ New material on studying (topics include concentration, emotional involvement, scheduling time to study)
		∞ Revised/expanded coverage of SQ3R
		∞ New material on marking up a textbook
6	Listening, memory, and note taking	∞ Revised section on notes, including new material on how to combine class and text notes into a master set
		∞ Revised material on memory, including expanded coverage of mnemonics
7	Test taking	∞ Added points/strategies on test taking and preparation
		∞ Revised section on learning from test mistakes
8	Wellness, money, and careers	∞ Expanded and updated section on eating habits and disorders
		∞ Drug and birth control information updated
		∞ New section on the value of money and the different ways in which people manage it
		∞ Section relating emotional and social intelligence to career success
		∞ New in-chapter exercise consisting of a self-assessment on the twenty successful intelligence "self-activators"
		∞ New opportunity to revisit successful intelligence self-assessments from chapter 1

Tips for Using Text Features and Exercises

Following are some ideas for how to use the features and exercises.

Successful Intelligence Self-Assessments: Have students complete the chapter 1 assessments in the first week of class. Encourage them to reflect on their answers and perhaps write a short journal-style essay detailing what they plan to improve as a result. Hand back their essays midway through the term to help students determine if they're on track.

Near the end of the term, have students complete the chapter 8 assessments. Then, direct students to their chapter 1 assessments and have them compare results. You may want to have them meet in pairs or groups to discuss changes, things that surprised them, things they expected, etc. Consider a journal assignment asking students to compare their chapters 1 and 8 results and ask them to discuss their growth.

Real Problems, Practical Answers. These question-and-answer features near the beginning of each chapter are ideal jumping-off points for discussing common student issues and questions. Begin your chapter coverage with the question posed and ask students to respond with examples of how they dealt with this problem or a similar one. To vary your approach, have students write journal entries giving their own answers to the question or have students evaluate the answer given in the feature.

Successful Intelligence Preview/Wrap-Up. These features "bookend" the chapter with successful intelligence – the preview is visual, the wrap-up more verbal. Have students look at the preview and respond in class discussion with their thoughts about the skills. Or, consider assigning a short writing response to the preview as homework before covering that chapter to ensure that students think about the topics ahead of time. Discuss the wrap-up in class to see what students retained from coverage. Have students write even more personalized versions of the wrap-up after chapter coverage ends.

Successful Intelligence Online. Each chapter describes a link to one podcast that can be accessed on the Companion Web site. Have students listen to the podcast and respond in writing, in group discussion, or in class discussion. Have students create their own successful intelligence tips in relation to a chapter topic other than the one featured in the podcast. Use podcast tips in your quizzes or discussion questions.

Get Analytical/Creative/Practical! Each chapter has one of each of these exercises within the chapter text (except for chapter 3, which has one combination exercise, since the learning assessments also appear in that chapter). Most are individual exercises, but some require pair or group interaction. However, you can bring in a teamwork element at any time if you have students discuss or work the exercises in pairs or groups. Assign these for in-class or homework; use them as discussion points; check student work on them to make sure that students are reading and comprehending chapter material.

Personal Portfolio: Prepare for Career Success. Have students get a folder or notebook in which to put each portfolio item through the term. Assign each along with chapter coverage, checking to see that they are completed. Consider building in some class time for students to discuss the assignments in pairs or as a class. At the end of the term, have students turn in the entire portfolio of work. Save time to talk about the portfolio as a whole and its value.

Multiple Intelligence Grids. These charts appear in chapters 5 through 8, showing multiple intelligence strategies linked with a chapter topic as well as ideas about how to use those specific strategies in another academic discipline (each discipline is matched to its chapter in the grid below). If any students are currently in a course matching the discipline shown, have them try strategies and report on their effectiveness.

Chapter and Main Grid Topic	Discipline Featured in the MI Grid
Chapter 5: Reading	Sociology (text by Macionis)
Chapter 6: Note Taking	Earth Science (text by Lutgens et al)
Chapter 7: Test Taking	Geometry (text by Musser et al)
Chapter 8: Stress Management	Child Development (text by Feldman)

Additionally, in the material for each of the involved chapters (5 through 8) in this manual you will find a photocopy-ready grid showing the MI strategies next to a blank column for students' own ideas. Have students use it to create their own MI strategies.

Personal Triumph Case Studies. These appear three times, at the ends of chapters 3, 6, and 8, and are linked to the *Successful Intelligence: Think, Create, Apply* exercises for those chapters. Two recur from the previous edition, and one (a returning student) is new. These riveting personal stories can be great discussion-starters. Have students read them at home and complete the linked questions and exercises. Then, invite group discussion about the stories and the question responses. Have students write their own Personal Triumph Case Studies – about themselves or about special people whom they know.

Successful Intelligence: Think, Create, Apply. This end-of-chapter exercise applies analytical, creative, and practical thinking to chapter material and is useful for homework. If you assign it ahead of coverage of the topic in class, you may be able to discuss the assignment as a class or in small groups.

Teamwork: Create Solutions Together. This group work exercise appears at the end of each chapter and may be used during class time. It is designed to help students develop the crucial skill of working with others. Some of the exercises require more than one meeting – they can be started in class and continued when the group meets outside of class.

Writing: Journal and Put Skills to Work. This writing exercise now has two parts. The journaling section will help students deepen their relationship with the material in the text through personal response – assign for outside of class. The practical writing section gives students writing-related tools they can use in school and out – you can assign as homework or have students work in class and then pair up to evaluate each other's materials.

Get Focused! Time and Test Taking. The materials in these two end-of-part sets of exercises are useful as in-class work or homework. They enhance student understanding of these two crucial skills – managing time and taking tests. You might work through one of these sections as you approach a midterm, final, or other important test.

Tips for Using Supplemental Resources

More and more instructors are turning to a variety of resources to teach their students in different ways. Today's students are often living in a media-saturated environment, and respond well to technology and audio/visual components of the presentation. Some instructors have the benefit of a "smart" classroom, where screen shots of documents or programs running on a laptop computer can be projected onto a screen for student viewing at the same time.

Whatever your skills and your setup in the classroom, you can benefit from using supplemental resources. The grid on the next page contains an overview of what is offered with the text. Beginning on page 27 of this introduction, you will find a more comprehensive list of supplements available. Look there for more details on all of the categories shown in the grid.

Special Note Regarding PowerPoints: This edition's PowerPoint slide collection has been designed to be more useful than ever! Each chapter's set is aligned with, and augments, the chapter material. All sets contain the following slides (in addition to chapter-specific slides) to provide continuity and enhance your presentation:

- Title page
- Chapter quote on successful intelligence
- Review of previous chapter's important points (for chapters 2-8)
- Question from "Real Problems, Practical Answers" feature
- Outlines of major chapter headings
- Successful Intelligence Wrap-Up
- Foreign word exploration
- End-of-chapter thought-provoking quote

In addition, you can customize the slide shows to suit your teaching style, adding or deleting slides as you wish or even adding content.

Special Note Regarding Online Instructor Resources: Author Joyce Bishop, a pioneer in online learning, has teamed with Prentice Hall to produce a one-of-a-kind online instructor faculty training site. Anytime you want, you can connect with the site to ask questions and share ideas and materials. Online faculty training sessions will be available.

This groundbreaking new resource also joins the Instructor Resource Center and available OneKey Course Management to round out the *Keys to Success* online offerings for instructors (details on p. 27 of this introduction).

Resource Overview

PowerPoints	Chapter-specific PowerPoints – available online. Visit the Instructor Resource Center (IRC) at http://vig.prenhall.com/catalog/main_content/0,1151,-500,00.html
Instructor's Manual	In addition to its paper form, this manual is downloadable from the Instructor's Resource Center (IRC), url as above.
Online Resources	In addition to the resources downloadable on the IRC, we offer ▪ Online instructor faculty training and communication site, managed by author Joyce Bishop, available through Course Compass ▪ OneKey Course Management system ▪ Research Navigator for instructor and student research support
Videos	Available videos include ▪ Faculty training videos, including a Successful Intelligence Faculty Development Workshop DVD featuring authors Joyce Bishop and Carol Carter ▪ PH Reference Library collections: Life Skills Pack, Study Skills Pack, Career Skills Pack (now available on DVD) ▪ Current issues videos from ABC News
Companion Web site	www.prenhall.com/carter Many features available in chapter-specific links, including ▪ Chapter objectives ▪ Downloadable podcasts featuring a successfully intelligent approach to a particular chapter topic ▪ Two cross-disciplinary exercises per chapter ▪ Glossary of chapter vocabulary ▪ Online quiz (students can e-mail their results) ▪ E-journal and practice essay questions ▪ Web links listing additional resources related to chapter topics
Pearson Student Success Supersite	www.prenhall.com/success Visit areas related to chapter topics for supplemental articles and activities.
Assessments	Available assessment options include ▪ LASSI ▪ Noel Levitz/RMS ▪ Robbins Self Assessment Library ▪ Readiness for Education at a Distance Indicator (READI)
Other Printed Resources	Particular resources complement chapter topics – for example, the *Prentice Hall Planner* is a great tie-in to time management, and the *10 Ways to Fight Hate* booklet works well with the diversity material

Your Course

Many students enter college without a strong sense of how to manage their time, coursework responsibilities, and attitudes – in short, how to manage *themselves*. Sometimes this is due to academic struggles or an overwhelming number of responsibilities, but even students who have the raw ability to succeed academically and the time to focus can falter. A student success course can prevent students from floundering and give them the best chance to succeed in school and beyond.

To ensure that your course planning is as simple and effective as possible—especially if you are new to this course—we offer a series of planning strategies gathered from users across the country.

1. Plan Early and Well

We cannot overemphasize the importance of planning well for your course. Being organized conveys to the students that their time is important and that you intend to spend it wisely. Being organized also teaches students, through concrete experience, how good planning makes things run more smoothly. It is an excellent context in which to discuss time management, goal setting, and organizational skills.

Your syllabus is a crucial means of communicating what topics you will cover and when; and what assignments, quizzes, projects, and so on, you will give and when. The syllabus can also establish clear classroom guidelines, such as grading, attendance, and participation guidelines. Handing out and discussing the syllabus early in the term helps establish expectations immediately. This revision contains a new discussion, in chapter 1, of the value and use of a syllabus.

2. Establish Clear and Important Goals

Before constructing your syllabus, establish your course goals. They will give you a road map on which to base specific choices such as materials and activities. Much of this may be dictated by your school, although there is often room for individual design. Here is a basic list of goals often cited for this course (written as though addressed to the student):

- Understand your responsibility for creating a successful college experience
- Strengthen higher-order thinking skills
- Connect with resources that support your academic, career, and personal goals
- Understand college rules, regulations, and systems
- Develop a personal academic plan
- Assess and understand current strengths and areas for growth using specific tools
- Set, pursue, and achieve academic and personal goals
- Develop problem-solving and decision-making skills
- Improve your ability to recall information
- Manage time more efficiently
- Read a textbook with improved understanding and retention
- Listen, with comprehension, to a lecture
- Take effective notes
- Prepare for and take tests
- Write an essay

- Become more culturally competent
- Learn communication and conflict-resolution strategies
- Assess and improve general wellness habits
- Develop strategies for managing stress
- Exhibit basic quantitative learning skills
- Explore career possibilities and aptitudes

3. Create an ACTIVE Learning Environment

Many instructors tell us that the best way to help students learn study skills is to create an active learning environment that allows for self discovery, a strong connection to the material being taught, and the added benefit of strong retention. As a general guideline for each class, we recommend 10 to 15 minutes of lecture or group facilitation, with the remaining class time devoted to activities, projects, role plays, guest speakers, and so on, and then a short wrap-up. One suggested plan for a 50-minute class period is:

- Five minutes to settle down and relay housekeeping messages.

- Five-minute review of last class. Discuss goals for today's class.

- Ten minutes to present new material during which you take questions.

- Twenty-five minutes to process material through activities and applications (each chapter of this instructor's manual has many from which to choose, in addition to those in the text).

- The final 5 minutes for summary, question and answer time, and students' evaluation of the knowledge and techniques they learned.

Four other suggestions follow:

A. Self Discovery (Assessments) – Students often know more than we give them credit for. At the beginning of each new topic, instead of jumping right in, query the students about their foundation of knowledge regarding the topic. They can share these in small groups, individually or anonymously on index cards given to you. This is self discovery at the front end of learning. Validating their current framework of knowledge empowers students to increase that information base.

On the back end of learning, have students assess what they gained. This can be done by having the students complete a 1-minute drill at the end of each class. Have them answer three basic questions: "What did you know about this topic before today?" "What did you learn about this topic today?" and "What didn't you understand about today's topic?" These questions also help instructors to assess how well students articulate their knowledge and can reveal a lack of understanding.

B. Reading Log –To motivate students to read and to think about what they've read, consider assigning a reading log to be submitted for each chapter you cover. Dede deLaughter, coordinator of academic support at the Oconee Campus of Gainesville State College, developed the following general questions for her reading log assignment:
1. What chapter did you read? List the number and title of the chapter.
2. Where did you do this reading assignment (living room, bedroom, library, outside, etc.)?

3. What was going on while this assignment was read (peace and quiet, TV, radio, roommate interruptions, etc.)?
4. What do you consider to be the most important points in the chapter?
5. On a scale of 1-10, with 1 being *not at all* and 10 being *extremely,* how effective do you think you are in this topic area? What is one way you can improve your effectiveness? Be very specific.
6. How would you describe the chapter(s) to a friend?

The text's Companion Web site has chapter-specific reading logs that you or your students can download. If you want to design your own reading logs, use the general questions above as a guide, adding chapter-specific questions for each chapter's log.

C. Group Activities – This class flourishes through group exercises. It is often one of the first classes a student takes in college, and is sometimes required for freshmen. Group exercises create community, helping to build friendships and break down barriers between races and genders. Community building benefits the class as you progress through the course and tackle tough topics such as diversity and sexuality.

Plan early for community by stocking up on posterboard and markers. A discount dollar store is a great place to purchase these items in bulk. Having a stock of posterboard allows you to pull students together in various groupings to brainstorm on topics throughout the text. Also, keep a ready list of creative ways to group students. This way it will be easy to group them for activities and ensure they are meeting new people in the classroom. Some grouping ideas include:

- birthday month
- birthday quarter
- first letter of middle name
- digits of phone number
- number of siblings
- multiple intelligence strength
- analytical, practical or creative strength or weakness

The *Teamwork* exercises in each chapter provide opportunities to apply many different topics in a group setting. Each chapter of this instructor's manual will have more group activities. In addition, encourage your students to form study groups and meet outside of class.

D. Field Trips and Guest Speakers – These provide a great opportunity for students to connect with academic resources outside the classroom. Guest speakers can include the college president, deans, department chairs, an academic advisor, the head of the tutoring center, someone from the health or wellness center, someone from the career or employment center, or a librarian. Field trips can include visits to the library, tutoring center, career center, or computer labs. Another option is to take advantage of campus presentations that students can attend outside of class time. Make attendance at such events extra credit or include it as a component of your grading system. For instance, students can take notes on a guest lecturer's speech or write a review and turn in their work product for a grade.

4. Develop a Comprehensive Course Syllabus

Here's where you put into concrete format everything that you want to achieve with this course. Consider the syllabus a written contract between you and your students. It needs to be as detailed as possible to eliminate any questions concerning grading systems, course assignments and certain policies, such as attendance.

Your syllabus also tells the students how to contact you for questions or support they may need. Indicate your office phone, e-mail address or other contact information, and office hours. Emphasize to students that contact is encouraged; all too often, office hours are underutilized by students.

Many colleges and universities require a syllabus for each class and also may require certain policies to be included as well. Check with your course coordinator or department chair to verify what policies or procedures must be included in your syllabus, or if there is a certain format that is expected to be followed. Consider the following points when constructing your syllabus.

A. Start with Course Length, Credit Hours, and Number of Class Meetings
The length of the course you teach will be determined by the length of the term at your school and the number of credit hours allotted for the course. Credit hours for this course can be as few as one or as many as three, and courses may meet weekly, bi-weekly, or three times a week.

B. Align Your Syllabus with Other Courses in a Learning Community Environment
This course provides a wonderful opportunity to create a learning community with other courses offered for freshmen. For example, if you were to create a learning community with this course and an introductory psychology course, students could learn to take notes while listening to psychology content on long- and short-term memory processes. Discuss ideas you may have with your department chair and other teachers in the learning community.

C. Promote Accountability with Clear Grading Policies
Students need a clear understanding of how their performance will be graded and what types of evaluative methods you will use. Because the information being taught is not consistently "content-driven," you may find that it is more effective to mix formal evaluations, such as objective tests, with other evaluative methods, such as grading chapter activities and exercises.

We suggest you provide a grading outline of all evaluations given during the term, including a detailed scale that indicates points per assignment, test, and so on. That way, you help students monitor themselves as they keep track of their performance. We also recommend that you discuss your grading system, especially your reasoning for weighting certain tasks with a heavier percentage.

D. Explain Classroom Policies That Affect Grades
While creating your grading system, we recommend that you include classroom policies as well as college policies. The following areas are highly suggested.

Attendance/Tardy Policy: Making attendance/tardiness a component of your grading system sends the message that being in class is important for success. Be clear about how tardiness and absences can affect a grade, such as how many excused absences are allowed, what constitutes an unexcused absence, and how many tardies are allowed before a grade drops.

For example, you may want to allow three excused absences in a 15-week course, with a policy that students will lose 2 percentage points per absence after the three excused absences. You may also want to establish that two tardy arrivals count as one unexcused absence.

There will be cases when you may have to stretch your policy for individual students whose circumstances are not within their control (public transportation, weather, family issues). By providing contact information, students have the ability to notify you as to their absence or tardiness when necessary.

Class Participation/Preparation: Determine class participation/preparation in various ways.

- Are students bringing their course materials to class each time?
- Are they taking notes, discussing in small groups, asking questions, responding?
- Do students submit homework on time in the expected format?

Although participation can be a very subjective area, it is important for a course with so much active learning. Participation helps students learn more effectively.

E. Lay Out the Schedule

The final task for syllabus development is to lay out the schedule for the full length of the course. A list or table provides a useful format for letting students know expectations for each class meeting – topic covered, reading required, in-class activities, assignments due, and so on.

Consider this sample syllabus for a 15-week, 3-credit course, contributed by instructor Martha Martin.

Community College of Baltimore County – Essex
Humanities and Arts Division
SDEV 101 – Achieving Academic Success
Spring 2007

Instructor: **Martha Martin**   Course Number: 27283
Phone: **443-555-2121**   Class Times: **Tues/Thurs 11:10 – 12:35**
E-mail: martha.martin@xyz.com   Location: A 203
Office Hours: Mon/Wed (11:00 - 12:30) or Tues/Thurs (2:15 - 3:00), Building E, Writing
Center, 3rd floor

Course Description:
Achieving Academic Success is designed to focus on those student behaviors and attitudes that
are most consistently identified with achieving success in college. The significance of a college
education is explored and the specific ways that The Community College of Baltimore County
Campus operates are discussed. Strategies for time management, test taking, memory and
recall, communication, and personal success are included.

Course Objectives:
Students who successfully complete SDEV 101 will be able to:
- Discuss how you are responsible for creating a successful and satisfying experience in
  college.
- Be knowledgeable about college policies and procedures.
- Be able to locate and utilize information in the college catalog and other resources to
  develop a personal academic plan.
- List and describe specific methods to improve your ability to recall information, manage
  time more efficiently, read a textbook with improved understanding and retention,
  prepare for and take tests, and take effective notes and listen, with comprehension, to a
  lecture.
- Learn methods of communication that facilitate listening to, speaking with, and resolving
  conflicts with peers, family members, and instructors.
- Identify strategies that help you to focus attention on the task at hand when reading,
  listening, and taking notes and tests.
- Assess your general health habits including substance abuse or physical abuse and
  methods to more effectively cope with and/or prevent excessive stress.
- Locate college resources to assist you in meeting your needs as a student at The
  Community College of Baltimore County.
- Discover your most developed and least developed learning styles.
- Develop decision-making skills for effective goal setting.
- Learn tools for creating new ideas, solving problems, and thinking critically.
- Strengthen skills to study, work, and live in a multicultural, diverse, and changing
  world.

Grading and Course Requirements:

<u>Grading</u>
The following percentages are used to calculate the final grade:

① Attendance - 10% ② Textbook Checks - 15%
③ Midterm - 15% ④ Portfolio - 15%
⑤ Final Exam - 15% ⑥ Chapter Quizzes (4) - 15%
⑦ Graduated Learning Plan Completion - 10% ⑧ Campus Event Reviews (2) - 5%

① Attendance - 10 %: Regular attendance is mandatory. Students who miss more than 4 class periods may automatically fail the course. Also, students are expected to arrive on time and stay for the full class period. Arriving late or leaving class early will also affect attendance grades. Whenever an absence is unavoidable, it is still the student's responsibility to find out about and complete all assignments missed while absent. In other words, if you are absent on the day that an assignment is given <u>you are still required</u> to turn in that assignment on time. While you may call or e-mail me, I also recommend exchanging telephone numbers with at least one other student in class so that you can find out about missed assignments. If you are absent on the day that an assignment is due, you must turn in that assignment the very next day that you attend class in order to avoid a late penalty. Perfect class attendance will be recognized with bonus points on the final exam.

② Textbook Checks - 15%: Assignments are given from the textbook. Please note the phrase "text check" on your syllabus. On these dates, your homework will be checked in your textbook. Grades are assigned as follows: 100%, 75%, 50%, 25% or 0%. Late assignments will receive a 10% grade reduction.

③ Midterm - 15% and ⑤ Final Exam - 15% and ⑥ Chapter Quizzes (4) - 15%:
There will be 4 chapter quizzes during the semester. There will be 2 exams during the semester: midterm and final. If you are absent on the day of a quiz or test, you will be expected to take it the day that you return to class. Please note these dates on the syllabus.

④ Portfolio - 15%: These assignments are written responses to each chapter. They are to be completed by the suggested schedule as seen below.

2/13, Portfolio #1 4/03, Portfolio #5
2/27, Portfolio #2 4/17, Portfolio #6
3/13, Portfolio #3 4/24, Portfolio #7
3/27, Portfolio #4 5/01, Portfolio #8

⑦ Graduated Learning Plan Completion - 10%: This assignment will be primarily completed in class with the assistance of a CCBC Advisor.

⑧ Campus Event Reviews (2) - 5%: The assignment is to attend any variety of campus events and/or workshops and write a brief description of the activity. These assignments may be turned in at any time throughout the semester. The last day they will be accepted is 5/10/2007.

Academic Honesty:

Students are expected to complete and submit their own work. Copying from the work of another student, or from any source either in print or online, is a serious offense and will result in the student receiving a zero for that assignment. In addition, the student may also automatically fail the course. Also, students who try to obtain and use information from other students about a quiz or test may automatically fail the course. Students who willingly allow other students to copy their work or who provide information about quizzes or tests may be subject to the same penalties as the students who receive the information.

Required Texts and Materials:

Keys to Success: Building Analytical, Creative, and Practical Skills for College, Career,
and Life, Brief 5ᵗʰ Edition
Authors: Carol Carter, Joyce Bishop, and Sarah Lyman Kravits

Other necessary items are:
- A notebook or notebook paper and a pocket folder
- Pens/pencils
- A highlighter
- A good college-level dictionary

Class Schedule

1/30 Introduction to the text, class, Getting to know you

2/01 Computer Lab: e-mail, CCBC Web site navigation

2/06 *Chap 1: Welcome to College*

2/08 Group project startup: team building

2/13 *Chap 2: Values, Goals, Time, and Stress*

2/15 Computer Lab: career/major resources

2/20 Graduated Learning Plan advisor presentation and text check

2/22 Computer Lab: Student Success Center, LASSI

2/27 *QUIZ #1: chapters 1-2* and *Chap 3: Diversity Matters* – section on *How You Learn*

3/01 *Chap 3:* Section on *Diversity and Communication*

3/06 Diversity panel presentation

3/08 *Chap 4: Critical, Creative, and Practical Thinking*

3/13 Continued coverage of Chap. 4, text check, and *QUIZ #2: chapters 3-4*

3/15 Midterm

3/20 *Chap 5: Reading and Studying*

3/22 Continued coverage of Chap. 5 and library tour

3/27 *Chap 6: Listening, Note Taking, and Memory*—section on *Listening/Note Taking*

3/29 *Chap 6:* Section on *Memory*

4/03 Presentations of group projects and text check

4/05 *QUIZ #3: chapters 5-6*

Spring Break

4/17 *Chap 7: Test Taking*

4/19 *Chap 8: Wellness, Money, and Careers*-- Section on *Wellness*

4/24 Presentation by counseling and health center

4/26 *Chap 8:* Section on *Money* with presentation on grants and scholarships by financial aid office

5/1 *Chap 8:* Sections on *Careers and Self-Activators*

5/3 Field trip to Career Center and text check

5/8 *QUIZ #4: chapters 7-8*

5/10 Review for final exam

5/17 9:00 am - **FINAL EXAM**

6. Set Yourself Up for Success in the First Week

Get up to speed. Your first week is often a combination of housekeeping (syllabus review, collection of student demographic information), welcoming and getting to know your students, and delving into the course with an icebreaker (or two). The chapter 1 material has some exercises that can serve as icebreakers. See, for example, the "Name Game" exercise on page 50 of this instructor's manual.

If you feel pressed for time and want to concentrate on getting to know students, have them take the syllabus home to "study." On day two or three (depending on how many new students you have), consider giving them a brief syllabus quiz. It opens the discussion about what is on the syllabus and allows students to begin asking questions regarding grading, attendance and assignments.

Chapter 1 has a sample syllabus which, along with your own, gives you two examples to use in this discussion. Having more than one syllabus for students to look at is especially helpful for inexperienced students who may not have much basis for comparison. Check out the "Syllabus Jeopardy" exercise in the chapter 1 material, on page 50 of this instructor's manual.

Use the Quick Start "pre-pendix" to get students in the groove. Quick Start lays out the information students need in order to be responsible and in control as they begin college. In combination with your student handbook, it is a great source of helpful details. Topics include:

- Policies and procedures (curriculum requirements, adding/dropping a course, etc.)
- Understanding the grading system
- Your school's computer system (with tips on effective use of e-mail)
- Helpful people (instructors, TAs, administrators, advisors, etc.)
- Helpful resources (organizations, student-centered services)
- Financial aid overview (types of aid, federal programs, advice on applying for federal aid)

You may want to look through Quick Start ahead of time and then, at the end of the first day, assign it as reading along with particular sections of the student handbook. After they've read it, ask your students what topics they consider most important (financial aid, calculating a GPA) and see if those topics warrant further discussion. Take a look at the "GPA Practice" exercise in the *Handouts* section of the chapter 1 materials, on pages 57-58 of this instructor's manual.

Set a goal. The most important goal for your first week is to answer, in a compelling way, this question for students: WHY THIS COURSE? You can start this discussion by asking your class, "If you were a manager of a small company and could only hire one person, what would their qualities be?" Write on the board what students volunteer. Then encourage students to ask themselves, how does how they behave as students relate to this picture of an ideal employee? Based on this consideration, have them rate their readiness for school and job success on a scale of 1-10. (More on this in chapter 1 following this introduction).

Make the connection with analytical, creative, and practical thinking. Tie the book's theme into your initial discussion by making the connection with successful intelligence – for yourself as well as for your students. Get in the successful intelligence mode with your coverage by:

- Thinking analytically about each chapter's content
- Engaging creative skills through community-building group activities
- Using practical thinking skills to evaluate the success of your choices and student progress and make decisions about how to proceed to the next topic in the syllabus

You may want to detail this plan for your students so they see more clearly, and can more easily model, the example you are setting.

Establish an interactive learning community. Set up, from the start, an environment that fosters relationships, encourages interaction, and values different opinions. Use questions like the following to open the floor to discussion relevant to the beginning of the course:

What will you get out of the course?
What do you want out of the course? Out of college? Life?
What are your greatest fears?
What are your strengths/weaknesses?
What is the difference between high school/college?
What is the syllabus/what are the expectations?
What are your goals and values?
What are the class agreements?
Who do you want to be in two years/four years?
What needs to change now to make that a reality?

This instructor's manual is just a starting point. We cordially invite you to our faculty training site where you can troubleshoot, share ideas, and build community with Student Success instructors across North America. The site is exclusively available to Keys to Success *Brief 5e adopters. See the next section on supplemental resources for more details.*

We hope our suggestions aid your teaching success. Please contact us at any time with questions, comments, and suggestions. You can reach us by telephone at 1-877-737-8510. You may also use e-mail to reach Carol Carter at caroljcarter@lifebound.com or Joyce Bishop at jbishop@gwc.cccd.edu.

Supplemental Resource Guide

INSTRUCTOR SUPPORT
Resources to simplify your life and engage your students.

Print

Instructor's Manual with Test Bank	0-13-512847-1
PowerPoint on CD	0-13-512895-1

Technology

"Easy access to online, book-specific teaching support is now just a click away!"

Instructor Resource Center - Register. Login. Open the door to a variety of print and media resources in downloadable, digital format, available to instructors exclusively through the Prentice Hall IRC.
http://vig.prenhall.com/catalog/main_content/0,1151,-500,00.html

"Expand your teaching skills and build community with other instructors with the first-of-its-kind Keys Online Faculty Training Course with author Joyce Bishop!"

Online Instructor Faculty Training - Faculty training anytime you want it. Ask questions. Share ideas. Troubleshoot. Join the *Keys* author online faculty training sessions, available to all adopters through Course Compass, and you'll learn what other faculty using *Keys* are doing; be able to share exercises, syllabi, and teaching strategies; and view online videos of Joyce explaining specific learning activities. This new "Key" to your teaching success is free—no matter what your course size or location--and accessible online.

"Teaching an online course, offering a hybrid class, or simply introducing your students to Technology just got a whole lot easier!"

OneKey Course Management - OneKey: All you and your students need to succeed. OneKey is Prentice Hall's exclusive new resource for instructors and students providing access to the best online teaching and learning tools—24 hours a day, 7 days a week. OneKey means all your resources are in one place for maximum convenience, simplicity and success. Visit www.prenhall.com/onekey and scroll through the gallery option to Student Success for additional information. Note the videos housed on our OneKey sites are now available on DVD (ISBN 013-514249-0).

"Reinforce strong research skills, encourage library use, and combat plagiarism with this tool!"

Prentice Hall's Research Navigator - Designed to help students with the research process-- from identifying a topic to editing the final draft. It also demonstrates how to make time at the campus library more productive. RN includes four databases of credible and reliable source material to get your research process started: The EBSCO/Content Select, New York

Times, Link Library, and The Financial Times. Visit www.researchnavigator.com for additional information.

Video Options

"Choose from a wide range of video resources for the classroom!"

Prentice Hall Reference Library: Life Skills Pack #0-13-127079-6 contains all 4 videos. Also available on DVD 013-5142474, or they may be requested individually as follows:
• Learning Styles and Self-Awareness, 0-13-028502-1
• Critical and Creative Thinking, 0-13-028504-8
• Relating to Others, 0-13-028511-0
• Personal Wellness, 0-13-028514-5

Prentice Hall Reference Library: Study Skills Pack #0-13-127080-X contains all 6 videos. Also available on DVD 0135142482 or they may be requested individually as follows:
• Reading Effectively, 0-13-028505-6
• Listening and Memory, 0-13-028506-4
• Note Taking and Research, 0-13-028508-0
• Writing Effectively, 0-13-028509-9
• Effective Test Taking, 0-13-028500-5
• Goal Setting and Time Management, 0-13-028503-X

Prentice Hall Reference Library: Career Skills Pack #0-13-118529-2 contains all 3 videos. Also available on DVD 013-5142504, or they may be requested individually as follows:
• Skills for the 21st Century – Technology, 0-13-028512-9
• Skills for the 21st Century – Math and Science, 0-13-028513-7
• Managing Career and Money, 0-13-028516-1

Faculty Video Resources
• Teacher Training Video 1: Critical Thinking, 0-13-099432-4
• Teacher Training Video 2: Stress Management & Communication, 0-13-099578-9
• Teacher Training Video 3: Classroom Tips, 0-13-917205-X
• Student Advice Video, 0-13-233206-X
• Study Skills Video, 0-13-096095-0
• Building on Your Best Video, 0-20-526277-5

Current Issues Videos
• ABC News Video Series: Student Success 2/E, 0-13-031901-5
• ABC News Video Series: Student Success 3/E, 0-13-152865-3

Faculty Development Series Workshops
• Carter: Faculty Development Workshop DVD, 0-13-199047-0

Assessment Options

"Through partnership opportunities, we offer a variety of assessment options!"
LASSI - The LASSI is a 10-scale, 80-item assessment of students' awareness about and use of learning and study strategies. Addressing skill, will and self-regulation, the focus is on both covert and overt thoughts, behaviors, attitudes and beliefs that relate to successful learning and that can be altered through educational interventions. Available in two formats: Paper 0-13-172315-4 or Online 0-13-172316-2 (Access Card).

Noel Levitz/RMS – This retention tool measures Academic Motivation, General Coping Ability, Receptivity to Support Services, PLUS Social Motivation. It helps identify at-risk students, the areas with which they struggle, and their receptiveness to support. Available in Paper or Online formats, as well as Short and Long versions. PAPER Long Form A: 0-13-072258-8; PAPER Short Form B: 0-13-079193-8; Online Forms AB&C: 0-13-098158-3.

Robbins Self Assessment Library – This compilation teaches students to create a portfolio of skills. S.A.L. is a self-contained, interactive library of 49 behavioral questionnaires that help students discover new ideas about themselves, their attitudes, and their personal strengths and weaknesses. Available in Paper, 0-13-173861-5; CD-Rom, 0-13-221793-7; and Online, 0-13-243165-3 (Access Card) formats.

Readiness for Education at a Distance Indicator (READI) - READI is a Web-based tool that assesses the overall likelihood for online learning success. READI generates an immediate score and a diagnostic interpretation of results, including recommendations for successful participation in online courses and potential remediation sources. Please visit www.readi.info for additional information. 0-13-188967-2.

Other Resources

"Teaching tolerance and discussing diversity with your students can be challenging!"
Responding to Hate at School - Published by the Southern Poverty Law Center, the Teaching Tolerance handbook is a step-by-step, easy-to-use guide designed to help administrators, counselors and teachers react promptly and efficiently whenever hate, bias, and prejudice strike.

"For a terrific one-stop shop resource, use our Student Success Supersite!"
Supersite - www.prenhall.com/success Students and professors alike may use the Supersite for assessments, activities, links, and more.

"For a truly tailored solution that fosters campus connections and increases retention, talk with us about custom publishing."
Pearson Custom Publishing – We are the largest custom provider for print and media shaped to your course's needs. Please visit us at www.pearsoncustom.com to learn more.

STUDENT SUPPORT
Tools to help make the grade now, and excel in school later

"We offer an online study aid to help students fully understand each chapter's content, assess their knowledge, and apply what they've learned."

Companion Web site – The site includes an online glossary of key terms, practice quizzes of objective and subjective questions, e-journaling activities, additional Personal Triumph case studies, reading logs, cross-disciplinary exercises, and audio files from the authors. Please visit the site for this text at www.prenhall.com/carter.

"Time management is the #1 challenge students face. We can help."

Prentice Hall Planner – A basic planner that includes a monthly & daily calendar plus other materials to facilitate organization. 8.5 x 11.

Premier Annual Planner - This 4-color planner, updated annually, includes sections on academic planning/resources, monthly planning (2 pages/month), and weekly planning (48 weeks; July start), which facilitate short-term and long-term planning. Spiral bound, 6 x 9.

"Journaling activities promote self-discovery and self-awareness."

Student Reflection Journal - Through this vehicle, students are encouraged to track their progress and share their insights, thoughts, and concerns. 8 1/2 x 11. 90 pages.

"Our Student Success Supersite is a one-stop shop for students to learn about career paths, self-awareness activities, cross-curricular practice opportunities, and more!"

Supersite - at www.prenhall.com/success.

"Learning to adapt to the diverse college community is essential to students' success."

10 Ways to Fight Hate - Produced by the Southern Poverty Law Center, the leading hate-crime and crime-watch organization in the United States, this guide walks students through 10 steps that they can take on their own campus or in their own neighborhood to fight hate every day. 0-13-028146-8.

"The Student Orientation Series includes short booklets on specialized topics that facilitate greater student understanding."

S.O.S. Guides – Connolly: *Learning Communities* 0-13-232243-9 and Watts: *Service Learning* 0-13-232201-3 help students understand what these opportunities are, how to take advantage of them, and how to learn from their peers while doing so. New to the series is Hoffman: *Stop Procrastinating Now! 10 Simple & SUCCESSFUL Steps for Student Success* 0-13-513056-5.

Pre- and Post- Course Assessments

One way to help students realize that what they do now sitting in this classroom will have a positive effect on their futures is to use pre- and post-course assessments. Ideally, you would give a pre-course assessment within the first week of starting the course, and a companion post-course assessment in the last week as a wrap-up. There are distinct benefits:

∞ Pre-course assessment helps students get an overview of the course as well as an idea of how they perceive their skills and aptitudes in key areas.

∞ Post-course assessment gives students a big-picture idea of all of the ground they have covered and goals they have accomplished, boosting self-esteem. Furthermore, it gives them a new snapshot of how they perceive their skills now after a semester of work, and a chance to compare that snapshot to the pre-course assessment to get an illustration of perceived growth.

∞ *Additional benefit to instructor.* Evaluating the trends in responses to the pre-course assessment helps you assess where students feel most confident and, conversely, most challenged. Evaluating the trends in responses to the post-course assessment helps you see where the course had the most significant effect.

Be sure to emphasize to your students, before each assessment, that the assessment measures how they perceive themselves – it is not a hard and fast measure of their ability in any area.

Assessments Included Here

The first and last chapter of the text contain two types of pre- and post-course assessments:

▪ Three successful-intelligence-based self-assessments – *Assess Yourself as an Analytical Thinker*, *Assess Yourself as a Creative Thinker*, and *Assess Yourself as a Practical Thinker* (pre-course versions found in the in-text exercises in chapter 1, and post-course versions in the *Personal Portfolio* exercise at the end of chapter 8)

▪ A self-assessment based on the self-activators that are characteristic of successfully intelligent thinkers (pre-course version found in the *Activate Yourself* end-of-chapter exercise in chapter 1, and post-course version as the *Get Analytical* in-text exercise in chapter 8)

Although these assessments appear in the text, they are reprinted here in ready-to-photocopy format for your convenience, should you need to recopy them for any reason.

PRE-COURSE: ASSESS YOURSELF AS AN ANALYTICAL THINKER

For each statement, circle the number that feels right to you, from 1 for "not at all true for me" to 5 for "very true for me."

1. I recognize and define problems effectively.   1 2 3 4 5

2. I see myself as "a thinker," "analytical," "studious."   1 2 3 4 5

3. When working on a problem in a group setting, I like to break down the   1 2 3 4 5
   problem into its components and evaluate them.

4. I need to see convincing evidence before accepting information as fact.   1 2 3 4 5

5. I weigh the pros and cons of plans and ideas before taking action.   1 2 3 4 5

6. I tend to make connections among pieces of information by categorizing them.   1 2 3 4 5

7. Impulsive, spontaneous decision-making worries me.   1 2 3 4 5

8. I like to analyze causes and effects when making a decision.   1 2 3 4 5

9. I monitor my progress toward goals.   1 2 3 4 5

10. Once I reach a goal, I evaluate the process to see how effective it was.   1 2 3 4 5

Total your answers here: _____

If your total ranges from 38–50, you consider your analytical thinking skills to be *strong*.

If your total ranges from 24–37, you consider your analytical thinking skills to be *average*.

If your total ranges from 10–23, you consider your analytical thinking skills to be *weak*.

PRE-COURSE: ASSESS YOURSELF AS A CREATIVE THINKER

For each statement, circle the number that feels right to you, from 1 for "not at all true for me" to 5 for "very true for me."

1. I tend to question rules and regulations.   1   2   3   4   5

2. I see myself as "unique," "full of ideas," "innovative."   1   2   3   4   5

3. When working on a problem in a group setting, I generate a lot 1   2   3   4   5
    of ideas.

4. I am energized when I have a brand-new experience.   1   2   3   4   5

5. If you say something is too risky, I'm ready to give it a shot. 1   2   3   4   5

6. I often wonder if there is a different way to do or see   1   2   3   4   5
    something.

7. Too much routine in my work or schedule drains my energy. 1   2   3   4   5

8. I tend to see connections among ideas that others do not. 1   2   3   4   5

9. I feel comfortable allowing myself to make mistakes as I test 1   2   3   4   5
    out ideas.

10. I'm willing to champion an idea even when others disagree 1   2   3   4   5
    with me.

Total your answers here: _____

If your total ranges from 38-50, you consider your creative thinking skills to be *strong*.

If your total ranges from 24-37, you consider your creative thinking skills to be *average*.

If your total ranges from 10-23, you consider your creative thinking skills to be *weak*.

PRE-COURSE: ASSESS YOURSELF AS A PRACTICAL THINKER

For each statement. circle the number that feels right to you, from 1 for "not at all true for me" to 5 for "very true for me."

1. I can find a way around any obstacle.   1 2 3 4 5

2. I see myself as a "doer," the "go-to" person, I "make things happen."   1 2 3 4 5

3. When working on a problem in a group setting, I like to figure out who   1 2 3 4 5

   will do what and when it should be done.

4. Because I learn well from experience, I don't tend to repeat a mistake.   1 2 3 4 5

5. I finish what I start and don't leave loose ends hanging.   1 2 3 4 5

6. I pay attention to my emotions in academic and social situations to see if   1 2 3 4 5

   they help or hurt me as I move toward a goal.

7. I can sense how people feel, and can use that knowledge to interact with   1 2 3 4 5

   others effectively in order to achieve a goal.

8. I manage my time effectively.   1 2 3 4 5

9. I find ways to adjust to the teaching styles of my instructors and the   1 2 3 4 5

   communication styles of my peers.

10. When involved in a problem solving process, I can shift gears as   1 2 3 4 5

    needed.

Total your answers here: _____

If your total ranges from 38-50, you consider your practical thinking skills to be *strong*.

If your total ranges from 24-37, you consider your practical thinking skills to be *average*.

If your total ranges from 10-23, you consider your practical thinking skills to be *weak*.

PRE-COURSE: ACTIVATE YOURSELF

Use this self-assessment to see how developed you perceive your self-activators to be *right now*.

1	**2**	**3**	**4**	**5**
Definitely Like Me	Somewhat Like Me	Not Sure	Somewhat Unlike Me	Not At All Like Me

Please circle the number which best represents your answer:

1. I motivate myself well.   1   2   3   4   5

2. I can control my impulses.   1   2   3   4   5

3. I know when to persevere and when to change gears.   1   2   3   4   5

4. I make the most of what I do well.   1   2   3   4   5

5. I can successfully translate my ideas into action.   1   2   3   4   5

6. I can focus effectively on my goal.   1   2   3   4   5

7. I complete tasks and have good follow-through.   1   2   3   4   5

8. I initiate action – I move people and projects ahead.   1   2   3   4   5

9. I have the courage to risk failure.   1   2   3   4   5

10. I avoid procrastination.   1   2   3   4   5

11. I accept responsibility when I make a mistake.   1   2   3   4   5

12. I don't waste time feeling sorry for myself.   1   2   3   4   5

13. I independently take responsibility for tasks.   1   2   3   4   5

14. I work hard to overcome personal difficulties.   1   2   3   4   5

15. I create an environment that helps me to concentrate on my goals.   1   2   3   4   5

16. I don't take on too much work or too little.   1   2   3   4   5

17. I can delay gratification in order to receive the benefits.   1   2   3   4   5

18. I can see both the big picture and the details in a situation.   1   2   3   4   5

19. I am able to maintain confidence in myself.   1   2   3   4   5

20. I can balance my analytical, creative, and practical thinking skills.   1   2   3   4   5

POST-COURSE: ASSESS YOURSELF AS AN ANALYTICAL THINKER

For each statement, circle the number that feels right to you, from 1 for "not at all true for me" to 5 for "very true for me."

1. I recognize and define problems effectively.   1   2   3   4   5

2. I see myself as "a thinker," "analytical," "studious."   1   2   3   4   5

3. When working on a problem in a group setting, I like to break down the   1   2   3   4   5

    problem into its components and evaluate them.

4. I need to see convincing evidence before accepting information as fact.   1   2   3   4   5

5. I weigh the pros and cons of plans and ideas before taking action.   1   2   3   4   5

6. I tend to make connections among pieces of information by categorizing them.   1   2   3   4   5

7. Impulsive, spontaneous decision-making worries me.   1   2   3   4   5

8. I monitor my progress toward goals.   1   2   3   4   5

9. Once I reach a goal, I evaluate the process to see how effective it was.   1   2   3   4   5

10. When something goes wrong, I work to find out why.   1   2   3   4   5

Total your answers here: _____

POST-COURSE: ASSESS YOURSELF AS A CREATIVE THINKER

For each statement, circle the number that feels right to you, from 1 for "not at all true for me" to 5 for "very true for me."

1. I tend to question rules and regulations.   1   2   3   4   5

2. I see myself as "unique," "full of ideas," "innovative."   1   2   3   4   5

3. When working on a problem in a group setting, I generate a lot   1   2   3   4   5

    of ideas.

4. I am energized when I have a brand-new experience.   1   2   3   4   5

5. If you say something is too risky, I'm ready to give it a shot.   1   2   3   4   5

6. I often wonder if there is a different way to do or see   1   2   3   4   5

    something.

7. Too much routine in my work or schedule drains my energy.   1   2   3   4   5

8. I tend to see connections among ideas that others do not.   1   2   3   4   5

9. I feel comfortable allowing myself to make mistakes as I test   1   2   3   4   5

    out ideas.

10. I'm willing to champion an idea even when others disagree   1   2   3   4   5

    with me.

Total your answers here: _____

POST-COURSE: ASSESS YOURSELF AS A PRACTICAL THINKER

For each statement, circle the number that feels right to you, from 1 for "not at all true for me" to 5 for "very true for me."

1. I can find a way around any obstacle.	1 2 3 4 5
2. I see myself as a "doer," the "go-to" person, I "make things happen."	1 2 3 4 5
3. When working on a problem in a group setting, I like to set up the plan and monitor how it is carried out.	1 2 3 4 5
4. Because I learn well from experience, I don't tend to repeat a mistake.	1 2 3 4 5
5. I finish what I start and don't leave loose ends hanging.	1 2 3 4 5
6. I pay attention to my emotions in academic and social situations to see if they help or hurt me as I move toward a goal.	1 2 3 4 5
7. I can sense how people feel, and can use that knowledge to interact with others effectively in order to achieve a goal.	1 2 3 4 5
8. I manage my time effectively.	1 2 3 4 5
9. I find ways to adjust to the teaching styles of my instructors and the communication styles of my peers.	1 2 3 4 5
10. When involved in a problem solving process, I can see when I'm headed in an ineffective direction and I can shift gears.	1 2 3 4 5

Total your answers here: _____

POST-COURSE: EVALUATE YOUR SELF-ACTIVATORS

To see how you use successful intelligence in your daily life, assess how developed you perceive your self-activators to be after completing this course.

1	2	3	4	5
Definitely Like Me	Somewhat Like Me	Not Sure	Somewhat Unlike Me	Not At All Like Me

Please circle the number which best represents your answer:

1. I motivate myself well.   1   2   3   4   5

2. I can control my impulses.   1   2   3   4   5

3. I know when to persevere and when to change gears.   1   2   3   4   5

4. I make the most of what I do well.   1   2   3   4   5

5. I can successfully translate my ideas into action.   1   2   3   4   5

6. I can focus effectively on my goal.   1   2   3   4   5

7. I complete tasks and have good follow-through.   1   2   3   4   5

8. I initiate action -- I move people and projects ahead.   1   2   3   4   5

9. I have the courage to risk failure.   1   2   3   4   5

10. I avoid procrastination.   1   2   3   4   5

11. I accept responsibility when I make a mistake.   1   2   3   4   5

12. I don't waste time feeling sorry for myself.   1   2   3   4   5

13. I independently take responsibility for tasks.   1   2   3   4   5

14. I work hard to overcome personal difficulties.   1   2   3   4   5

15. I create an environment that helps me to concentrate on my goals.   1   2   3   4   5

16. I don't take on too much work or too little.   1   2   3   4   5

17. I can delay gratification in order to receive the benefits. 1   2   3   4   5

18. I can see both the big picture and the details in a situation.   1   2   3   4
5

19. I am able to maintain confidence in myself.   1   2   3   4
5

20. I can balance my analytical, creative, and practical thinking skills.   1   2   3   4
5

Welcome to College
Opening Doors to Success

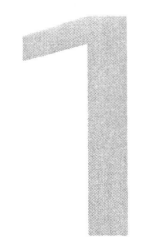

BRIEF CHAPTER OVERVIEW

This re-envisioned chapter delivers what so many instructors told us they wanted to see – a more comprehensive introduction to **successful intelligence**, the theme of *Keys to Success*. While retaining the essentials that get students motivated and moving at the beginning of the term, the chapter combines enhanced information about successful intelligence with expanded self-assessments on analytical, creative, and practical thinking that previously appeared in chapter 4.

In addition, the topics of emotional and social intelligence are introduced comprehensively here, setting up a context for when the text revisits these concepts at strategic points throughout the chapters.

One of the toughest issues teachers face in this course is that many students believe they already know how to do well in college and think the class will be a waste of time. Still another issue is some students' underlying sense of insecurity about college. They wonder whether they'll be able to make it, but are often afraid to admit their concerns. The concept of successful intelligence, introduced comprehensively and reinforced throughout the term, will encourage both types of students to see the value of this course.

Note the successful intelligence skills your students will build in chapter 1:

Analytical	Creative	Practical
■ Evaluating your starting point as you begin college	■ Creating new ideas about college goals	■ How to follow the code of academic integrity
■ Analyzing how successful intelligence can help you achieve goals	■ Developing a fresh understanding of your ability to grow	■ How to work with others effectively
■ Considering how specific actions promote success in college	■ Creating ways to benefit from failure	■ How to become a lifelong learner

CHAPTER ONE OUTLINE

Where Are You Now – and Where Can College Take You?

How Can Successful Intelligence Help You Achieve Your Goals?

- Defining Successful Intelligence
- How This Book Helps You Build Successful Intelligence

What Actions Will Prepare You for College Success?

- Be Responsible
- Get Motivated
- Practice Academic Integrity
- Understand and Manage Learning Disabilities
- Learn From Failure and Celebrate Success

How Can You Work Effectively With Others?

- Value Diversity
- Develop Emotional and Social Intelligence
- Know How to Work With Others in Groups

How Can The Things You Learn Now Promote Life Success?

COMMUNICATE CONTENT
TOPICS COVERED IN THE CHAPTER

[Chapter and part intro: PowerPoint slides 1, 2, 3]

The *Real Questions, Practical Answers* Discussion Starter Question:
How can I make the transition to college easier? [PowerPoint slide 4]

> Think about transitions – brainstorm several from the class and list them on the board. (Ideas include single to married, high school to college, middle school to high school, working to retired, childless to children, and married to widowed or divorced.) Take a vote and decide on a common transition that either all students have experienced or agree is difficult. Ask students to brainstorm the difficult characteristics of the transition and the exciting parts of it. Explain that the text will help students approach the transition to college in many different ways.

(For more discussion starters, see p. 49 of this IM chapter.)

 ## Question 1: Where Are You Now – and Where Can College Take You?

The whole point of this section – and the most important point to hit as you begin – is that this course, and college, are of value to students now and in the future. They need to understand that the work and experience are worth their time. [see PowerPoint slides 5, 6]

Ask students to express their thoughts and feelings about what they expect from the course. Do they see its value? Are they there because it is required? Do they expect it will be "easier" than their other discipline-specific courses? Besides the value in letting them weigh in and open up, their answers will reveal their attitude, which can help you make decisions about when and how you approach certain topics through the term.

For some ideas about how to emphasize that their work and focus in this course will reap benefits, go through the "life success goals" (in text) enhanced by a college education:

- Increased employability and earning potential (point out the visuals in Keys 1.1 and 1.2 to illustrate points)
- Preparation for career success
- Smart personal health choices
- Active community involvement/appreciation of different cultures
- Self-knowledge

Finally, remind students that they should step back from time to time and ask themselves: "Why is this topic/assignment/class important? How will it help me achieve my goals? How can I use it in my other classes?" This may help them connect more effectively with what is going on in the classroom.

(At the beginning of your work with the students, consider using the "Name Game" exercise on p. 50 of this IM chapter.)

 ## Question 2: How Can Successful Intelligence Help You Achieve Your Goals?

[Section outline: PowerPoint slide 7]
This part of the text consists of a newly revised and comprehensive introduction of our theme and framework – Successful Intelligence. Start out by querying your students about their concept of *intelligence* – what do they think it means? Who has it? Are you stuck with the level you are born with? Use their concepts as a jumping-off point to communicate these principles of successful intelligence:

- Intelligence is more than analytical skills/IQ

- Intelligence is NOT a fixed quantity; research has shown that it can grow and develop with effort and practice

Defining Successful Intelligence
Have a student read aloud the story about the two boys and the bear that appears in the text. It is a great illustration of the power of creative and practical intelligence (most students already understand the power and importance of analytical intelligence).

Follow up the story with a definition of successful intelligence – the kind of intelligence used to achieve important goals (focusing on action instead of recall and analysis). Introduce the three aspects of successful intelligence **[see PowerPoint slide 8]**:
- Analytical thinking (critical thinking)
- Creative thinking
- Practical thinking

The text has two useful examples that illustrate how all three work in conjunction. Help students understand that because all three skills are necessary for success, <u>all kinds of learners – especially ones not strong in analytical skills – can take encouragement from this framework that they have the potential to grow and succeed.</u>

Use the text points to show students where, in their copies of this textbook, they will build successful intelligence throughout their reading and work ("How this book helps you build successful intelligence").

<u>Note</u>: Now is a good time to make sure students are clear on the fact that "practical intelligence" is <u>more than just "knowing how to do something"</u> – it includes self-knowledge, emotional and social intelligence, and an ability to apply what you have learned from experience.

(Consider using the "Self-Perception Exploration" exercise on p. 50 of this IM chapter.)

Pre-course assessments. This chapter has four valuable assessments that work best when given at the beginning of the term. Three of these assessments are in the chapter 1's *Get Analytical!*, *Get Creative!*, and *Get Practical!* exercises, and concern each of those thinking skills. The fourth assessment is at the end of the text and helps students see how developed they are in the "self-activators" – qualities/skills that Sternberg sees as characteristic of successfully intelligent thinkers.

 Question 3: What Actions Will Prepare You for College Success?

The ideas in this section are intended to combat the feeling of helplessness that can accompany the first days and weeks of school, especially for freshmen. When students can feel like they have some control over what's going on, they build a foundation and proceed with more confidence. The idea that they are responsible for their success can be both scary and empowering. **[See PowerPoint slide 9.]**

Be Responsible and Accountable. Responsibility, control, self-directed learning – these are hot topics in classrooms all over the country, and some states have developed guidelines for self-directed learning that state schools are instructed to support with curriculum, materials, and resources. Students need to understand that they are in charge of making their own way, step by step, toward goals and academic excellence.

Students might have an intimidating vision of what defines a "responsible student." Ask the class and see what response occurs. If they aim too high, bring them down to earth by mentioning the building blocks of responsible student behavior – and note how basic they are:

- Read materials ahead of class.
- Attend class.
- Have a positive attitude.
- Take notes.
- Complete assignments on schedule.
- Listen and participate in class discussion.
- Study for tests.
- Communicate with instructors and students.
- Seek help if you need it.

If you have discussed Quick Start in class, or even if you have just had students read it, you can connect its details with this material on responsibility.
(Consider using the "GPA Practice" exercise on pp. 57-58 of this IM chapter.)

The text brings up the topic of the syllabus here. The syllabus is such a valuable tool for students, but many put it in a pile of papers and don't often use it to their advantage. If you have not already done so, you may want to do a walk-through of your course syllabus at this point, in the context of responsibility.

(Consider using the "Syllabus Jeopardy" exercise on p. 50 of this IM chapter.)

Get Motivated. Under the umbrella of motivation are the topics of self-esteem and facing fears. A difficulty for many students, especially those who are at risk, is self-perception and fear. They may have accepted labels that came from former teachers, grades, or SAT scores. Students with great capability may think they are "not smart," while those with a very narrow set of abilities (especially those with strong memory skills, but weak higher-order thinking skills) may think of themselves as very smart. The power of negative labels is often so strong that students stop trying. Conversely, the first set of grades that damages the "smart" person's self-perception may convince them to take only those courses that require memory skills.

(Consider using the "Teamwork: Create Solutions Together -- Motivators" exercise from the end of the text chapter, discussed on p. 49 of this IM chapter.)

Fear may prevent students from taking risks, such as talking with a roommate about problems in the relationship, or taking a difficult course that helps the student explore their talents. Fear can sap motivation and affect learning. Strategies for dealing with fears:
- Acknowledge specific fears.
- Decide which ones are real, which conceal something deeper, and which are unfounded.
- Develop a plan of attack.
- Talk about fears with people you trust.

(Consider using either or both of two student-generated handouts – "Common Reasons Why Students Don't Do Well in School," on p. 59 of this IM chapter, and "Top Ten Difficulties Going from High School to College," on p. 60 of this IM chapter, to inspire discussion.)

Practice Academic Integrity. This topic is more and more in the forefront of everyone's attention in the academic community. Computer technology, telephone technology, and the Internet have brought a new dimension to plagiarism and cheating. Instructors are seeing a wide range of behaviors from copying material directly from Web sites to text-messaging answers on cell phones during exams. **[See PowerPoint slide 10.]**

Be direct with students, and be specific. We recommend that you:

- Define academic integrity using the Center for Academic Integrity's five aspects (as shown in the text).

- Highlight your school's integrity policy. Photocopy it from the student handbook, hand it out, give students two minutes to read it, and lead a discussion about it.

- Make very clear, in your syllabus and verbally, what your expectations are for your course, including consequences for plagiarism or other kinds of cheating.

- Emphasize the value of integrity. Emphasize to students that reinforcing integrity now will forge positive behaviors for the rest of college and the workplace as well.

- Be true to your word. If you (the instructor) discover cheating, follow through with the consequences you have established.

Understand and Manage Learning Disabilities. This may be a sensitive topic for some students. On the other hand, you may have students present who have disabilities and are willing to be open and forthright with the class. Encourage a positive outlook from the entire class.

You may want to plan your coverage of this topic with your particular class in mind – more need might require more time, less need might mean more cursory coverage. Some coverage is useful no matter what, because there's always a chance that someone has problems that have gone undiagnosed, and this material may make them think and even encourage them to explore the situation further.

Learn from Failure and Celebrate Success. We believe (and other instructors we've talked to agree) that one of the strongest assets any teacher of this course has is his or her own experience. This is a great place to introduce a failure of your own – tell the story, and emphasize what you learned from it. Go through the three steps to learning from failure:

- Analyze what happened
- Come up with creative ways to make a change
- Put the plan into action

This plan, similar to the plan for facing fear, will give students a taste of the problem-solving plan to come in chapter 4.

(Consider using the "Self-Esteem, Motivation, and Learning" exercise on p. 51 of this IM chapter.)

(Consider using the "A Shield and a Symbol for Life" on pp. 54-55 of this IM chapter for a way to get students thinking about their personal big-picture goals for academic success.)

Question 4: How Can You Work Effectively With Others?

[Section overview: PowerPoint slide 11]
On the topic of **knowing how to work with others**, bring up the idea that "no person is an island." Note that the growing capability of communication among people, both locally and globally, has increased interaction with others in countless ways, both visible and invisible.

Ask students to volunteer examples of teamwork in their lives. Give school, work, and life examples to show that teamwork is essential for success (family scenarios, sports or news teams, medical teams performing surgery, etc.)

Value of diversity. Given the reality of growing diversity in school, work, and life, the section starts with a discussion of the value of diversity. Clarify the two aspects of diversity:

- Differences among people (many types listed in the text)
- Differences within ourselves (personality traits, strengths and weaknesses, etc.)

Emotional and social intelligence. Here the text introduces the up-to-the-minute topics of social and emotional intelligence, based on Daniel Goleman's work. Keys 1.4 and 1.5 have clear and comprehensive information about the definitions of each. Emphasize the value of these qualities in working with others, and let students know that they will see them referenced in other parts of the text. **[See PowerPoint slide 12.]**

Know how to work with others in groups. The text gets practical here, with helpful strategies about working with others. You may want to go through the list of study group success strategies found in this section.

(Consider using the "Who Can Help You?" exercise on p. 56 of this IM chapter.)

 Question 5: How Can The Things You Learn Now Promote Life Success?

[Section overview: PowerPoint slide 13]

This short but inspiring last section in the chapter helps students think more broadly about what they are working to accomplish in college, discussing the value of **lifelong learning** and illustrating the changes taking place now that will affect what students learn and the choices they make in school, at work, and in their lives.

- Knowledge in nearly every field is doubling every two to three years.

- Technology is changing how you live and work.

- The global economy is moving from a product-and-service base to a knowledge-and-talent base.

- Workers are changing jobs and careers more frequently.

With these points, you can get back to the chapter-opening idea of the value of their work in this course.

[Successful Intelligence Wrap-Up: PowerPoint slide 14]
[End-of-chapter foreign word: PowerPoint slide 15]
[End-of-chapter thought-provoking quote: PowerPoint slide 16]

****

CREATE COMMUNITY

DISCUSSION STARTERS

1. Ask students to think of how they got into college. Did their practical or creative intelligence play a part?
2. Ask students who have worked in a job how they've had to apply their analytical, creative, or practical intelligence
3. Present to students this Teacher Challenge: "You have a teacher in a required course that is difficult to understand because he or she has an accent that is unfamiliar to you. The teacher lectures quite a bit and has warned that much of the test will be based on the lecture. So far, your class notes aren't very clear. You're not sure what to do. Develop a plan of action to ensure that you can get through the class successfully."

GROUP EXERCISES

Teamwork: Create Solutions Together – *Motivators*

This exercise, found at the end of chapter 1 in the text, is a group brainstorming exercise. Follow the directions in the text, asking students to pass papers with motivation blockers listed. Students are to generate ways to overcome the blockers. To summarize the activity, students are to jot three specific actions in their text that they will commit to taking.

Who Can Help You?

Every school is unique and offers its own particular range of opportunities. Ask students to investigate your school, using their student handbook or other literature as well as legwork and the school's Web site to personally call, e-mail, or visit locations.

- First, give each student a copy of the *Who Can Help You?* handout on p. 56 of this IM chapter and have them make a check mark by the resources that they think will be most helpful to them.
- Work together as a class. Each member of the class should choose one or more different resources, making sure no two people within a group explore the same resource. (If there are additional important resources on your campus that are not listed on the handout, be sure to include them.)
- Instruct group members to investigate their resources and fill in the information on the grid located on the handout.
- After each person has completed his or her investigation, meet again in groups to exchange information. Have students brainstorm a way to combine all the information together (for example, by using a copy machine to create one document out of all the index cards, or perhaps a volunteer could use a computer to create a table of the information). This exercise allows campus investigation of resources available to students at your school. The end result will be a comprehensive resource guide for your entire class.

Self-Perception Exploration

To demonstrate the effect of labels, try this exercise. Divide the class into groups of four or five. Take any classic brain-teaser puzzle of medium difficulty (see, for instance, www.puzzlemaster.com), and place a copy face down in the center of each group's table. Tell half the groups, privately, that highly-trained engineers took three minutes to solve the puzzle. Tell the remaining groups, privately, that average 10-year-olds solved the problem within 30-40 minutes. Normally, the groups that compare themselves to the smartest people will give up more readily than those comparing themselves with the 10-year-olds. Discuss the results with the class and analyze why they gave up or refused to do so. Ask whether they had any negative thoughts about their ability to complete the task and have them write down what they said to themselves. Now ask if they would say that same thing to another person in the group or to someone they care about.

Name Game

One of the keys to retention is helping students develop a sense of connection with the college. A first step in this direction is to have everyone learn the names of everyone in the class. To do this, we recommend that you play a name game. There are several variations on this theme. The simplest is to have students form a circle. The first student states his or her name, the second student says his or her name and then repeats the first student's name, and so on, until the last person repeats all the names. Any group larger than 30 will take too long and will be too difficult to remember, so you should consider breaking the class into groups (takes approximately 10 minutes).

Variations of the Name Game:

- Have students couple their name with an adjective or location that starts with the same sound as the first letter of their name. "Hi, I'm Buffalo Bob." "Hi, I'm Kingston Kunal."

- Divide students into pairs and have them interview each other. Have them find out interesting, memorable things about their partners. At the conclusion of the exercise, have them introduce their classmates. (This exercise takes a bit longer.)

Syllabus Jeopardy

This quick game can ensure that students understand key parts of your syllabus. Divide into three or four teams. Craft answers from your syllabus. You can create categories, such as Grading and Attendance policies, About the Course, Class Rules, Assignment Schedules, and so on. One student from each team has to respond to a statement such as, "Three of these count as one absence." Students answer in a question format, such as "What is a tardy?" If you like, you can give extra-credit points to the "team" that wins. There is a similar game available online at the text's Companion Web site.

Optional follow-up: Give a short syllabus test that counts for a grade at the end of the first week of class.

Self-Esteem, Motivation, and Learning

This exercise helps students analyze how they talk negatively to themselves when they haven't met certain internal standards. ("I should have ....." "Why didn't I...?") Students can become their own worst enemy, berating themselves harshly and unnecessarily.

Have students each write one negative phrase on a slip of paper, a phrase they have said to themselves recently. They should not include their names. Collect them quickly and read them aloud to the class. Ask a few rhetorical questions: How would you feel if someone else said these things to you? Would you speak that way to people you care about? Four strategies can help students improve their thinking:

- Stop negative talk in its tracks and change it to positive talk.

- Take a moment every day to pay yourself a general compliment.

- Replace words of obligation (I should) with words of personal intent (I will).

- Note your successes.

POP CULTURE LINKS

Movies: Look to movies for images of success, responsibility, and hard work. Think about referencing films like the original Rocky, any documentary about climbing Mt. Everest (such as Everest: The Other Side), Walk the Line, Coal Miner's Daughter, Hoop Dreams. Ask students about the movies they know that have inspirational stories.

Music: What music do you find motivating? Tell students about what music you play when you work, when you exercise, or any other time that you need a boost to keep you in forward motion. Ask them for their own examples. Discuss what about the music is motivating – is it the words, the rhythm, the tune? You may even want to have a listening day where each student brings in a song that is special to him or her and explains why it is significant and powerful. **Extra-special idea if you or a tech-savvy student have the capability: Make a class CD containing everyone's significant songs, and hand it out toward the end of the term.

SUCCESSFUL INTELLIGENCE EXERCISES

Get Analytical! *Assess Yourself as an Analytical Thinker*
Assign for in-class activity or homework. As students begin this text and course they will need to have a clear understanding of analytical thinking and their own skills in this area. Encourage them to take this first of many self-assessments seriously. Remind them that looking at themselves clearly will help them see places to improve. Tell students that they will not be graded and you will not necessarily know the outcome of the self-assessments in the textbook. After a short pep talk, have students circle the numbers from 1 for "not at all true for me" to 5 for "very true for me."

Get Creative! *Assess Yourself as a Creative Thinker*

Assign as homework. As noted above, encourage students to take this self-assessment seriously. Have them complete each item, circling 1 for "not at all true for me" to 5 for "very true for me."

Get Practical! *Assess Yourself as a Practical Thinker*

Assign for in-class activity or homework. This is the third in the series of self-assessments relating to successful intelligence. Have them complete each item, circling 1 for "not at all true for me" to 5 for "very true for me."

HOMEWORK

In-text exercises: All three successful intelligence exercises (*Get Analytical*, *Get Creative*, and *Get Practical*) can be assigned for homework.

Foreign word response: Every chapter of the textbook ends with a foreign word that implies a response to successful intelligence and the application of skills learned in the chapter. Approach these words positively. We know many are hard to pronounce, but it is important link to the global martketplace concepts in the text and incorporates diversity in our approach to teaching and understanding others. In this first chapter, it is "egyszer volt budán kutyavásár." The phrase is Hungarian and the text includes an English interpretation of the meaning. Have a student read the meaning out loud. A possible homework assignment related to this word includes assigning a responsive essay. Essay prompts can include: "Write a short essay describing your goals and dreams for your college future" or "How are you planning to take initiative this school year with your college responsibilities" or "What skills have you learned so far in school that have helped you this far." Write these prompts on the board or on PowerPoint slides so students can copy them into journals or onto paper.

End-of-chapter exercises:
- **Successful Intelligence: Think, Create, Apply** – Students are to complete the self-assessment assignment based on Robert Sternberg's *self-activators*. After self evaluation, students are to pick five self-activators that need development and write an e-mail or journal entry to remind themselves that they are working with focus on that particular area.
- **Writing: Journal and Put Skills to Work** – Students can complete the journal entry as homework. Students are to journal about their decisions to attend college and goals for the experience. The real-life writing assignment – Initial impressions – is an enjoyable exercise, because students can return to it at the end of the term and compare their first impressions with their actual experiences.
- **Personal Portfolio:** This assignment is the first of a series of handouts available in this Instructors Manual. They are to be distributed to students and kept either in a folder by the teacher or by students themselves. Emphasize that these portfolio assignments are designed for their use in the future. Encourage students to complete them neatly. You may decide not to write on them, but make comments on a separate sheet of paper or on the back, allowing the students to keep them neat for presentation to future employers. You may consider using the accompanying handout on p. 61 of this manual.

QUOTES FOR REFLECTION

Use these quotes to generate discussion, start class, or offer as a short exercise. Have students reflect on what any or all of the following quotes mean to them in a short paper or presentation.

I know the price of success: dedication, hard work, and an unremitting devotion to the things you want to see happen.
Frank Lloyd Wright

My motto was always to keep swinging. Whether I was in a slump or feeling badly or having trouble off the field, the only thing to do was keep swinging.
Hank Aaron

A journey of a thousand miles must begin with a single step.
Lao Tzu

Dig a well before you are thirsty.
Chinese Proverb

When I rest I rust.
German saying

The things taught in schools and colleges are not an education, but the means of an education.
Ralph Waldo Emerson

The thing always happens that you really believe in; and the belief in a thing makes it happen.
Frank Lloyd Wright

Here is the test to find whether your mission on earth is finished: If you're alive, it isn't.
Richard Bach

HANDOUTS

The following are exercises with handouts, or handouts that you can use on their own. Integrate them into your lesson plan as you see fit, or follow the suggestions in the "Communicate Content" section.

- A Shield and a Symbol for Life (exercise with handout)
- Who Can Help You? (handout to accompany group exercise on p. 56)
- GPA Practice (handout)
- Common Reasons Why Students Don't Do Well in School (handout)
- Top Ten Difficulties Going from High School to College (handout)
- Personal Portfolio handout to accompany chapter 1 Personal Portfolio exercise

A Shield and a Symbol for Life

Materials:

1. Have example symbols ready.
2. Handout: *A Shield and a Symbol for Life*

Process:

In this exercise, students create a symbol that will assist them in remembering and reaching their goals. Grab their attention by showing students pictures of different symbols (stop sign, garbage can, traffic light, happy face, etc.). Elicit the meaning of the symbols. Lead into a discussion on how symbols can be a quick reminder to perform a certain task. Ask the students to make up a symbol to remind someone to put the cap back on the toothpaste (share different responses). Hand out *A Shield and a Symbol for Life* and have them complete it. Once finished, have students present their symbols.

Name _____ Date _____

A SHIELD AND A SYMBOL FOR LIFE

Directions:
1. Answer the questions in the shield.
2. Add any related information to the given topics.
3. Create a symbol that will help you recall the information in your shield.

Hint: Your symbol should be a simple picture that inspires you to succeed!

Education

Where am I coming from?

Why am I here?

Where do I want to be?

Success

How am I going to get where I want to be?

What do I need to do to get there?

Self-Esteem

How will I maintain a positive atmosphere?

How am I going to believe?

Preparation for Change

What will I need to do to adjust?

Name _____Date _____

WHO CAN HELP YOU?

The following checklist shows resources that your school may offer to students. First, make a check mark by the resources that you think will be most helpful to you. Use the blank spaces at the bottom to fill in resources your school offers that are not listed here.

_____ Advisors and counselors   _____ Adult education center   _____ Library

_____ Support groups/hotlines   _____ Instructors   _____ Administration

_____ Career/job placement office   _____ Clubs/organizations   _____ Bulletin boards

_____ Academic centers   _____ Student health center   _____ School publications

_____ Student government   _____ Housing and transportation   _____ Tutoring

_____ Wellness/fitness centers   _____ Financial aid office   _____ Int'l. student office

_____ Services for students with disabilities _____ English as a second language _____ _____

_____ _____ _____ _____ _____ _____

Then, use the grid to fill in information on the resources you are assigned to investigate.

Resource	Who provides it?	Where can you find it?	When is it available?	How can it help you?	How do you ask for it?	Phone # and/or e-mail address

Name _____Date _____

GPA PRACTICE

How does the grading system work?

Letter grades are given a numerical value, called "grade points," that are multiplied by the number of credits you receive for the class in which you earn that grade.

Grade	Grade points per credit
A	4.0
B	3.0
C	2.0
D	1.0
F	0.0
W	0.0

Note: *Always* talk with your instructor before you withdraw.

To determine your grade point average (GPA):

1. List the grade you make in each class.
2. Determine the grade points for each grade.
3. Multiply this number by the semester hour credits for each class. For example, if you received a B (3 grade points per credit) in a 3 credit hour class, you calculate: 3 x 3= 9 grade points.
4. Add all of your grade points for all courses you took in the term.
5. Divide the total grade points by your total class hours.
6. This is your GPA or grade point average.

Practice using the following sheet.

Use sample report cards to practice calculating a grade point average (GPA).

1. Add semester hour credits.
2. Add total grade points.
3. Divide the total grade points by the total semester hours credit. Your result is the GPA.

Calculate the GPA for the following report cards. For the first, grade points per semester hour are entered for you. For the second, enter grade points per semester hour in addition to total grade points.

Class	Semester Hours Credit	Grade Received	Grade Points per Sem. Hour	Total Grade Points
English	3	B	3	_____
Physics	3	D	1	_____
Economics	3	A	4	_____
Chemistry	5	C	2	_____
Psychology	3	F	0	_____
Total	_____			_____

Class	Semester Hours Credit	Grade Received	Grade Points per Sem. Hour	Total Grade Points
English	3	A	_____	_____
Math	3	F	_____	_____
Comm.	2	B	_____	_____
History	3	C	_____	_____
Art	4	W	_____	_____
Total	_____		_____	_____

Total and divide. Show your work!

Deborah Maness, Pre-Curriculum Instructor, Wake Technical Community College, Raleigh, North Carolina.

Common Reasons Why Students Don't Do Well in School

1. Sleeping late.

2. Absences.

3. Partying instead of studying.

4. Looking at the book instead of studying and learning.

5. Losing books, assignments, and papers.

6. Procrastinating on assignments.

7. Tuning out in class.

8. Taking classes out of sequence.

9. Overloading with too many classes.

10. Accepting too many tasks out of school -- friends, clubs, religious organizations, work hours.

11. Not using time well – wasting minutes/hours.

12. Slow reading.

13. Lack of understanding of material.

14. Weak vocabulary.

15. Lack of support groups – babysitters, study help.

16. Family distractions – sick children, bad relationships.

17. Lack of transportation – and alternatives.

18. Not reading assignments.

19. Not willing to learn – to put forth effort/hard work.

20. Poor note-taking skills.

Student-generated under the instruction of
Deborah Maness, Pre-Curriculum Instructor, Wake Technical Community College, Raleigh, North Carolina.

Top Ten Difficulties Going from High School to College

1. I feel unprepared to be so responsible for myself.

2. All this free time – what exactly am I supposed to be doing?

3. I find the workload overwhelming.

4. I don't know how to organize my time.

5. I'm not good at meeting new people. Making friends is difficult for me.

6. I no longer have my mother and/or father to do some of my work for me.

7. I do not like to tell people about my struggles in the classroom.

8. I couldn't get the courses I want to take.

9. I can't handle failure. What do I do if I'm failing a course at the end of the term?

10. I get too distracted – how can I focus?

Student-generated under the instruction of
Deborah Maness, Pre-Curriculum Instructor, Wake Technical Community College, Raleigh, North Carolina.

PERSONAL PORTFOLIO ACTIVITY # 1
SETTING CAREER GOALS

❶ First, brainstorm everything that you wish you could be, do, have, or experience in your career 10 years from now - the skills you want to have, money you want to earn, benefits, experiences, travel, anything you can think of. List, draw, or cut out pictures from magazines.
❷ Next, group all of these ideas into 3 different groups: Priority 1, Priority 2, Priority 3.
❸ Finally, answer the questions below.

Priority 1	Priority 2	Priority 3

What do your priority lists tell you about what is most important to you?

_____
_____
_____
_____

What wishes are you ready to work toward right now?

_____
_____
_____
_____

Circle or highlight the three highest-priority wishes. Write down any trade-offs you will have to make today to make these wishes come true.

_____
_____
_____
_____

CONSIDER COMPREHENSION

REVIEW WITH STUDENTS BEFORE YOU BEGIN THE NEXT CHAPTER:

- What are the three parts of successful intelligence and how can I build "intelligence"?
- How do fears and self-perception affect esteem, motivation, and learning?
- What does it mean to be a successfully intelligent student?
- Definitions for *emotional intelligence, successful intelligence* and *diversity*.

Chapter One Vocabulary Quiz Answer Key
(Quiz appears on following page)

1. G
2. A
3. J
4. C
5. H
6. D
7. O
8. F
9. M
10. I
11. L
12. E
13. N
14. K
15. B

CHAPTER ONE VOCABULARY QUIZ

1. ____ global marketplace

2. ____ inert intelligence

3. ____ analytical thinking

4. ____ creative thinking

5. ____ practical thinking

6. ____ syllabus

7. ____ persistence

8. ____ motivation

9. ____ self-esteem

10. ____ academic integrity

11. ____ diversity

12. ____ emotional intelligence

13. ____ social intelligence

14. ____ learning disability

15. ____ lifelong learners

B. Individuals who continue to build knowledge and skills as a mechanism for improving their lives and careers

C. Involves generating new and different ideas and approaches to problems

D. A comprehensive outline of course topics and assignments

E. The ability to perceive, assess, and manage one's own emotions

F. A goal-directed force that moves a person to action

G. An interconnected marketplace, where companies all over the world compete for business

H. Putting what you have learned into action in order to solve a problem or make a decision

I. Following a code of moral values, prizing honesty and fairness in all aspects of academic life

J. Commonly known as critical thinking, involves evaluating information

K. A neurological disorder that interferes with one's ability to store, process, and produce information

L. Differences among people as well as within each person

M. Belief in your value as a person that builds as you achieve your goals

N. The ability to understand and manage the complexity of social interaction

O. The act of continuing steadfastly in a course of action

A. Passive recall and analysis of learned information

CHAPTER ONE ASSESSMENT

Multiple Choice
Circle or highlight the answer that seems to fit best.

1. College graduates, on the average,
    a. have a greater chance of being unemployed than high school graduates.
    b. earn approximately $20,000 more per year than individuals with a high school diploma.
    c. are less likely to have well paying, highly skilled jobs.
    d. have decreased employability and earning potential.

2. Which of the following is the BEST example of *successful intelligence?*
    a. Scoring high on an IQ test
    b. Effortlessly recalling vocabulary words for an exam
    c. Passing your exams with high scores
    d. Creating and implementing an action plan to reach an educational goal

3. Which of the following is the BEST example of applying analytical thinking to career exploration?
    a. Evaluating results of interest inventories with a career counselor
    b. Creating a dream career
    c. Considering what major will be the quickest to complete
    d. Asking the academic advisor to select which career would be the best fit for you

4. *Syllabus* can be defined as
    a. an outline of course topics and assignments, including due dates.
    b. the topic and page listings found at the beginning of your texts.
    c. a college-wide list of important dates and deadlines for each term.
    d. a schedule of class offerings.

5. Motivation is
    a. externally driven by others in your life.
    b. a goal-directed force that moves individuals to action.
    c. the act of continuing to pursue a course of action, regardless of obstacles or challenges, never considering a mid-course change.
    d. the primary building block of academic success.

6. To get motivated, a successfully intelligent student requires
    a. the drive to create and pursue a plan of action that involves analytical, creative, and practical actions needed to achieve a goal.
    b. a reward if he/she studies for a test and achieves the academic goal he/she set for that test.
    c. ignoring past mistakes.
    d. strong encouragement from people he or she respects.

7. Self-esteem is
    a. the belief in yourself that helps you stay motivated to achieve your goals.
    b. defined as analytical, creative and practical intelligence.

      c.   only needed when you are starting something new.

      d.   none of the above.

8.   Choosing to act with integrity has which effects?

      a.   It adds to your self-esteem as you follow academic guidelines.

      b.   It forces you to learn assigned material.

      c.   It makes you part of a community of students who respect one another and behave ethically.

      d.   All of the above

9.   We as individuals often interact, both at school and work, with others who have a variety of backgrounds and personal experiences. These differences reflect cultural

      a.   ethnocentricity.

      b.   ethnicity.

      c.   heritage.

      d.   diversity.

10.   According to Daniel Goleman, what two combined components define social intelligence?

      a.   Social awareness and social facility

      b.   Personal awareness and societal ease

      c.   Social awareness and social etiquette

      d.   Social acceptance and social ability

11.   Which is a characteristic of a lifelong learner?

      a.   Keeping an open mind during new experiences and learning from diversity

      b.   Continually increasing your knowledge

      c.   Taking risks to reach goals

      d.   All of the above

12.   When facing your fears, which of the following actions is most helpful?

      a.   Acknowledge your fears and work to overcome them.

      b.   Talk about your fears.

      c.   Think about other, happier thoughts.

      d.   None of the above

13. The benefits of working with one or more people include all of the following EXCEPT
    a. increased motivation.
    b. increased ability to find ways to work with different kinds of people.
    c. waiting until the last minute to benefit from the group.
    d. increased awareness and understanding of how practical intelligence contributes to success in group activities.

14. One can learn from failures and mistakes by
    a. analyzing what happened.
    b. coming up with creative ways to improve the situation.
    c. getting upset and frustrated.
    d. a and b only.

15. Which is NOT a key to motivation?
    a. Making a commitment
    b. Developing positive habits
    c. Buying yourself expensive incentives
    d. Building your self-esteem

True/False

Determine whether the statement is true or false, and circle or highlight the answer.

1. Successful intelligence requires critical, practical, and analytical skills.
   True
   False

2. The skills needed in the global marketplace can be acquired only after gaining the basics by attending college.
   True
   False

3. Earning a college degree will guarantee that you will find and keep a highly-skilled, well-paying job.
   True
   False

4. *Successful intelligence* appears to predict life success more than traditional IQ tests because it focuses on what you *do* to achieve your goals, rather than just recall and analysis.
   True
   False

5. *Persistence* is the act of continuing to stay focused on an action.
   True
   False

6. Academic integrity promotes getting good grades over learning.
   True
   False

7. You can learn from failure by analyzing what happened and creating ways to improve the situation.
   True
   False

8. Attention Deficit Disorder (ADD) is not categorized as a learning disability.
   True
   False

9. Diversity refers to the differences among or within individuals.
   True
   False

10. Being a lifelong learner is an important characteristic of career success.
    True
    False

Fill in the Blank

Insert the word or phrase that BEST completes the sentence.

1. College is the ideal time to acquire skills that will serve you in the _____ _____.

2. College students who analyze and evaluate information, generate new and different approaches to solving problems, and make action plans to solve a problem are using _____ _____.

3. To be prepared for college success, you will need to be _____ as well as _____ to achieve your goals.

4. Academic integrity can be defined as following a code of moral values, prizing _____ and _____ in all aspects of academic life.

5. _____ refers to the differences between ourselves and others, but also the differences within individuals.

6. Emotional intelligence is a set of _____ and _____ competencies that allows individuals to understand and manage the complexity of social interactions.

7. _____ learning refers to the ability to maintain the kind of flexibility that will enable you to adapt to the demands of the global marketplace.

8. _____ intelligence is passive recall and analysis of learned information rather than goal-directed thinking linked to real-world activities.

9. Being honest, responsible, trustworthy, fair, and respectful are fundamental values for students with _____ _____.

10. _____ thinking means taking unique approaches to problems and seeing the world from a different perspective.

Short Answer

1. Briefly explain the three components of successful intelligence.

2. What are the benefits of being able to successfully work in groups?

3. Define *syllabus*. What information will a syllabus provide for a student?

Essay

1. How is the global marketplace changing the challenges for workplace success in today's world?

2. Explain Robert J. Sternberg's view of intelligence and why he believes intelligence is not a fixed quantity. Then, explain whether or not you agree with him, and support your position with at least two personal examples.

4. How can acknowledging fears increase your self-esteem? Discuss a time in your life when you had to "face your fear." What was the outcome?

5. What was your score on the analytical thinker assessment? How do you plan to improve your score? Be specific.

Word Exploration

Define this phrase: *egyszer volt budán kutyavásár* (edge-zehr volt bu-darn ku-tcho-vah-shahr)

What does this word mean to you? How does it apply to your life?

Chapter One Assessment Answer Key

Multiple Choice

Test Item Assesses This Learning Objective/Topic

1. b   Where Are You Now--and Where Can College Take You?
   Life success goal: Increased employability and earning potential

2. d   How Can Successful Intelligence Help You Achieve Your Goals?

3. a   How Can Successful Intelligence Help You Achieve Your Goals?
   Defining successful intelligence

4. a   What Actions Will Prepare You for College Success?

5. b   What Actions Will Prepare You for College Success?
   Get motivated

6. a   What Actions Will Prepare You for College Success?
   Get motivated

7. a   What Actions Will Prepare You for College Success?
   Get motivated: Build self-esteem

8. d   What Actions Will Prepare You for College Success?
   Practice academic integrity

9. d   How Can You Work Effectively With Others? *Value diversity*

10. a.   What Actions Will Prepare You for College Success?
    Develop emotional and social intelligence

11. d   How Can The Things You Learn Now Promote Life Success?

12. a   What Actions Will Prepare You for College Success?
    Get motivated

13. c   How Can You Work Effectively With Others?
    Know how to work with others in groups

14. d   What Actions Will Prepare You for College Success?
    Learn from failure and celebrate success

15. c   What Actions Will Prepare You for College Success?
    Get motivated

True/False

Test item assesses this learning objective/topic

1. F   Successful Intelligence Preview

2. F   Where Are You Now – And Where Can College Take You?

3. F   Where Are You Now – And Where Can College Take You?
   Life success goal: Increased employability and earning potential

4. T   How Can Successful Intelligence Help You Achieve Your Goals?
   Defining successful intelligence

5. T   How Can Successful Intelligence Help You Achieve Your Goals?

Defining successful intelligence

6. F   What Actions Will Prepare You for College Success?
Academic integrity

7. T   What Actions Will Prepare You for College Success?
Learn from failure and celebrate success

8. T   What Actions Will Prepare You for College Success?
Understand and manage learning disabilities

9. T   How Can You Work Effectively With Others? *Valuing diversity*

10. T   How Can the Things You Learn Now Promote Life Success?

Fill in the Blank

	Test item assesses this learning objective/topic
1. *global marketplace*	Where Are You Now – And Where Can College Take You?
2. *successful intelligence*	How Can Successful Intelligence Help You Achieve Your Goals?
3. *responsible and accountable*	What Actions Will Prepare You For College Success?
4. *honesty and fairness*	Marginal definition of academic integrity
5. *Diversity*	How Can You Work Effectively With Others? *Valuing diversity*
6. *personal and social*	How Can You Work Effectively With Others? *Develop emotional and social intelligence*
7. *Lifelong*	How Can The Things You Learn Now Promote Life Success?
8. *Inert*	What Actions Will Prepare You for College Success?
9. *academic integrity*	What Actions Will Prepare You For College Success? *Practice academic integrity*
10. *creative*	How Can Successful Intelligence Help You Achieve Your Goals?

Values, Goals and Time
Managing Yourself

BRIEF CHAPTER OVERVIEW

This chapter discusses self-management skills. First, it explores what values are and how personal values affect students' choices in setting goals, managing time, and managing college stress. These skills form a foundation for success in college and in life.

The chapter has four main headings: Values, Goals, Major Selection, and Time Management. It is essential that students are able to differentiate between values and goals, as they are closely related and easily confused. Values drive goals, so clarifying values will help students realize their goals more effectively. Goals that clash with values often result in stress. The time management strategies introduced in the text do work, but often students aren't sure they're worth using. Assign homework and in-class work so students have opportunities to apply time management skills. Revisit the self-management topics later in the course--especially after the first wave of tests and before finals.

Note the successful intelligence skills your students will build in chapter 2:

Analytical	Creative	Practical
▪ Examining your values	▪ Developing ideas for how to reach a goal	▪ How to set effective goals
▪ Analyzing how you manage time	▪ Creating ways to avoid procrastination	▪ How to achieve a goal
▪ Considering what goals are most important to you	▪ Brainstorming what majors interest you	▪ How to manage a schedule

CHAPTER TWO OUTLINE

Why Is It Important to Know What You Value?

- How Values Affect Your Educational Experience
- Values and Cultural Diversity

How Do You Set and Achieve Goals?

- Set Long-Term Goals
- Set Short-Term Goals
- Prioritize Goals
- Work to Achieve Goals

How Can You Begin to Explore Majors?

- Short-Term Goal #1: Use Self-Assessments to Identify Interests and Talents
- Short-Term Goal #2: Explore Academic Options
- Short-Term Goal #3: Establish Your Academic Schedule
- Be Flexible As You Come to a Decision

How Can You Effectively Manage Your Time?

- Identify Your Time-Related Needs and Preferences
- Build a Schedule
- Use Scheduling Techniques
- Fight Procrastination
- Be Flexible
- Manage Stress by Managing Time

COMMUNICATE CONTENT
TOPICS COVERED IN THE CHAPTER

[Chapter intro with chapter 1 review: PowerPoint slides 1, 2, 3]

The *Real Questions, Practical Answers* Discussion Starter Question:
How can I choose a major that is right for me? [PowerPoint slide 4]

Read the questions from student Courtney Mellblom aloud together (assign paragraphs, ask for a volunteer, or read yourself). Ask for a show of hands from students on majors: **How many of you have declared a major? How many of you are just not sure yet, but have an idea? How many of you have NO CLUE what you want to study?** Make a chart on the board of those who are sure, not sure and no idea, using tick marks, not names. This will give visual students an idea of where they fall within the larger class grouping on major decision. Reemphasize that this course should help those who have no clue and affirm those who are already declared.

Ask those students who are sure of their major how they decided what to major in: **How much impact did your parents have in declaring your major? How much impact did high school or college courses have in deciding your major?** At this point, it is good to share your own story. How did you, as an instructor, decide what to major in? Give students a few silent minutes to read the professional answer to Courtney's question. (If they have already read it, ask them to go back and underline or highlight parts of the professional answer they feel are significant.)

After silent reading, solicit responses: **What part of the advice do you think is right on? What part encouraged you as you search for your major? Those of you who have no clue about a major, how do you feel now? Does the professional advice help you at all?** (Be prepared for negative answers – take them in flow and encourage students that the text will begin to address their negative feelings and, hopefully, take them in a positive direction.)

(For more discussion starters, see p. 79 of this IM chapter.)

Question 1: Why Is It Important to Know What You Value?

[Section outline: PowerPoint 5]

One of the main reasons students drop out of college is because of poor self-management skills. Poor self-management refers to a mismatch between a person's values and their goals, a lack of clear and concise goals, and misuse of time—any and all of which can lead to stress. This chapter and your teaching can keep students from falling victim to this trap.

Values help us to understand what we want out of life, build "rules" for life, and find people who inspire us. Value decisions are difficult and take time. This chapter provides many opportunities for classroom dialogue because of the inherent questioning involved in establishing values and goals. **[See PowerPoint slides 6 and 7.]** Review the questions in the text with the class:

- Where did the value come from?
- What other different values could I consider?
- What might happen as a result of adopting this value?
- Have I made a personal commitment to this choice?
- Have I told others about it?
- Do my life goals and day-to-day actions reflect it? **[See PowerPoint slide 8.]**

(Consider using the "Discovering What is Important" exercise and handout on p. 85 of this IM chapter.)

The section on values and diversity is important to cover. Often, a diversity panel in the classroom is effective. Consider inviting a group of students representing different interest groups and nationalities into the classroom. Facilitate an even exchange and question and answer period – everyone will benefit if this is done with a willingness to learn and explore each other's cultures.

(Consider using the "Values Observation" exercise on p. 79 of this IM chapter.)

 # Question 2: How Do You Set and Achieve Goals?

[Section outline: PowerPoint slide 9]

Let students know that establishing individual goals helps make them achievable. By stating them or writing them down, they've taken the first step in achieving the goal. Talk about the two categories of goals and how they reinforce one another. **[See PowerPoint slide 10.]**

(Consider using the "Goal Setting Now and Later" exercise on p 81 of this IM chapter.)

(Consider using the "Setting Goals" exercise and handout on p. 86 of this IM chapter.)

1) <u>Long-term goals</u> – goals with large scope, intended to be attained over a relatively long period of time – 6 months or longer.

   Examples: To earn a college degree, to achieve proficiency in a trade, to run a marathon, to write a book.

   Writing out a goal statement helps a student clarify the goal. Writing goals along with value statements is a very significant experience for students and will help them grasp one key to this chapter: the difference between values and goals! Goals should reflect personal values or the clash will cause stress.

2) <u>Short-term goals</u> – goals with a narrow focus, intended to be attained over a short period of time – a day, a week, two weeks, a month.

Examples: To pass a class, to earn a good grade on a proficiency exam, to run three times a week, to write an essay.

<u>Short-Term Goals Build the Path Toward Long-Term Goals</u>. Emphasize that knowing the long-term goal is only the beginning. Say, for instance, a student wants a particular grade point average in a course by midterm. He or she needs to set and prioritize short-term goals – including completing assignments on time, making particular grades on quizzes, being in class – to make this long-term goal a reality.

Show students how to **prioritize** goals. When prioritizing, it is important to consider values, personal situation and time commitments. Point out:

- Priorities focus your energy on what's most important at any given moment.
- Priorities help you organize your goals, paying attention to the most important first.
- Priorities mean power – you choose and control what is important.

There is practical advice at the end of this chapter for getting "unstuck" if you hit a roadblock in working to achieve goals. **[See PowerPoint slide 11.]**

(Consider using the "Goals Exercise" exercise on p. 80 of this IM chapter.)

(Consider using the "Teamwork: Create Solutions Together – Multiple Paths to a Goal" exercise from the end of the text chapter, described on p. 79 of this IM chapter.)

 # Question 3: How Can You Begin to Explore Majors?

[Section outline: PowerPoint slide 12]
There are numerous resources on your campus for major and career explorations – faculty, advisors, other students, and friends to name a few. Advisors or career counselors make excellent guest speakers at this point in the course. Encourage students to use the Internet and college catalog to explore majors available at your school.

The text outlines three short-term goals for exploring a major:

1. <u>Use self-assessments to identify interests and talents</u>. Consider the questions:
   - What are my favorite courses?
   - What do these courses have in common?
   - What subjects interest me when I read?
   - What activities do I look forward to?
   - Am I a "natural" in any academic or skill area?
   - What do people say I do well?
   - How do I learn most effectively?

2. <u>Explore academic options</u>. Practical advice includes talking to the people who can help and visiting the department. Consider the questions:
   - When do I have to declare a major?
   - What are my options in majoring?
   - What majors are offered at my school?
   - What minimum grade point average does the department require before it will accept me as a major?
   - What GPA must I maintain in the courses included in the major?
   - What prerequisites are required?
   - What courses will I be required to take and in what sequence?
   - Should I consider a minor?

3. <u>Establish your academic schedule</u>. Set timing for short-term goals, identify dates connected to your goal fulfillment, and be flexible as you come to a decision.

(Consider using the "Online Majors Exploration" exercise on p. 80 of this IM chapter.)

(Consider using the "Exploring Career Goals" exercise and handout on p. 87 of this IM chapter.)

 Question 4: How Can You Effectively Manage Your Time?

[Section outline: PowerPoint slide 13]
A primary goal of time management is reaching goals. Look at time management not as a have-to task but as an important part of getting what you want out of school and life. **[See PowerPoint slide 14.]** Go through these points from the text:

1. Identify Your Time-Related Needs and Preferences. Let students know that self-knowledge sets the stage for scheduling and prioritizing. When you know what times of day or length of study sessions work best for you, you can make effective decisions about how to plan your time. The steps:
   - Create a personal time "profile."
   - Evaluate the effects of your profile.
   - Establish what schedule preferences suit your profile best.

2. Build a Schedule. This process is an extension of goal-setting skills set to smaller increments of time that helps students manage what they do on a day-to-day basis, and ensures that they'll advance toward their long-term goals.

Example: If the long-term goal for the term is to pass 12 credit hours, the short-term goals that determine the schedule may be to attend classes, establish periods to study individually and with a study group, schedule reasonable breaks, and get adequate sleep. The result: a controlled schedule and achievable goals.

To help students get a more accurate read on how they spend their time, assign the "Discover How You Spend Your Time" exercise from the end of the text chapter. Give them a week to complete and then discuss results as a class or in small groups or pairs.

(In conjunction with the "Discover How You Spend Your Time" exercise, consider using the "Making and Measuring Predictions" exercise on p. 81 of this IM chapter.)

(Consider using the "Time Management Game" exercise on p. 80 of this IM chapter.)

3. **Choose a Planning Tool That Works**: The key to successful scheduling is to keep track of tasks by <u>writing them down</u>. Writing everything down helps free the brain from unnecessary clutter and reduces stress. One look at a planner will remind students of their obligations. Different tools work for different students. It doesn't matter if it's a notepad, daily planner, or a PDA.

To illustrate the advantages of a planning tool, have students bring syllabi from each of their courses. Give them 1 ½ minutes to find out what date and time they will have midterms and their first papers due in each of their classes. The students will have to plow through all syllabi to give you an answer (unless they have some type of planning tool in front of them). They are also likely to feel time stress.

The text contains points on what to put in a schedule and how students can align a schedule to mesh with their goals.

4. **Work the Planning Tool**: It doesn't matter how sophisticated the tool is, students who don't have the discipline to use the tool won't benefit. Talk about using the planner to keep track of events and commitments and schedule tasks and activities that support your goals. As an application, have them record the date, time, and place of their midterms and the due dates of their first papers in their planners, calendars, or PDAs. Then assign them the task of developing a short-term plan to prepare for one course's midterm exam

Remind them of the scheduling techniques in the text – including to-do lists, monthly and yearly calendars, taking the time to plan, and avoiding time traps.

5. **Prioritize**: To avoid feeling overwhelmed by responsibilities, good time managers prioritize by evaluating and choosing what's most important at any given time.

Example: Suppose you have a meeting and a study group that overlap one night and you want to go for a run. You know you can't do all three things, so you have to decide what is *most important*. Let's say you need help in the class, you don't have official duties at the meeting, and you'll have more time to work out tomorrow. More than likely, you'll choose the study group. But if you are on the track team and they have a big meet soon, you may opt for the run!

(Consider using the "Conflicting Priorities" exercise on p. 81 of this IM chapter.)

Remind students to prioritize their schedules according to a system of most important to least. Use a 1, 2, and 3; or A, B, and C; or color coding system (note to students: Keep it simple!).

5. **Fight – and Avoid – Procrastination:** Ask students whether they procrastinate, and how they do it (i.e., what they do to avoid doing what they don't want to face). Ask what happens when they procrastinate. Explain why people procrastinate--unrealistic or intimidating goals, no goals at all, lack of self-belief, and fear. All anti-procrastination strategies can be summed up with the phrase "act early and plan for the worst." **[See PowerPoint slides 15-16.]**

Some others in more detail:

- think about the positive effects of completing the task
- ask for help
- don't expect perfection of yourself
- set reasonable goals
- use positive self-talk

- take the first step
- break the task into smaller parts
- reward yourself when the task is accomplished

Explain to students: "Some people believe that they work better under pressure. They say that they are thinking about the task in the meantime. If you fall into this category, it is important that you recognize that you must leave time to do a quality job. If the quality of your work is affected, then you may need to rethink your strategy."

6. **Be Flexible**. Change will always happen. Students need to be able to adjust, overhaul, or throw out plans in response to life's ups and downs.

(Consider using the "Fighting Procrastination" exercise on p. 82 of this IM chapter.)

7. **Manage Stress by Managing Time**. College students are often stressed over so many things, and statistics show that stress levels on campus are rising. **[See PowerPoint slide 17.]**

Make sure students know the definition of stress – stress is a reaction to pressure. Help them understand that <u>any time management technique is a stress reducer</u>. Having tasks and upcoming exams hanging over their heads is one of the biggest stressors for students; when they manage time well, they take some of that pressure off. The text recommends:
- Being realistic about time commitments
- Putting sleep and down time on your schedule
- Actively managing your schedule
- Focusing on one assignment at a time
- Checking things off

Further information on stress appears in the wellness material in chapter 8, but this chapter makes a clear connection between effective time management and reduced stress.

[Successful Intelligence Wrap-Up: PowerPoint slide 18]
[End-of-chapter foreign word: PowerPoint slide 19]
[End-of-chapter thought-provoking quote: PowerPoint slide 20]

****

CREATE COMMUNITY

DISCUSSION STARTERS

1. <u>Values</u>: To help students prioritize values, try this simple activity. You'll need a chalkboard and students will need a pencil and paper. Draw a circle on the board. Explain to the students that the circle represents their life. Inside the circle, they should write what they value most (my integrity, happiness, family, spiritual life, health). Next, draw a circle around the first circle. Inside that space, ask students to write additional things they value, but ones that are not as important as the first items (time for vacations, time to socialize, autonomy). Finally, draw a third circle around the first two. In the space between the second and third circles, ask students to list those values that they want as a part of their life, but are not crucial to their happiness (learn about other cultures, be of service to your community, develop new ways to express yourself). If there is time, share the results in pairs or in small groups.
2. <u>Goals</u>: Ask students to share their goals for the day, week, or month aloud with the class. Sharing goals aloud builds community and helps the students hold each other accountable for goals.
3. <u>Majors</u>: Refer to the initial discussion about majors.
4. <u>Time</u>: Ask students whether they procrastinate, and what form of procrastination they use (i.e., what they do to avoid doing what they don't want to face).

GROUP EXERCISES

Teamwork: Create Solutions Together – *Multiple Paths to a Goal*

This exercise, found at the end of chapter 2 in the text, puts students in groups to brainstorm academic goals. Students are to pick one of the goals after brainstorming together and explore multiple paths to the goal. Clearly explain the process of this group exercise so that students know that they need to devote individual attention to the goal BEFORE they come back together to share goal-achieving strategies. Make sure students have the text open during this activity so they can review the process of setting a timetable, being accountable, and getting unstuck.

Values Observation

A very simple yet effective exercise for values observation is to simply distribute large posterboards and markers to student groups. (You are encouraged to use creative methods to form groups, including organizing by zip code, by birth month, by letters in middle name, and so on, so that students are constantly mixing and not grouping themselves.) On one posterboard write the word VALUES across the middle in large letters. On another, write the word GOALS and on a third write TIME-WASTERS. Simply distribute the posterboards, have student brainstorm and write. After a period of a few minutes, have students pass the posterboard to the next group. Each group should write on each posterboard.

When finished, collect posterboards and read them aloud. Make observations about what appears on each. This exercise may show that students are still confused about the distinction between values and goals. In addition, it may show that they same item may appear on each posterboard.

Goals Exercise

Try this after your class completes the *Get Creative!* in-text exercise: Have students pair up. Ask them to share feedback on each other's paths to the goals they laid out in the exercise. Write questions such as these on the board, overhead transparency or PowerPoint, and ask students to talk through them (and any others that they come up with):

- Is the path realistic?
- Is the path complete?
- Is the goal clearly defined?
- Are the goals clearly prioritized?

When you call students back to attention, have each group share with the class the results of the conversation and mutual evaluation.

Online Majors Exploration

Ask students to select three majors of interest to them. Have students visit the Student Success Supersite for more majors and career exploration. Ask them to compare information gained at the site to what they already know. Have students with common interests gather in groups and compare information.

Time Management Game

This game requires a large open area and five small balls or beanbags. It simulates the challenges of managing a typical college course load. Tell the class the purpose of the exercise. Everyone stands in a circle in an open area. Hold one ball or beanbag and keep the rest close by in a large pocket or bag. Explain that the exercise will happen twice, and that the ball cannot be thrown to someone who's already touched it. Throw a ball gently to one person in the circle. That person must throw the ball to a second person. The ball will keep in motion, going from person to person with no one person catching the ball twice until it returns to the instructor. Then you say, "After the ball returns to me, we will throw it again in exactly the same order. Remember from whom you got it and to whom you throw it."

As the ball goes around the circle again, you may want to comment on how the group is doing. Once the ball is returned to you, throw the ball again. After about two throws, pull out a second ball and warn the class to "Keep the same order." Throw the second ball to the first recipient. The third, fourth, and fifth balls follow. Often, after the second ball, chaos ensues. If this happens, stop the game and start over. After two or three tries, either the group is able to send all five balls around or you'll need to stop the game.

Discussion: Ask why the game was so difficult the second time. Students typically point out that there was more than one ball in play and they weren't expecting that. Note that each ball represents one class in a college schedule, and that the unexpected often happens in college. If time permits, lead the students in a discussion about what helped them to keep the balls in play successfully and how those attributes can help one keep one's college schedule in order during the semester. Hopefully, they will see that focus, preparedness, balance, and expecting the unexpected all lead to college success.

Goal Setting Now and Later

(Contributed by Judy Wallins, Director of the University of Idaho's Tutoring and Academic Assistance Center, University of Idaho)

Using the chapter guidelines, have students prepare a list of goals for their lives and for college, including short-term academic goals for the term. Collect the goal statements and put them away until week 4 or 5 of class (after the first set of exams). Redistribute the goal statements to the students. Most students now have a better grasp of their goals and are ready to critique their first list. I put some of the first goal statements on an overhead or handout (without identifying their authors, of course) and we review them together in class discussion, making suggestions about improving them. I reemphasize the importance of goals being self-generated versus driven by the expectations of others. We find ourselves discussing values, priorities, and the difference between attainable and unattainable goals all over again.

For some, the original goals are valid, but most rewrite their goals, narrowing and fine-tuning them. At midterm and just before finals, I redistribute the goal statements and my students rewrite them again each time. Once they are satisfied with their long-term goals, they rarely change them throughout the term, but they do tend to change their short-term goals often.

Conflicting Priorities

Using the example in the time management "Prioritize" discussion on p. 77 of this manual, ask students to consider what they would do if all three priorities seemed equally important (you're the president of the club, you have an upcoming track event, and you need help in the class). Have the students break into groups and brainstorm ways to decide between these three equally important events.

Possible answers:

- Find a tutor to work with you on your class material.

- Get up a half hour earlier to exercise tomorrow.

- Delegate your duties to your vice-president and discuss the meeting over breakfast.

- Rearrange your weekly schedule so this won't happen.

Making and Measuring Predictions

(*Use this in conjunction with the "Discover How You Spend Your Time" journaling exercise at the end of the text chapter.*)
Before beginning the journal exercise, have the class make predictions about how much time an average student in their class spends per week watching television, on the telephone or instant messaging, and sleeping. After students complete the chart for the exercise, elicit students' responses on time spent watching television, telephone/instant messaging, and sleeping. Find the class averages, and compare them to the predictions.

Fighting Procrastination (*Contributed by Prof. Joe Martin*)

To get students' attention, make them an offer: "How would you like to have more free time to spend with your friends, have fun, and do the things that you love to do?" Often, students already have enough time to do those things, but they are mismanaging it. Using the time monitor chart from the graded work assignment (or you can have students estimate in class), have students calculate how they are currently spending their time on necessities (for instance, students have to sleep, attend class, and shower). Then add up their total time allotted for necessities and subtract the total from the total number of hours available in a week. Students discover they have a lot more "free hours" in a week than they originally thought. "What happens to all of the remaining hours?" is the million dollar question.

Ask students how they "choose" to spend their time outside of the classroom, and write their responses on the board. Typically, students will generate between 20 and 30 "time burning" activities (if not more). The power of this exercise is revealed when students realize that the choices they make about their time have a direct influence on the results they experience in college.

POP CULTURE LINKS

Movies: In The Pursuit of Happyness, Will Smith portrays Chris Gardner, the main character, as he brings to life the true story of a father-son family struggling courageously to step up from the bottom rung of the ladder in 1980s San Francisco. Ask students to comment on Chris' zealous pursuit of the best life possible for his son. How did Chris establish these goals for himself? What drove him to achieve them?

Music: There's a classic tune by Harry Chapin called "Cat's in the Cradle." It tells the tale of a man who valued other things over spending time with his son, and when he is old and wants to connect with his son, now grown, he finds that his son values other things over connecting with his father. He regrets what he valued earlier, because he then sees the negative consequences. Consider using this song – play the tune, or distribute the lyrics – to talk about values and their effects.

SUCCESSFUL INTELLIGENCE EXERCISES

Get Analytical! *Explore Your Values*
Assign for in class activity or homework. Ask students to share their top value aloud in class if they are willing. Make a chart on the board and see if the class has any values in common. This is a definite discussion starter! Ask students to survey their parents' values at home and report back to the class any similarities or differences. Ask students to ask significant others about their values and share in class if they are similar or different. Ask the class: Is it important to you that your significant other (spouse, partner, girlfriend, boyfriend) share similar values? Ask the class: What have you learned about your own values after completing this exercise?

Get Creative! *Map Out a Personal Goal*

Assign for in class activity or homework. This exercise can also be shared as a group activity. Have students agree on a personal goal and collaborate on developing a plan. Distribute posterboards to class and have them write up the plan and post it in the classroom. Alternately, encourage them to develop plans for goals that are specific to success for the semester or in the specific class, for example: studying for exams, finding a study group, completing all homework on time, etc.

Get Practical! *Make a To-Do List*

Assign for in class activity or homework. This exercise is best done individually. Have students spend time thinking through this list and not haphazardly filling it in. Encouraging student to take *Get Practical!* exercises seriously early in the semester will build a concrete foundation for achieving success. Review the coding system possibilities for selecting to-do list priorities as students can be confused by the options. For example: using a highlighter, numbering, starring items that must be done today, etc.

HOMEWORK

In-text exercises: All three successful intelligence exercises (Get Analytical, Get Creative and Get Practical) can be assigned for homework.

Foreign word response: Ask students to write a responsive essay on the word "paseo." Ask them to journal and creatively brainstorm how they can define their version of "paseo" this semester (see examples listed in text).

End-of-chapter exercises:

- **Successful Intelligence: Think, Create, Apply** – This is a personal reflection exercise for students. When assigning this homework, make sure to point out that they will use all three successful intelligence skills in analyzing, creatively considering, and practically planning their extracurricular activities. They are to think through all of the options available on campus and set action plans for involvement.

- **Writing: Journal and Put Skills to Work** – Encourage students to complete the journal exercise, estimating and recording time spent on activities. Ask students to use the planner pages included in the text to record activities throughout the week. Students can complete the follow-up questions ("Where do you waste the most time?", "What are you willing to change, and why?") as a homework assignment essay. Real-life writing is an additional essay assignment which asks students to write a research report on academic areas of interest. It may be helpful to provide each student with a course catalog (often available from various college offices) to aid in this writing assignment.

- **Personal Portfolio:** This assignment encourages students to choose three characteristics that employers seek in employees and set them as goals for the coming year. Students need to map out a plan for progress and include a series of smaller goals that will lead to developing one of the listed skills. You may consider using the accompanying handout on p. 88 of this manual.

QUOTES FOR REFLECTION

Use these quotes to generate discussion, start class, or offer as a short exercise. Have students reflect on what any or all of the following quotes mean to them in a short paper or presentation.

The tragedy of life doesn't lie in not reaching your goal. The tragedy of life lies in not having a goal to reach.
> *Marian Wright Edelman*

Even if you're on the right track, you'll get run over if you just sit there.
> *Will Rogers*

The great thing in this world is not so much where we are, but in what direction we are moving.
> *Oliver Wendell Holmes*

The essential conditions of everything you do must be choice, love, and passion.
> *Nadia Boulanger*

Great minds have purposes; others have wishes.
> *Washington Irving*

Goals are dreams with deadlines.
> *Diana Scharf Hunt*

Haste, haste, has no blessing.
> *Swahili proverb*

Don't start your day unless you have finished it on paper first.
> *Jim Rohn*

Exhaust the little moment. Soon it dies. And be it cash or gold it will not come again in this identical disguise.
> *Gwendolyn Brooks*

HANDOUTS

The following are exercises with handouts, or handouts that you can use on their own. Integrate them into your lesson plan as you see fit, or follow the suggestions in the "Communicate Content" section.

- Discovering What is Important – Values Exercise (handout)
- Setting Goals (handout)
- Exploring Career Goals (handout)
- Personal Portfolio Handout to accompany chapter 2 Personal Portfolio exercise

Name _____Date _____

DISCOVERING WHAT IS IMPORTANT

1. Look at the list of words below and circle the five that are most important to you.

beauty	creativity	courage	education	excitement
faith	fame	family	friends	finances
happiness	health	helping others	honesty	leisure time
love	music	popularity	power	reading
skill	time alone	vacations	wealth	wisdom

2. Now mark out two--and two more--so that you only have one word left. Does this word describe what is most important to you?

3. Is this involved with your short- and long-term goals?

4. How will you make this a priority in your life?

Deborah Maness, Pre-Curriculum Instructor, Wake Technical Community College, Raleigh, North Carolina.

Name _____Date _____

SETTING GOALS

Think about a goal that you want to achieve.
The goal may be personal, academic, or work-related.
Complete the following questions to help you take action toward this goal.

1. State the goal.

2. What skills do you have that you will use to work toward this goal?

3. Is this goal something that you can achieve on your own or are there factors beyond your control? Make a list of these factors.

4. How will you achieve this goal?
   List several steps that will help you achieve this goal (short-term goals).

5. What is your time frame for achieving these steps? Put dates beside each step above.

6. What will you do if you experience a setback?

Deborah Maness, Pre-Curriculum Instructor, Wake Technical Community College, Raleigh, North Carolina.

Name _____Date _____

EXPLORING CAREER GOALS

Part 1
State your intended major: _____

State your career goal (the job you want): _____

Part 2
Using your college Web site, go to the college catalog and list all of the required courses for your major in a neat outline.

Part 3
Using the text Web site, www.prenhall.com/success, click on "Career Path."
Click on "Career Profiles" on the left-hand side of the next screen.
Choose a career category from the drop down box.
Choose a title from the next drop down box.
Print the Career Profile Questionnaire.
Read this questionnaire and mark information that you find helpful.
Staple your questionnaire to this sheet.

Deborah Maness, Pre-Curriculum Instructor, Wake Technical Community College, Raleigh, North Carolina.

PERSONAL PORTFOLIO ACTIVITY # 2
PLAN FOR SUCCESS: CAREER GOALS – KNOWLEDGE AND SKILLS

No matter what career goals you ultimately pursue, certain knowledge and skills are useful in any career area. Consider this list of the general skills employers look for in people they hire:

Acceptance	**Critical Thinking**	**Leadership**
Communication	**Flexibility**	**Positive Attitude**
Continual Learning	**Goal Setting**	**Teamwork**
Creativity	**Integrity**	

Choose three of these that you want to focus on developing this year. Map out a practical plan by indicating a series of smaller goals that will lead to developing these skills. *(See the example in your text.)*

Skill: _____

By *six weeks* from now: I will _____

By *four months* from now: I will _____

By *the end of this year*: I will have _____

Skill: _____

By *six weeks* from now: I will _____

By *four months* from now: I will _____

By *the end of this year*: I will have _____

Skill: _____

By *six weeks* from now: I will _____

By *four months* from now: I will _____

By *the end of this year*: I will have _____

CONSIDER COMPREHENSION

REVIEW WITH STUDENTS BEFORE YOU BEGIN THE NEXT CHAPTER:

- Define *value* again – this is often very difficult, because students confuse values with goals! Review an example, such as value: independence and financial success; goal: to obtain a degree in business and start a company. Give examples of values and have students call out goals. Reverse the exercise and give examples of goals and have students identify the value.
- Give examples of good time management strategies.
- Definitions for *values*, *cultural competence*, and *procrastination*.

Chapter Two Vocabulary Quiz Answer Key
(Quiz appears on following page)

1. G
2. J
3. A
4. I
5. B
6. H
7. D
8. C
9. F
10. E

CHAPTER TWO
VOCABULARY QUIZ

1. ____ values

2. ____ cultural competence

3. ____ goal

4. ____ prioritize

5. ____ major/concentration

6. ____ curriculum

7. ____ procrastination

8. ____ perfectionism

9. ____ stress

10. ____ paseo

A. An end toward which effort is directed; an aim or intention

B. An academic subject area chosen as a field of specialization, requiring a specific course of study

C. Gauging one's self-worth solely by one's ability to achieve

D. The act of putting off a task until another time

E. A Spanish term meaning siesta or rest

F. Physical or mental strain or tension produced in reaction to pressure

G. Principles or qualities that you consider important

H. The particular set of courses required for a degree

I. To arrange or deal with in order of importance

J. The ability to understand and appreciate differences and to respond to people of all cultures in a way that values their worth, respects their beliefs and practices, and builds communication and relationships

CHAPTER TWO ASSESSMENT

Multiple Choice
Circle or highlight the answer that seems to fit best.

1. Values play an important part in achieving goals because they help you
    a. understand what you want out of life.
    b. build "rules" for life.
    c. find people who inspire you.
    d. all of the above.

2. Being able to understand and appreciate differences in people of all cultures is
    a. cultural competence.
    b. values.
    c. cultural intelligence.
    d. cultural misunderstanding.

3. The BEST way to achieve goals is to
    a. carefully formulate and execute a goal-achievement plan.
    b. think carefully about what others feel are ideal goals.
    c. determine how your values support your planned goals.
    d. translate your wants and needs into a mission statement that you feel passionate about.

4. Once you set a goal, which of the following is MOST likely to help you to achieve that goal?
    a. Your sense of humor
    b. Your impulsiveness
    c. Your willingness to examine your values
    d. Your self-management skills

5. Prioritizing goals requires you to
    a. make quick decisions about what's unimportant.
    b. evaluate what you are working toward and decide which goals are most important.
    c. weigh the pros and cons of achieving each goal.
    d. brainstorm new ways to implement your goals.

6. Short-term goals are steps that help you to
    a. improve your study habits.
    b. finish your tasks more quickly and more efficiently.
    c. create day-to-day activities that help to implement your long-term goals.
    d. avoid procrastination.

7. When courses are offered at various times, which factor is NOT a time- management consideration in course scheduling?
    a. The time of the class and how it fits with your schedule preferences
    b. Your work schedule and other time commitments
    c. Your body rhythms
    d. Who else will be in the class

8. Planners are designed to
    a. help you schedule and remember events and commitments.
    b. stress you out.
    c. help you create more study time.
    d. be used occasionally, such as at the start and end of the term.

9. The quote from the study skills library at Cal Tech states that the procrastinator believes he/she can complete a task at the last minute easily. This can lead to
    a. perfectionism.
    b. counterproductive behavior that reinforces procrastination.
    c. optimism.
    d. great results.

10. People tend to procrastinate because
    a. they want to be perfect.
    b. they are afraid of their limitations.
    c. they are not sure what to do next.
    d. all of the above

11. All of the following strategies will help you cope with stress EXCEPT
    a. being realistic about time commitments.
    b. waiting until the last minute to complete a task.
    c. putting sleep and down time on your schedule.
    d. focusing on one assignment at a time.

12. When prioritizing your tasks to be completed in a day, you should always
    a . schedule lower priority items around your top priority items as they fit.
    b. complete your routine tasks first.
    c. stay motivated by doing what you like even if it isn't urgent.
    d. do the easiest tasks first so you will have more time for the harder ones.

13. You're considering ecology as your major. You've looked through the course catalogue and learned that there is an ecology major available at your school. Examining the course catalogue is an example of a(n)
    a. long-term goal.
    b. intermediate goal.
    c. immediate goal.
    d. short-term goal.

14. When exploring majors, it is important to
    a. learn how and when to declare a major.
    b. assess your skills and interests.

    c. consider your interest in the subject matter and your comfort level with the department.

    d. all of the above

15. Which is NOT a way to reduce stress levels?
    a. Getting plenty of sleep
    b. Avoiding time with friends
    c. Scheduling classes around time preferences
    d. Taking a walk before a big test

True/False
Determine whether each statement is true or false and circle or highlight the correct answer.

1. Values are principles or qualities that you don't consider important.
    True
    False

2. Spending time with others who share the same values as you can help you clarify and define your goals.
    True
    False

3. Values, once established, are permanent for life.
    True
    False

4. Cultural misunderstanding won't interfere with relationships.
    True
    False

5. An example of a long-term goal is earning a degree.
    True
    False

6. Stating goals out loud is more effective than writing them down.
    True
    False

7. Short-term goals help you to manage long-term goals.
    True
    False

8. Thinking practically and exploring your major early can help you achieve your academic goals more efficiently, both in terms of time and money.
    True
    False

9. Procrastination can be useful because it can motivate you to get things done in a hurry, which is a necessary time management skill.

True
False

10. Stress levels among college students have decreased dramatically.
    True
    False

Fill in the Blank
Insert the word or phrase that BEST completes the sentence.

1. Joining organizations where the activities reflect your values will broaden your
   _____ _____.

2. _____ is a unique set of values, behaviors, tastes, knowledge, attitudes, and habits
   shared by a specific group of people.

3. When you identify something you want, you set a _____.

4. Basing your long-term goals on values increases your _____ to succeed.

5. The act of putting off a task until another time is _____.

6. Physical or mental strain produced in reaction to pressure is ____.

7. Principles or qualities that you consider important are considered your _____.

8. The ability to understand and appreciate differences and to respond to people of all cultures
   in a way that values their worth is called _____ _____.

9. When you arrange or deal with things in order of importance, you are _____.

10. An academic subject area chosen as a field of specialization requiring a specific course of
    study is called your _____.

Short Answer

1. What are the advantages of using a planner? How would it help you manage your school commitments?

2. Why is down time important in your schedule?

3. Why do so many students procrastinate? If you procrastinate, why do you think you do it?

Essay

1. What are your current stressors? Identify your top three and place them in order of most stressful to least. Describe your plan to deal with these top three stressors. Be specific.

2. What academic goal have you set for yourself this term? Describe two short-term goals that will help you achieve this goal. Show how these short-term goals support the larger goal.

3. List your top core values. First, discuss the main influences on your core values. Second, describe how your core values will affect how you set and achieve your academic goals.

4. Describe three areas in your life when you tend to procrastinate. What's your plan to overcome this problem?

Word Exploration

Define this word: *paseo* (pass-*eh*-o)

What does this word mean to you? How does it apply to your life?

Chapter Two Assessment Answer Key

Multiple Choice

Test Item Assesses This Learning Objective/Topic

1. d.   Why Is It Important to Know What You Value?
2. a   Why Is It Important to Know What You Value?
          Values and cultural diversity
3. a   How Do You Set and Achieve Goals?
4. d   How Do You Set and Achieve Goals?
5. b   How Do You Set and Achieve Goals?
          Prioritize goals
6. c   How Do You Set and Achieve Goals?
          Work to achieve goals
7. d   How Can You Manage Your Time Effectively?
          Identify your time-related needs and preferences
8. a.   How Can You Manage Your Time Effectively?
          Keep track of events and commitments
9. b   How Can You Manage Your Time Effectively? *Fight procrastination*
10. d   How Can You Manage Your Time Effectively? *Fight procrastination*
11. b   How Can You Manage Your Time Effectively?
          Manage stress by managing time
12. a   How Can You Manage Your Time Effectively?
13. d   How Can You Begin to Explore Majors?
14. d   How Can You Begin to Explore Majors?
15. b   How Can You Manage Your Time Effectively?
          Manage stress by managing time

True/False

Test Item Assesses This Learning Objective/Topic

1. F   Why Is It Important to Know What You Value?
2. T   Why Is It Important to Know What You Value?
3. F   Why Is It Important to Know What You Value?
4. F   Why Is It Important to Know What You Value?
           Values and cultural diversity
5. T   How Do You Set and Achieve Goals?
6. F   How Do You Set and Achieve Goals?
7. T   How Do You Set and Achieve Goals?
8. T   How Can You Begin to Explore Majors?
9. F   How Can You Manage Your Time Effectively?
           Fight procrastination
10. F   How Can You Manage Your Time Effectively?
           Managing stress by managing time

Fill in the Blank

Test Item Assesses This Learning Objective/Topic

1. *educational experience* Why Is It Important to Know What You Value?
           How values affect your educational experience
2. *Culture*   Why Is It Important to Know What You Value?
           Values and cultural diversity
3. *goal*   How Do You Set and Achieve Goals?
4. *motivation*   How Do You Set and Achieve Goals?
5. *procrastination* How Can You Manage Your Time Effectively?
           Fight procrastination
6. *stress*   How Can You Manage Your Time Effectively?
           Manage stress by managing time
7. *values*   Why Is It Important to Know What You Value?
8. *cultural competence* Why Is It Important to Know What You Value?
           Values and cultural diversity
9. *prioritizing* How Can You Manage Your Time Effectively?
           Prioritize goals
10. *major*   How Can You Begin to Explore Majors?

Diversity Matters
How You Learn and Communicate

BRIEF CHAPTER OVERVIEW

This chapter is one of self-discovery for students. Understanding how you learn is a valuable tool for the rest of college and for life – it helps students play to their strengths and overcome or build weaker areas. The chapter offers two self-assessments and scoring guides: one based on Howard Gardner's Theory of Multiple Intelligences (Multiple Pathways to Learning), and another based on the Myers-Briggs Type Indicator® (the Personality Spectrum). Helping students identify both their Gardner MI and their Personality Spectrum is essential for students' comprehension of later material and exercises in the text.

The new inclusion of diversity and communication in this chapter helps students understand that the different ways that people learn and communicate are as much a part of human diversity as ethnic origin or religion. This material expands on chapter 2's discussion of cultural competence, focusing on people with different values, cultural backgrounds, preferences, communication styles, and personality traits as well as the more obvious differences of race and ethnicity.

Diversity material can be sensitive. Here are just a few ideas for coverage:
- ∞ Focus on journaling and papers to keep individual responses private.
- ∞ Encourage low-key group discussions.
- ∞ Invite one or more guest speakers (people from cultural organizations, counselors, deans) who can talk about experiences.

Gauge what you cover, and how, to best suit your students and what they respond to.

Note the successful intelligence skills your students will build in chapter 3:

Analytical	Creative	Practical
▪ Analyzing the eight Multiple Intelligences	▪ Creating new ways to develop your abilities	▪ How to choose and use your best study strategies
▪ Investigating how you relate to others	▪ Developing a new vision of yourself as a learner	▪ How to adjust to an instructor's teaching style
▪ Evaluating the assumptions that underlie prejudice and stereotypes	▪ Creating new ideas about what diversity means	▪ How to relate to others with cultural competence

CHAPTER THREE OUTLINE

Why Explore Who You Are as a Learner?

- Your Unique Intelligence Can Change and Develop
- Assessments Can Help You Learn About Yourself
- Self-Knowledge Is an Important, Lifelong Goal

What Tools Can Help You Assess How You Learn and Interact With Others?

- Assess Your Multiple Intelligences with *Pathways to Learning*
- Assess Your Style of Interaction with the *Personality Spectrum*

How Can You Use Your Self-Knowledge?

- Classroom Benefits
- Study Benefits
- Workplace Benefits

How Can You Develop Cultural Competence?

- Value Diversity
- Identify and Evaluate Personal Perceptions and Attitudes
- Be Aware of Opportunities and Challenges That Occur When Cultures Interact
- Build Cultural Knowledge
- Adapt to Diverse Cultures

How Can You Communicate Effectively?

- Adjust to Communication Styles
- Know How to Give and Receive Criticism
- Manage Conflict
- Manage Communication Technology
- Choose Communities that Enhance Your Life

COMMUNICATE CONTENT
TOPICS COVERED IN THE CHAPTER

[Chapter intro with chapter 2 review: PowerPoint slides 1, 2, 3]

The *Real Questions, Practical Answers* Discussion Starter Question:
How can I maximize what I do well? [See PowerPoint slide 4.]

> The questioner asks for advice concerning teachers who teach with a different method than one learns with. Read the question out loud with the class. Ask how many students can relate to the question. Often, many students have this concern. Even if they have not had this problem with a teacher in the past, an experience similar to the student in the text may be just around the corner.
>
> You may want to comment here that some students may naturally learn in ways that do not mesh with your *own* teaching style. It is good, then, for you to pay attention to what they say on this topic
>
> Review the professional's answer as a class. Ask the class if they have any additional suggestions. Ask the class if they have ever tried any of the suggested helpful strategies. Offer the professional's help as a suggestion for present struggles they may be having. Challenge the class to try one of two of the suggestions this term and report the results back to the class.

(For more discussion starters, see p. 109 of this IM chapter.)

 Question 1: Why Explore Who You Are as a Learner?

[Section overview: PowerPoint slide 5]
Important note: Make sure you take the assessments yourself before you begin covering this material, so that you speak from experience.

The main point of this section is to challenge students to consider themselves seriously as a learner. Address other labels they have given themselves or how others have labeled them during their educational careers. It is always great to share personal stories if you have been labeled in the past. Be open and honest with your students – they will value your transparency. Emphasize how self-awareness informs educational and career choices. It also means students can take more responsibility for their own education.
The first two sections address the changing uniqueness of individuals.

Your unique intelligence can change and develop. The focus of this section is a key point: Students, and all people, CAN and DO grow and develop in their abilities, skills, and strengths. Everyone is born with a unique set of abilities, but change is always possible. Highlight the rubber band metaphor in the text to drive this point home.

Assessments help you learn about yourself. The introduction on assessments is meant to encourage students to give them a chance. Assessment tools *are* valuable! It is good to address misconceptions students may have about assessment tools. Ask them:

- Do you like to take these types of tests?
- What do you think about them?
- Do others make fun of them?
- What is the general public's opinion about them?

Idea: Perhaps you could bring in some magazines that contain assessments, such as *Glamour, Men's Health,* or *Allure.* Show them to the class and ask them to compare and contrast these assessments and the ones in the text. (Listen for points such as "created by a professional," "results can be practically applied," "assessing an important skill," and so on.)

 # Question 2: What Tools Can Help You Assess How You Learn and Interact With Others?

[Section overview: PowerPoint slide 6]
Overview of Assessments: The chapter covers two assessments, but many others exist. The two in this chapter have different focus areas:

- Learning preferences—assesses potential and strength in areas of ability (Multiple Pathways to Learning)

- Personality traits—helps you understand how you respond to information, thoughts, and feelings, as well as to people and events (Personality Spectrum)

Important Note: How to differentiate these two assessments from each other and from the Successful Intelligence terminology is one of the most important things for you as an instructor to understand and communicate to your students.

First of all, note the distinction *between* these two assessments. Please be sure to emphasize it several times in class. It is the only way students will understand the difference in these assessments! **[See PowerPoint slide 6.]**

Second of all, note how the two assessments differ from the Successful Intelligence theory. The chart on the next page should help you clarify all of the distinctions. **[For a Multiple Intelligences/Successful Intelligence comparison, see PowerPoint slide 7.]**

	Robert Sternberg's Successful Intelligence (SI) Theory	Multiple Pathways to Learning (assessment based on Howard Gardner's Multiple Intelligences Theory)	Personality Spectrum (assessment based on the Myers-Briggs Type Indicator®)
Consists of...	THINKING PROCESSES	DOMAINS	TYPES/DIMENSIONS
Focuses on...	How people PROCESS and APPLY information to learn and achieve goals	How people INTAKE information to learn	How people INTERACT with others
Key terms are...	Analytical thinking, Creative thinking, Practical thinking	Verbal-Linguistic, Musical, Logical-Mathematical, Visual-Spatial, Bodily-Kinesthetic, Interpersonal, Intrapersonal, Naturalist	Thinker, Organizer, Giver, Adventurer

With this important information in mind, return to introducing the assessments. Consider writing, in very large letters, *MI* and *PS* at the front of the room. Emphasize that these are two important assessments that will be done during class time. Make important points:

- There are no right or wrong answers.
- It is not a test.
- A high score is not "better," it just reflects an area of strength; a low score is not "bad," it simply reflects a less dominant area.
- Finally, and most importantly: The assessments are scored *differently* (more on this under each assessment description that follows).

Assure students who are intimidated by personality type tests that these are well-written and you will be available to answer questions as students complete the assessments.

Howard Gardner's Multiple Intelligences Assessment: The MI information, which comes first in this chapter, includes an assessment by author Joyce Bishop based on Howard Gardner's theory of Multiple Intelligences. His theory changed the way people perceive intelligence and learning. Review some of Gardner's biographical information from the text. Have a student read the first paragraph under the topic question aloud to the class.

Before you have the class begin the assessment, review the icons located on Key 3.1. Ask students to brainstorm together why the editors chose the specific icons and how they are related to the MI characteristics listed in the columns. Be sure to highlight that the assessment evaluates the *levels* to which each of your student's eight intelligences are developed. EVERYONE has some of each of the intelligences listed. **[See PowerPoint slide 8.]**

Begin the assessment in class, carefully explaining how to score each item. **Be sure to point out that each item should be rated *individually* on a scale of 1 to 4.** In other words, it is OK to rate all of the items a 4 if they fit you. **[See PowerPoint slides 9 and 10.]**

(Through the remainder of your coverage of this material, consider using any of the MI-based handout exercises found on pp. 116-131 of this IM chapter.)

Joyce Bishop's Personality Spectrum: Also by Joyce Bishop, this assessment is based on the Myers-Briggs Type Indicator® and on the related Keirsey Sorter. Have the students complete the assessment in class, making sure to highlight the differences as noted above. Mapping the Personality Spectrum on the scoring diagram will help students see how they are balanced or skewed in one or two directions. Highlight Key 3.3 with students: Ask a specific student who tested high in each area to read the characteristics of their personality type aloud, then ask them whether they think that the list of traits suits them. Encourage students to read the trait lists to parents and close friends and ask them if they agree with the assessment outcomes. **[See PowerPoint slide 11.]**

<u>Heads up</u>! The Personality Spectrum assessment *differs* in how it is scored. <u>Items in each section of the Personality Spectrum are given a 1 to 4, but each number can only be used one time.</u> Several students will likely do this wrong, so be prepared with blank copies of the Personality Spectrum so students can try again. **[See PowerPoint slides 12 and 13.]**

(Consider putting together "Personality Spectrum Teams" to continue through the term, starting after students complete this assessment. Description is found on p. 111 of this IM chapter.)

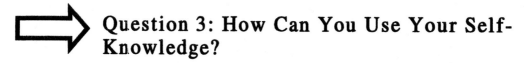

Question 3: How Can You Use Your Self-Knowledge?

[Section overview: PowerPoint slide 14]
The goal here is to <u>put everything students have learned to work</u>, and show them how they can use it in all aspects of their lives.

It is easy, and common, for students to take an assessment like this, think "oh, that was fun/boring/useless," and forget about it. <u>Taking this information past the scoring point is the key to making sure that they put what they've learned to good use.</u> Discuss the significance their learning styles have for **classroom**, **studying**, and **workplace** situations (see corresponding text sections).

(To get students thinking about how to use what they've just learned about themselves, consider using the "Teamwork: Create Solutions Together – Ideas about Personality Types" exercise from the end of the text chapter, described on pp. 109-110 of this IM chapter.)

- **Classroom benefits** – discuss how self-knowledge helps students assess and adjust to their instructors' teaching styles. Various styles are mentioned in Key 3.4. Use your own style – and any experiences you've had where your style didn't suit some students – as an example.
- **Study benefits** – talk about how students can choose study techniques that work with their styles, and that particular choices can help them with material that is especially tough for them. Focus their attention on Keys 3.5 and 3.6, which detail study techniques that correspond with each intelligence and Personality Spectrum dimension.

(Consider using the "Multiple Intelligences and Study Success" exercise on pp. 110-111 of this IM chapter.)

- **Workplace benefits** – Better performance, better teamwork, and better career planning – all in all, more wise choices for the future – are potential outcomes of comprehensive self-knowledge. Point out Key 3.7 and ask students to review the majors and internships listed within their strongest multiple intelligences. Ask them if their chosen major is listed. Ask them if they have ever considered one of the majors listed. Ask them if the list confirms the area where they think they will major.

⟹ Question 4: How Can You Develop Cultural Competence?

[Section overview: PowerPoint slide 15]

Consider who your students are, how well they know one another, and how long they've been in class together to determine how to approach this topic. Some students may have extensive experience with diverse people. For others, college may be their first true experience.

Exploring differences in how people learn (levels of ability in the Multiple Intelligences, Personality Spectrum, or successful intelligence) can serve as an effective entrée into diversity because students aren't typically as sensitive about their unique learning preferences as they might be when discussing race, gender, sexual preferences, or creed. Still, the topic illustrates how an understanding of differences can improve relationships and can serve as a springboard for discussion about other types of diversity. **[See PowerPoint slide 16.]**

(Consider using the "Classroom Diversity" exercise on p. 111 of this IM chapter to get things started.)

Cultural Competence

Make sure students understand that diversity is a reality and that they will need cultural competence to succeed in college, work, and in life. As an introduction, review the five actions that make up cultural competence, as described in the text:

1. Value diversity. Ask students what they perceive are positive effects of learning in a diverse classroom and living in a diverse world. Ideas may include:

- Opportunities to learn from the ideas, arts, and practices of others

- Increased understanding and acceptance of the variety of human experience

- Increased open-mindedness

- Less self-centeredness ("my way is the only way")

- Stronger relationships

- New experiences

2. Identify and evaluate personal perceptions and attitudes. Here, you'll discuss the concepts of prejudice and stereotypes. First make sure everyone is clear on the definitions:

Prejudice is a preconceived judgment or opinion formed without just grounds or sufficient knowledge.

Stereotypes are standardized mental pictures or assumptions made, without proof or critical thinking, about the characteristics of a person or group of people.

Help students understand that stereotypes often form the basis for prejudice. Point out Key 3.9 and remind students that stereotypes can be either negative or positive – and that either way, they are inaccurate. See if students have other examples. How about how students view others from a rival school? How they view themselves as part of your school? These questions can help you highlight some easily-revealed stereotypes.

Emphasize that stereotypes communicate disrespect and prevent relationships from growing. For example, if someone judges you based on your appearance, you most likely won't feel inspired to help them get to know you on a more detailed and personal level.

(To help students begin to examine themselves, consider assigning the "Personal Differences Assessment" on pp. 133-134 of this IM chapter).

3. Be aware of opportunities and challenges that occur when different cultures interact. This area incorporates discrimination and hate crimes (two of the most significant challenges). Gauge how well your class will handle these topics – if it might prove too touchy, you can stick to a more general brainstorming session regarding opportunities (the positives) and challenges (the negatives) of intercultural interaction.

4. Build knowledge about other cultures. Turn students' attention toward taking positive action. Remind them that the best way to solve a problem is to address the cause, not the effect. Therefore, combating prejudice is the key to taking things in a more positive direction. **[See PowerPoint slide 17.]**

Getting to know more about other cultures is just one of many positive action steps. Ask students to use their creative intelligence to generate other ideas. Fill in with ideas from the text if you need to (the parts of cultural competence are all action steps). (*Consider the "Ten Ways to Fight Hate" supplement to inspire ideas.*) As an example, you could mention how Rev. King chose nonviolent but assertive communication to build cultural knowledge and awareness and to trigger change.

(Consider using the "Personal Diversity" exercise on p. 112 of this IM chapter.)

5. Adapt to diverse cultures. Here's where students take what they've learned through the discussion and use their practical intelligence to put it to work. The chapter contains a list of ideas that your students could add to, if time permits.

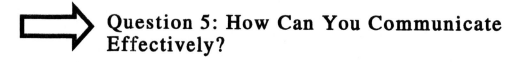 **Question 5: How Can You Communicate Effectively?**

[Section overview: PowerPoint slide 18]
Everyone communicates with a different style. Although there are many ways to discuss communication style, the text presents four general styles that align with the dimensions of the Personality Spectrum. Review the styles with students, ask them to recall their dominant Personality Spectrum dimension(s), and ask them to think about whether the communication styles for that dimension (or those dimensions) match up with how they tend to communicate with others. **[See PowerPoint slide 19.]**

(Consider using the "Communication Style" exercise on p. 112 of this IM chapter.)

Manage Criticism

Giving and receiving constructive criticism isn't easy. Define constructive criticism for the students and give examples of both constructive and nonconstructive criticism. The text contains a couple of helpful examples.

You may want to give, and ask for, personal examples of one or the other to drive home the point. Emphasize that criticism must have a goal that is focused on help and improvement. Criticism that is meant to demean has only negative effects.

Managing Conflict

(Note: Consider inviting a counselor who can provide scenarios and strategies for dealing with communication and relationship issues.)

Dollar Bill Demonstration: Ask two students to come forward and face each other. Hold a dollar bill vertically between them. Ask each student to describe, in turn, what he or she sees. Both are looking at a dollar bill and both are right in their descriptions. They simply have a different point of view.

Conflict cannot often be avoided, but it can be handled effectively. Ask for student suggestions about effective conflict resolution. Augment what students say with these hints:

- Be assertive, not aggressive or passive (use text information to explain the three possibilities).
- Use "I" messages when speaking – frame communication in terms of your own needs.
- Reflect back what the other person has said. Ask whether you heard correctly.
- Look for solutions instead of addressing "right" or "wrong."
- Stay away from the extremes – avoidance (passivity) or escalation (aggression).
- Be willing to take a break and discuss it later.
- Don't match an attack with an attack.

(If your students tend to be young and live in on-campus housing, try the "What Would You Do?" exercise on p. 132 of this IM chapter.)

Manage Communication Technology

Many of today's students are immersed in technology – if allowed in class, you may want to ask students to exhibit items (computer, cell phone, PDA, MP3 player, etc.). As much as technology promotes interpersonal communication, it also presents unique challenges.

Emphasize the ways in which texting, IM-ing, and "friending" on communication Web sites like MySpace or Facebook can be superficial, deceptive, and/or time consuming (examples in the text include potential for miscommunication on IM and the time drain of e-mailing friends). Focus on the value of in-person communication.

Important overarching idea: Let communication technology *enhance* in-person communication, not replace it. Explore with students the idea of matching communication strategies to particular situations – i.e., knowing when to use e-mail, when to pick up the phone, and when to speak to someone in person.

Choose Communities That Enhance Your Life

This makes a nice wrap-up to this chapter. Ask students to volunteer what communities they are a part of, and to say how these communities help them, educate them, support them. Emphasize that we don't achieve anything alone, and that we are more likely to find positive energy and success when we surround ourselves with people who foster that energy and success.

[Successful Intelligence Wrap-Up: PowerPoint slide 20]
[End-of-chapter foreign word: PowerPoint slide 21]
[End-of-chapter thought-provoking quote: PowerPoint slide 22]

****

CREATE COMMUNITY

DISCUSSION STARTERS

1. **Map a Learning Path:** Show students several examples of maps--a campus map, a topographic map or globe, an aerial map, a precinct voting map, a hiking map, and so on. All these maps show different aspects of the same location (preferably your campus). Draw the analogy to self assessments. Various learning assessments give students different views of themselves that can guide them through the learning process. What they'll be doing with the learning material is to begin mapping their learning path. This will be easily done if the maps are accessible via the Internet and shown on a screen in the classroom. Use the maps to open dialogue about assessments: Are you interested in knowing how you learn? Have you had bad experiences with assessments in the past? Do you feel that they put you in a box, and you can't get out, or do you feel like they help you understand your perceptions better? Do you ever complete the simple personality tests in tabloid magazines? Do you take them seriously or not? Why should we take the MI and PS tests seriously?

2. Ask students to spend 1-2 minutes writing about what "living in a diverse world" means to them (topics may include different backgrounds, cultures, values). Discuss their answers. Broaden the definition, if necessary, to include topics like talents and abilities, religious practice, perspectives, lifestyle choices, etc.

3. Throw out a diversity-related statistic about your school (differences in how long it takes students to graduate, race/ethnic percentages in the student body, religious group membership, etc.). Invite reaction and discuss. Note any level of surprise, and ask why. Ask about potential effects of this statistic.

GROUP EXERCISES

Teamwork: Create Solutions Together – *Ideas about Personality Types*

This exercise, found at the end of chapter 3 in the textbook, requires students to gather in groups based on their Personality Spectrum type. Students refer to the list of ideas to brainstorm for their particular type.

As a variation on the procedure recommended in the text, try the following: Post the four different personality types (organizer, adventurer, giver, and thinker) on butcher paper at the four corners of the room.

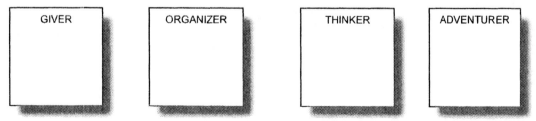

Instruct the students to review their completed Personality Spectrum assessment and scores. When finished, have each student move to the appropriate corner of their most dominant personality type. On notebook paper or on other sheets of butcher paper, have each group list characteristics of that type with special attention to these areas:

- Strengths
- Growth areas
- Stress (what causes them stress)

- Teachers that motivate/inspire them
- Teachers that confuse/annoy them
- Career interests

For example: (Students should fill the paper with numerous examples.)

GIVER Strengths: sensitive, Caring Motivations: Learning how to	ORGANIZER *Growth Areas: Hard to say no* Overly sensitive Stress: People who are too spontaneous	THINKER Needs time, to consider possibilities Conflict causes stress	ADVENTURER Strengths-- spontaneous energetic Career interest- - counselor

...ve a sp... ...ch group...

Some common scenarios: The givers share freely, the thinkers won't talk at the beginning, the organizers spend time deciding who should write the list, and the adventurers will have to be reminded to keep on task. You may want to share these with students and see if they concur – they may get a kick out of it if they find that their groups repeated these scenarios!

Important: Go in the following order – adventurers, organizers, givers, thinkers. Let the dynamic group set the pace! After each group presents the list, engage the class in discussing which characteristics are positive, negative, or potentially both.

Multiple Intelligences and Study Success

This exercise should show students what teaching/learning methods work and don't work for them, and how to cope when the learning environment doesn't match how they learn. Split students into groups according to their dominant multiple intelligences (if students scored equally in more than one, have them choose a group in a way that will even out the groups as much as possible). Ask them to explore the effects on learning when they are in classes that match and don't match their dominant intelligence. Then have them devise three techniques to help when the match isn't a good one.

1. Positive Study Effects: Each group should identify classes they felt maximized their dominant learning intelligence. What were the results of maximizing their intelligence? For instance…
   - Was the information in these classes easier to remember?
   - Did they retain the information longer?
   - Did they save study time in this class more than in other classes that didn't tap their strongest intelligence?
2. Negative Study Effects: Next group members should discuss classes where their strengths were (or are) used little, if at all. Notice the types of classes. What were the effects?
3. Take Responsibility for Study Success: Have groups outline three specific ways to convert information they receive in classes that don't tap into their dominant intelligence into formats that activate their strongest intelligences. If time allows after the exercise, review the PowerPoints with MI descriptions and study strategies so groups can compare the strategies they developed to the text suggestions.

- Verbal-linguistic – <u>The Hours</u> (about writer Virginia Woolf)
- Logical-mathematical – <u>Good Will Hunting</u> (about a janitor who's a math whiz)
- Intrapersonal – <u>Born on the 4th of July</u> (about a war vet who, with time and thought and exploration, discovers true self-knowledge)
- Giver – <u>Parenthood</u> (about the ways in which parents give to their children)
- Organizer – <u>Ocean's 13</u> (the gang pulling off the Vegas heist are expert organizers)
- Thinker – <u>Linus Pauling, Crusading Scientist</u> (a documentary about one of the 20th century's greatest thinkers)
- Adventurer – <u>Die Hard</u> or sequels (about a classic risk-taking character)

To promote discussion on diversity, you can take your pick of movies that treat the ups and downs of human difference – <u>Glory</u> (the black experience in the Civil War), <u>Schindler's List</u> (the Jewish experience in World War II), <u>Philadelphia</u> (the homosexual experience in the face of AIDS), and <u>The Pursuit of Happyness</u> (the experience of someone economically disadvantaged) are just a few titles. Documentaries are worth your consideration and can be especially affecting on topics like these, whereas a fictional film may seem to skirt reality.

Music: Music of all kinds can support the strength of learners dominant in musical intelligence, and may also be useful for learners dominant in logical-mathematical or naturalist intelligence (both tend to be strong in patterns, also found in music). Discuss different ways in which music can be helpful – writing tunes or words to help remember concepts, using music as background to study time, filling in new words to familiar tunes, and so on.

To illustrate the concept of diversity, try bringing in 5-10 songs from totally different musical genres (jazz, country, R&B, hip hop, klezmer, folk, rock, gypsy, classical, etc.). Try featuring a song to illustrate the concept of communication – what does the song communicate, both in words and in sound? What feelings and ideas do your students take away from it?

SUCCESSFUL INTELLIGENCE EXERCISES

Get Analytical, Creative and Practical! *Maximize Your Classroom Experience*
This activity combines all three successful intelligence skills. Students are asked to think carefully about their instructor's style and brainstorm possible solutions if problems exist. Finally, they are asked to think of a practical solution. As a teacher, be attentive to what students list as problems between the instructor and student. In addition, hold students accountable to implementing their solutions. When you discuss this exercise, set up a later date on which to have them share (on paper or in class discussion) the results from their practical solutions.

HOMEWORK

In-text exercises: There is only one exercise in this chapter that combines all three (*Get Analytical, Get Creative,* and *Get Practical*). It can be assigned for homework, along with the completion of both assessments, if there is limited time in class.

Foreign Word Response: Ask students to write a responsive essay on the word "oruko lonro ni." Ask them to elaborate on names and labels assigned to them during past experiences, in school or out, by their parents, siblings, friends or coworkers, instructors, or themselves. Make sure students include their Multiple Intelligence and Personality Spectrum outcomes as aspects of their personal diversity in their essay.

End-of-chapter exercises:
- **Successful Intelligence: Think, Create, Apply** – Ask students to read Joyce Bishop's *Personal Triumph Case Study*. Then have them complete the exercise, being careful to follow the three separate steps.
- **Writing: Journal and Put Skills to Work** – Students can complete the journal entry – a brainstorming exercise where students are asked to name and discuss 10 details about themselves, focusing on facts that can't be seen at a glance – as homework. The real-life writing assignment has students create, and send, an e-mail that asks a question of an advisor. Then they must create two more versions of it, for an instructor and for a friend, to build skills in targeting their writing style to specific recipients. Also useful as a homework assignment.
- **Personal Portfolio:** Student often enjoy completing this assignment. It is fun to put together a cohesive picture of both assessments, combining both multiple intelligences with Personality Spectrum dimensions. There is a wheel shown in Key 3.9 for this exercise, or utilize the copy-ready portfolio handout on p. 135 of this instructor's manual chapter.

QUOTES FOR REFLECTION

Use these quotes to generate discussion, start class, or offer as a short exercise. Have students reflect on what any or all of the following quotes mean to them in a short paper or presentation.

Know thyself.
> *Inscription at Delphi*

What lies behind us and what lies before us are tiny matters compared to what lies within us.
> *Ralph Waldo Emerson*

If we are to achieve a richer culture, rich in contrasting values, we must recognize the whole gamut of human potentialities, and so weave a less arbitrary social fabric, one in which each diverse human gift will find a fitting place.
> *Margaret Mead*

We could learn a lot from crayons: some are sharp, some are pretty, some are dull, some have weird names, and all are different colors…but they all have to learn to live in the same box.
> *Unknown*

The remarkable thing is we have a choice every day regarding the attitude we will embrace for that day.
>   *Charles Swindoll*

The most important single ingredient in the formula of success is knowing how to get along with people.
>   *Theodore Roosevelt*

Injustice anywhere is a threat to justice everywhere.
>   *Martin Luther King Jr.*

HANDOUTS

Faculty members tell us the MI assessment is one of the most important aspects of the course. As a special feature for this chapter, we offer handout activities to teach each of the different intelligence types. This will help students see where their strengths lie, understand why they have struggles in some areas, and try to strengthen those weaker areas. Exercises relating to diversity and communication also appear in the list.

Many of these exercises have description pages for the instructor that precede the photocopy-ready handout. Integrate the exercises into your lesson plan as you see fit, or follow the suggestions in the "Communicate Content" section.

- Verbal-Linguistic Exercise – Howard Gardner's Eight Types of Intelligences
- Logical-Mathematical Exercise – Situation Puzzles
- Bodily-Kinesthetic Exercise – Build Me Your Strengths
- Visual-Spatial Exercise – Draw a Symbol
- Interpersonal Exercise – Use Multiple Intelligences to Get the Point Across
- Intrapersonal Exercise – Convince Yourself!
- Musical Exercise – Write Me a Song Lyric
- Naturalistic Exercise – Categorize Me
- What Would You Do? (handout)
- Personal Differences Assessment (handout)
- Personal Portfolio Handout to accompany chapter 3 Personal Portfolio exercise

HOWARD GARDNER'S EIGHT TYPES OF INTELLIGENCES

Read the text coverage on multiple intelligences and fill in the following definitions:

1. Verbal-Linguistic:

_____

_____

2. Logical-Mathematical:

_____

_____

3. Bodily-Kinesthetic:

_____

_____

4. Visual-Spatial:

_____

_____

5. Interpersonal:

_____

_____

6. Intrapersonal:

_____

_____

7. Musical:

_____

_____

8. Naturalist:

_____

_____

Situation Puzzles

Materials:
- Handout: *Situation Puzzles*

Activities:
1. Break into groups, or work as a class if your group is very small.
2. If you have several groups, assign one situation puzzle to each. Give the appropriate answer to ONE person in each group, with instructions not to reveal it (or, if the class is working as one group, you keep the answers to yourself).
3. Instruct the students that they must work toward the answer by asking the answer-holder yes-or-no questions ONLY.
4. Give students a time limit on their process – and go.

Closure: Have students ponder the course of their thinking. Did they arrive at the conclusion gradually, like scaling a mountain? Did the answer come to them suddenly, like a lightning bolt? Did any groups not get very far at all?

Benefits for this exercise. Students will . . .
1. Go into in-depth analysis of a puzzle.
2. Experience the value of hearing and understanding the insights of others in the process of working toward an answer to a question.
3. Understand how easy it is to move down the wrong path when pursuing an answer (it is likely that one or more groups will "bark up the wrong tree" for a while during the exercise).

**Answers to Situation Puzzles:
- The backpack is a parachute that failed to open.
- The man is a dwarf/little person and can only reach to the 10th floor button.
- The man had the hiccups and the bartender scared them out of him.
- Sunday is a horse.
- The man is a justice of the peace, marrying the women to other men.

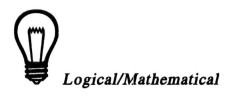

Logical/Mathematical

SITUATION PUZZLES

1. A man is lying alone and face-down in an enormous field with a backpack on his back. He is dead. How did it happen?

2. A man lives on the thirteenth floor of an apartment building. In the morning, he takes the elevator to the ground floor and goes to work. In the evening, if someone else is in the elevator, he goes directly to the thirteenth floor. However, if he is alone, he goes to the tenth floor and walks up three flights. Why?

3. A man walks into a bar and asks for a glass of water. The bartender pulls out a gun and points it at him. The man says "Thank you" and leaves. Why?

4. A woman left on Sunday, traveled for three days, and returned on Sunday. How?

5. A man marries twenty-five women in his town but is not brought up on charges as a polygamist. Why?

Build Me Your Strengths

Materials:
- Handout: *Build Me Your Strengths*
- Prepared bags with construction paper, scissors, glue, yarn, newspaper, marker, clay (you can supplement with other art supplies).

Activities:
1. Hook (as an attention getting activity)
   - Ask students if anyone has ever used a hammer.
   - Ask students if anyone can play baseball, football, ice-skate, etc.
   - Ask about an iron, electric drill, blender, etc.
2. Lead in to a discussion on the different intelligences by talking about why some people are better at certain things than others.
3. Hand out *Build Me Your Strengths*/prepared bags

Closure: Review the eight different types of intelligences by asking for a volunteer to share his or her building.

Benefits for this exercise: Students will
1. Have a chance to experiment with hands-on manipulatives.
2. Understand that this lesson was designed for the bodily/kinesthetic learner.

Name _____Date _____

BUILD ME YOUR STRENGTHS

Directions:

1. List five of your strengths.

    1. _____   4. _____

    2. _____   5. _____

    3. _____

2. Pick one of the strengths that you wrote down.
3. Build a three-dimensional structure that illustrates the strength that you picked (you can only use the materials that you have in the bag).
4. Be prepared to share your three-dimensional model with the class.

Questions to Think About:

What is your strength?

_____

Why do you think this is a strength of yours?

_____

_____

How did you go about constructing your model?

_____

_____

_____

Draw a Symbol

Materials: <u>Handouts</u> – *Semantic Web: 8 Different Types of Intelligences* and *Draw a Symbol*

Activities:
1. <u>Hook</u>: Ask the students what they like to do in their free time (construct a semantic web on the board or overhead projector).
2. Talk about the different ways you can organize the information that you constructed during the hook activity (concept map, sequential organizers, plot diagrams, Venn diagrams, semantic web, chart, etc.).
3. Handouts – *Semantic Web: 8 Different Types of Intelligences* and blank *Semantic Web*

Closure: Review the eight different types of intelligences by sharing the picture symbols the students create.

Benefits of the lesson: Students will
1. Become familiar with the different ways to visually organize their information.
2. Be aware that picture symbols might assist in the understanding of specific terms.
3. Understand that this lesson was designed for the visual-spatial learner.

SEMANTIC WEB: 8 DIFFERENT TYPES OF INTELLIGENCES

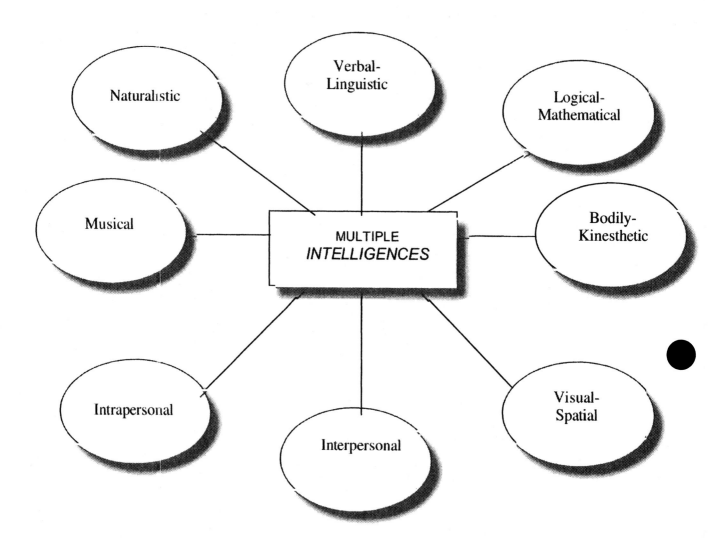

Name _____ Date _____

DRAW A SYMBOL

Directions. Draw a symbol to represent each of Gardner's Intelligences.

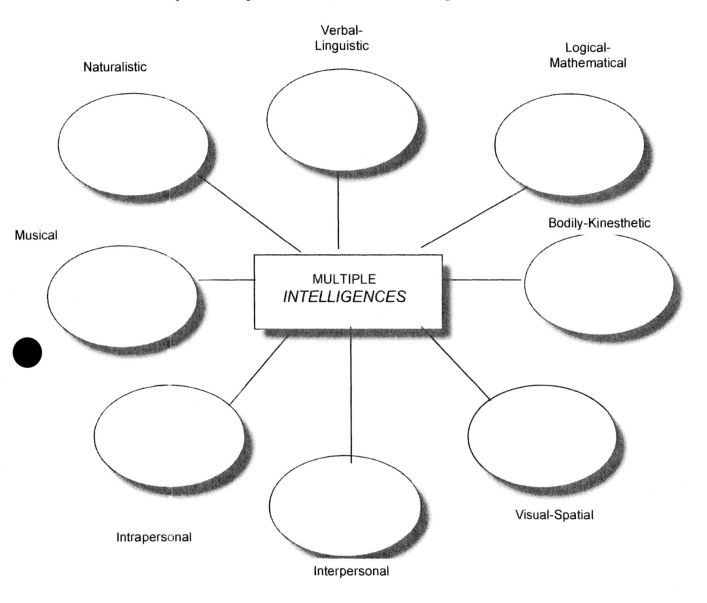

Use Multiple Intelligences to Get the Point Across

Materials: <u>Handout</u> – *Procrastination*

Activities/Assignments:
1. <u>Hook</u>: Ask students if they ever had to give an oral presentation (focus on the delivery of the presentations). Ask students to compare an oral presentation to teaching.
2. <u>Lead</u> in to a discussion on the multiple intelligences by talking about how and why people make different presentations. Why/when would a speaker focus on a logical-mathematical angle? A visual angle? Why/when would a speaker use a musical or naturalist component to a presentation?
3. <u>Prepare the setup</u>: Depending on the size of your class, divide students into eight groups or singles and *privately* assign a different multiple intelligence area to each (no student or group should know what MI any other student or group has). In a class with 8 students, each will have a different MI area; with more students, there will be a mix of singles and pairs/groups; with a large class, 8 pairs or groups.
4. <u>Goal</u>: **Let students know that they will be giving short presentations about procrastination using a particular MI angle**. They will use the handout as their source material, and create a presentation based on the multiple intelligence that they have been given – in other words, their presentations must somehow reflect the strengths or the needs of that particular multiple intelligence. Their audience must guess the MI each group or person is using.
5. <u>Logistics</u>: Give students the *Procrastination* handout. Let them know that each student or group will have 2 minutes to present during the next class period. Give them class time to begin to talk over their presentations, and instruct them to continue their work outside of class. Finally, schedule a period of time in the next class day to see the eight presentations.

Closure: Review the different types of intelligences shown through the different ways to discuss procrastination. Discuss the benefits of seeing different perspectives and strengths.

PROCRASTINATION

The procrastinator is often remarkably optimistic about his ability to complete a task on a tight deadline. ...For example, he may estimate that a paper will take only five days to write; he has fifteen days; there is plenty of time, no need to start. Lulled by a false sense of security, time passes. At some point, he crosses over an imaginary starting time and suddenly realizes, "Oh no! I am not in control! There isn't enough time!"

At this point, considerable effort is directed toward completing the task, and work progresses. This sudden spurt of energy is the source of the erroneous feeling that "I work well only under pressure." Actually, at this point you are making progress only because you haven't any choice. ...Progress is being made, but you have lost your freedom.

Barely completed in time, the paper may actually earn a fairly good grade; whereupon the student experiences mixed feelings: pride of accomplishment (sort of), scorn for the professor who cannot recognize substandard work, and guilt for getting an undeserved grade. But the net result is *reinforcement*. The procrastinator is rewarded positively for his poor behavior ("Look what a decent grade I got after all!"). As a result, the counterproductive behavior is repeated time and time again.

William Sydnor,

California Polytechnic State University at San Luis Obispo

NOTES _____

_____

_____

_____

_____

_____

Convince Yourself!

Materials: <u>Handout</u> – *Convince Yourself!*

Activities:
1. <u>Hook</u>. Pick a fictitious character and start eliciting everything the class knows about that character (Aladdin, Garfield, Mickey Mouse, etc.). Have the students individually associate an intelligence that best describes the fictitious character.
2. Lead into a discussion about inheriting $1,000,000.
3. Handout – *Convince Yourself!*

Closure: Review the eight different types of intelligences by sharing the essays composed by the individual students.

Benefits of the lesson: Students will
1. Be able to self-reflect and make their own connections on the multiple intelligences.
2. Understand that this lesson was designed for the intrapersonal learner.

Name _____Date _____

CONVINCE YOURSELF!

Directions: Someone in your family has recently passed away. You have been invited to attend the reading of the will. To your surprise, you have just inherited $1,000,000. However, the awarding of the inheritance is contingent upon convincing the executor of the will that you have contributed to society through each of Howard Gardner's multiple intelligences.

Take a few moments to reflect on how you are going to convince the executor. Write your response in the space provided.

_____

_____

_____

_____

_____

_____

_____

_____

_____

_____

_____

_____

_____

_____

_____

_____

_____

_____

_____

Write Me a Song Lyric

Materials: Handout—*Music and the Intelligences*

Activities:
1. <u>Hook</u>: Have music playing as the students enter the class. Ask the students what kind of music they like to listen to (try to elicit types, rather than names of specific bands or songs). Lead into a discussion on what music gave to us when we were children (abc's, songs, socialization).
2. Talk about what music gives to individual people (relaxation, enjoyment, dancing, pleasure, knowledge, etc.).
3. Assign, or have students choose, one intelligence each. Distribute the handout—*Music and the Intelligences* – and have students complete it.

(Please note that although "Row, Row, Row Your Boat" may appear to be an elementary selection because it is a children's song, the familiarity makes it easier for students to understand this mostly underdeveloped intelligence.)

Closure: Review the eight different types of intelligences by sharing the song lyrics created by the students.

Benefits of the lesson: Students will
1. Begin to make the connection with how they were taught academics at a younger age, and how it might benefit their lives today.
2. Understand that this lesson was designed for the musical learner.

Name _____ Date _____

MUSIC AND THE INTELLIGENCES

Directions. Using the _____ (assigned) intelligence, make up a song lyric to the tune of *Row, Row, Row Your Boat.* Be sure to include the following information:

1. Name the intelligence you are working on.
2. Define the intelligence you are working on.

Chorus:
Eight Intelligences (row, row, row your boat)
Is what Gardner believes (gently down the stream)
He thinks people learn differently (merrily, merrily, merrily, merrily)
'Cause that's what individuals need (life is but a dream)

_____

_____

_____

_____

_____

_____

_____

Chorus:
Eight Intelligences (row, row, row your boat)
Is what Gardner believes (gently down the stream)
He thinks people learn differently (merrily, merrily, merrily, merrily)
'Cause that's what individuals need (life is but a dream)

Categorize Me

Materials: <u>Handout</u> – *Categorize me*

*Note: Schedule this activity after students have a fairly good working knowledge of the eight intelligences.

Activities:
1. Give everyone the handout. Then discuss that you will explore the characteristics of the eight intelligences through real people and characters.
2. For each intelligence, have the class brainstorm a list of real people (preferably well-known enough that others would recognize them) and characters (TV shows, films, animation, advertisements, etc).
3. Working from the lists, think of similarities among each group, and use those ideas to come up with words or phrases that indicate categories or characteristics that apply to each group. You may choose to go completely through the process for each intelligence one at a time, or you may want to brainstorm the eight lists and then go back and do categories and patterns afterwards.

Benefits of the lesson: Students will think in terms of patterns and categories, dominant skills of the naturalistic learner.

Name _____ Date _____

CATEGORIZE ME

Directions: Brainstorm people or characters that demonstrate strength in each intelligence. From thinking about how they are similar, come up with categories (based on their common characteristics) in which they would fit.

INTELLIGENCES	PEOPLE/CHARACTERS	CATEGORY(IES)
Verbal-Linguistic		
Logical-Mathematical		
Bodily-Kinesthetic		
Visual-Spatial		
Interpersonal		
Intrapersonal		
Musical		
Naturalistic		

Case Study: What Would You Do?

Read the following case scenario and spend 3-5 minutes writing a response to the question. In pairs or in small groups, share your thoughts and work to form the best resolution possible. Share the results with the class.

Roommate Trouble

Christof is attending a university in the Midwest. He is socially liberal, has many friends of both genders from all types of backgrounds, and doesn't hesitate to invite them back to his dorm room. Some of his friends smoke cigarettes and on at least two occasions his friends have used illegal drugs in the room. Kenta--a somewhat shy, studious person who is socially conservative--is Christof's roommate. Kenta prefers to relax in the dorm room without other people around. He doesn't approve of cigarettes or other drugs. In fact, his grandfather died of lung cancer due to cigarette smoking. He also feels uncomfortable around some of his roommates' friends, especially the ones who talk about hooking up with girls all the time. Kenta has not dated much, but feels Christof's friends treat women with disrespect. Christof is puzzled. When he and Kenta are alone, they enjoy each other's company. However, he can feel Kenta's disapproval when his friends are around. He thinks Kenta works too hard and needs to "loosen up." Kenta is feeling pushed out of his personal space, and is frustrated and angered by the situation.

Question: Is there a resolution that can work for both roommates? What options would you suggest? Walk through your solution(s) step-by-step.

Personal Differences Assessment

Answer the following on a separate piece of paper to begin thinking about your assumptions. These answers are for your eyes only. Honest answers will give the best indication of your perspective on these topics – and will help you consider whether you want to examine and perhaps adjust that perspective.

1. When I walk into a room of predominantly white people and notice that there are only a few black people, I think . . .
2. Our society has taught me to feel that homosexuals are generally . . .
3. When I walk into a room and notice a person in a wheelchair or on crutches, I think . . .
4. Our society has taught me to feel that Jewish people are generally . . .
5. Our society has taught me to feel that white people are generally . . .
6. When I see a woman out alone with a group of men, I think . . .
7. Our society has taught me to feel that white people are generally . . .
8. When I see a man out alone with a group of women, I think . . .
9. Our society has taught me to feel that black people are generally . . .
10. When or if someone close to me said that they were in love with someone of the same sex, I thought, or I would think . . .
11. Our society has taught me to feel that heterosexuals are generally . . .
12. Our society has taught me to feel that Muslims are generally . . .
13. If my child came home and said, "My new boy- or girlfriend is Jewish," I would think . . .
14. Our society has taught me to feel that handicapped people are generally . . .
15. When I see a black man and a white woman out on what appears to be a date, I think . . .
16. Our society has taught me to think that native Americans are generally . . .
17. Our society has taught me to feel that able-bodied people are generally . . .
18. If I thought I was attracted to someone of the same sex, I think I would . . .
19. When I see a white man out with a black woman on what appears to be a date, I think . . .
20. Our society has taught me to think that Asians are generally . . .
21. If a blind person asked me out on a date, I would . . .
22. I think women that ask men out are generally . . .
23. Our society has taught me to feel that Arabs are generally . . .
24. Our society has taught me to feel that men are generally . . .
25. Our society has taught me to think that Eastern religions (Buddhism, Hinduism, Taoism, Shintoism, etc.) are generally . . .
26. Our society has taught me to feel that women are generally . . .
27. Our society has taught me to think that lesbians are generally . . .
28. If a person tells me he or she has AIDS, I think . . .
29. If a close friend of the same sex told me he or she was in love with me, I would . . .
30. If I see two people of the same sex together with a child, I think . . .
31. When I listen to a person who has trouble with English or speaks with a noticeable accent, I think . . .
32. I think that people who come from large cities are generally . . .
33. I think that people who come from small, rural communities are generally . . .

34. If I were in a room with a group of people who aren't speaking English, I would feel . . .
35. Our society has taught me to feel that Hispanics are generally . . .
36. If a close friend of mine told me that he or she was a regular caller and believer of the Psychic Network, I would think . . .
37. If I am told someone is very wealthy, I think . . .
38. If I am told that someone is very poor, I think . . .
39. If a person I'm talking to reveals that he or she has suffered from, or is suffering from a mental illness, I would . . .
40. If I am in a room that is predominantly made up of elderly people, I feel . . .
41. When I walk into a room of predominantly black persons and notice there are only a few white people, I think . . .

Reprinted with permission. Mary Bixby, Ed.D., Learning Resource Specialist
University of Missouri-Columbia

PERSONAL PORTFOLIO ACTIVITY # 3
SELF-PORTRAIT THINK LINK

Because self-knowledge helps us make the best choices about our future, a self-portrait is an important step in your career exploration. Use this exercise to put everything together in one comprehensive picture. Design your portrait in "think link" style, using words and shapes to describe your intelligence, personality, abilities, career interests and other important aspects of who you are.

Below is one way you can begin to envision your think link. Another example appears in the text with this Personal Portfolio exercise. There are many other ways you could design it. Be creative! Design a think link that reflects, both in appearance as well as content, who you are.

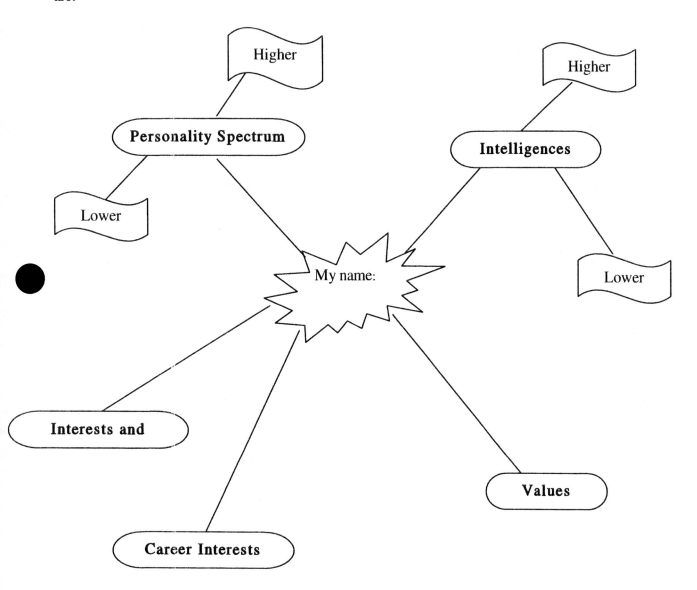

CONSIDER COMPREHENSION

REVIEW WITH STUDENTS BEFORE YOU BEGIN THE NEXT CHAPTER:

- What are assessments? ("The obtaining of information about a person's skills and potentials...providing useful feedback to the person." Howard Gardner, *Multiple Intelligence: New Horizons.* New York: Basic Books, 2006, p. 180.)
- What are the two assessments in this chapter and how are they different? (Gardner's MI: how we learn, Bishop's Personality Spectrum: how we react to the world)
- What is "cultural competence" and how do you define *prejudice, discrimination, stereotype*?
- Styles of communication and methods for giving and receiving criticism, managing conflict, and managing communication technology

Chapter Three Vocabulary Quiz Answer Key
(Quiz appears on following page)

1. E
2. I
3. A
4. G
5. K
6. B
7. J
8. C
9. L
10. F
11. D
12. H

CHAPTER THREE VOCABULARY QUIZ

1. _____ stereotype

2. _____ intelligence

3. _____ prejudice

4. _____ constructive criticism

5. _____ logical-mathematical intelligence

6. _____ bodily-kinesthetic intelligence

7. _____ visual-spatial intelligence

8. _____ interpersonal intelligence

9. _____ intrapersonal intelligence

10. _____ discrimination

11. _____ naturalistic intelligence

12. _____ Personality Spectrum

A. Preconceived judgment or opinion formed without just grounds or sufficient knowledge

B. Ability to use the physical body skillfully

C. Ability to relate to others, noticing their moods, motivations, and feelings

D. Ability to identify, distinguish, categorize, and classify species or items

E. A standardized mental picture that represents an oversimplified opinion

F. Actions that deny people equal treatment (employment, housing)

G. Criticism that promotes improvement or development

H. A tool based on the Myers-Briggs temperaments

I. An ability to solve problems or create products that are of value in a culture

J. Ability to understand spatial relationships and to perceive images

K. Ability to understand logical reasoning and problem solving

L. Ability to understand one's own behavior and feelings

CHAPTER THREE ASSESSMENT

Multiple Choice
Circle or highlight the answer that seems to fit best.

1. No matter what age you are,
   a. you cannot grow in certain academic areas.
   b. you can still learn and grow academically with effort.
   c. your IQ will remain fixed..
   d. your opportunities will depend on your GPA.

2. Howard Gardner defines intelligence as an ability to
   a. manage one's own emotions and understand the emotional reactions of others.
   b. solve problems or create products that are of value in a culture.
   c. apply self-knowledge in new settings.
   d. excel in verbal, logical, and mathematical skills.

3. Self-knowledge can help you
   a. understand how you respond to circumstances.
   b. make adjustments that will help you cope and grow.
   c. only a
   d. a and b

4. The ability to sense the moods and feelings of others is a strength of which intelligence?
   a. Intrapersonal
   b. Interpersonal
   c. Giver
   d. Organizer

5. In a group of students with various learning preferences, who of the following is using his or her strengths most effectively?
   a. A logical-mathematical learner who leads group discussions
   b. A bodily-kinesthetic learner who coordinates the schedule for the group
   c. A visual-spatial learner who brings chart and graphs to illustrate a point
   d. A musical learner who creates an outline of the lecture notes

6. If your instructor's teaching style is traditional lecture and you are an interpersonal learner, you might choose to
   a. adapt by sitting in a different location in class.
   b. ask the instructor to recommend charts, graphs, or photos to illustrate the concepts.
   c. join a study group to review and discuss issues with other students.
   d. focus on the abstract concepts to get the "big picture."

7. The Personality Spectrum assessment will help you to identify
   a. areas of intelligence, such as verbal-linguistic, bodily-kinesthetic, visual-spatial, logical-mathematical, and musical.
   b. four personality types that reveal the kinds of interactions that are most (and least) comfortable for you.
   c. your intelligence quotient.
   d. your visual, aural, reading/writing, kinesthetic abilities.

8. The traditional college classroom format is best for the
   a. verbal-linguistic learner.
   b. logical-mathematical learner.
   c. Thinker and Organizer
   d. all of the above.

9. According to the Personality Spectrum, what is NOT a primary characteristic of an Organizer?
   a. Loyalty
   b. Efficiency
   c. Dependability
   d. Ability to change

10. Ali has a strong interpersonal intelligence. She enjoys her history class but does not like memorizing facts and repetition. What would be a good study strategy for Ali?
    a. Think of concepts, interpretations, or theories that link the facts together.
    b. Use flash cards with a study group.
    c. Create a rhythm out of the words.
    d. Use notes as the basis for tables and graphs.

11. Shannon's most developed intelligences are naturalistic and bodily-kinesthetic. What career choice would be *least* suited to her based on these abilities?

    a. Telemarketer
    b. Landscaper
    c. Yoga instructor
    d. Massage therapist

12. The ultimate goal of cultural competence is to
    a. interact successfully with all kinds of people.
    b. understand diversity.
    c. learn to speak many languages.
    d. try different kinds of ethnic foods.

13. The BEST way to deal with your own prejudices and discriminatory actions is to
    a. focus on the positive aspects of individuals, groups, and cultures.
    b. build cultural knowledge.
    c. confront your own attitudes that define people based on group membership.
    d. avoid it.

14. What would be the BEST response if someone started giving you constructive criticism?
    a. Evaluate the criticism for truthfulness, then talk about it without being

defensive.
    b. Calmly walk away from the person.
    c. Even out the discussion by telling the person about his or her faults.
    d. Tell others about that person's faults.

15. Which is NOT an example of discrimination?
    a. Being fired from a job because you speak with an accent
    b. Not being hired because of a pregnancy
    c. Not being picked up by a cab because of skin color
    d. Thinking that your group is better than all other groups

True/False
Determine whether the statement is true or false, and circle or highlight the answer.

1. Each person has his or her own way to take information in and process it.
    True
    False

2. It is unlikely that an instructor will tailor the way he or she teaches to meet the learning preferences of every student in the classroom.
    True
    False

3. Gardner believes your levels of intelligences cannot grow or recede during your life.
    True
    False

4. Using self-assessments to gain an understanding of how you learn and interact with others can help you perform more effectively in college but will not help you at work.
    True
    False

5. An Adventurer is likely to respond well with an instructor who teaches with a traditional lecture format.
    True
    False

6. A naturalist is a person who looks for ways in which items fit or don't fit together into patterns.
    True
    False

7. Family members rarely learn intolerance from one another.
    True
    False

8. It's usually harder to label a group of people than to ask questions or really get to know them.
    True
    False

9. It is important to consider different communication styles because it helps you to relate more effectively to others who don't communicate as you do.
    True
    False

10. Organizer-dominant communicators tend to give a lot of detail and want to ensure that they have explained things clearly.
    True
    False

Fill in the Blank
Insert the word or phrase that BEST completes the sentence.

1. A learning _____ is a tool that identifies the processes one uses to take in, retain, and use information.

2. The *Personality Spectrum* assessment adapts and simplifies the Myers-Briggs Type Indicator® and the Keirsey Sorter categories by organizing them into four personality types: Thinker, Organizer, Giver and _____.

3. Instructors who use demonstrations, experiments, props, and class activities teach with an _____-_____ _____.

4. A strength in one or more _____ may lead to a major, an internship, or even a lifelong career.

5. When an instructor tackles topics in no particular order he or she uses a _____ _____ teaching style.

6. Respecting and accepting differences among people means you _____ _____.

7. A ____ _____ occurs when the motivation to commit a legal wrongdoing is prejudice and hate and when violence against another person(s) is involved.

8. Excluding someone or denying a person an opportunity because of religious differences is an example of _____.

9. The successfully intelligent response to discrimination and hate and the next step toward cultural competence is to gather_____.

10. An effective way to communicate with others is to recognize their communication patterns and then make an _____ in your own pattern to minimize misunderstandings.

Short Answer

1. Identify and describe your dominant intelligence (or your two most dominant, if two are fairly equal). How can you improve the way you use this intelligence to succeed in school?

2. Identify the teaching styles that you believe work best with your learning preferences and briefly explain why they work best.

3. Describe why "I" statements are so important to successful communication with a close friend or partner.

Essay

1. Consider a course you are taking now. How can you use your analytical, creative, and practical thinking skills to apply your newfound knowledge about your learning preferences to your work in the course?

2. Describe a time when a person or a group of people made an assumption about you that was not true. On what was the assumption based? Did it lead to any form of discrimination? Explain.

3. Summarize the advantages and disadvantages of communicating online. How can your words be interpreted differently online than when you are communicating face to face?

Word Exploration

Define this phrase: *oruko lonro ni* (o-roo-ko lon-ro nee)

What does this phrase mean to you? How does it apply to your life?

Chapter Three Assessment Answer Key

Multiple Choice

Test Item Assesses This Learning Objective/Topic

1. b   Why Explore Who You Are as a Learner?
Your unique intelligence can change and develop

2. b   Why Explore Who You Are as a Learner?
Assessments can help you learn about yourself

3. d   Why Explore Who You Are as a Learner?
Self-knowledge is an important, lifelong goal

4. b   What Tools Can Help You Assess How You Learn and Interact with Others?
Assess your multiple intelligences with Pathways to Learning (Key 3.1)

5. c   What Tools Can Help You Assess How You Learn and Interact with Others?
Assess your multiple intelligences with Pathways to Learning (Key 3.1)

6. c   How Can You Use Your Self-Knowledge?

7. b   What Tools Can Help You Assess How You Learn and Interact with Others?
Assess your style of interaction with the Personality Spectrum

8. d   What Tools Can Help You Assess How You Learn and Interact with Others?
Assess your style of interaction with the Personality Spectrum

9. d   What Tools Can Help You Assess How You Learn and Interact with Others?
Assess your style of interaction with the Personality Spectrum

10. b   What Tools Can Help You Assess How You Learn and Interact with Others?
Assess your multiple intelligences with Pathways to Learning

11. a   What Tools Can Help You Assess How You Learn and Interact with Others?
Assess your multiple intelligences with Pathways to Learning

12. a   How Can You Develop Cultural Competence?

13. c   How Can You Develop Cultural Competence?
Identify and evaluate personal perceptions and attitudes

14. a   How Can You Communicate Effectively?
Know how to give and receive criticism

15. d   How Can You Develop Cultural Competence?
Be aware of opportunities and challenges that occur when cultures interact

True/Fase

Test Item Assesses This Learning Objective/Topic

1. T   Why Explore Who You Are as a Learner?
        Your unique intelligence can change and develop

2. T   Why Explore Who You Are as a Learner?
        Your unique intelligence can change and develop

3. F   What Tools Can Help You Assess How You Learn and Interact
        with Others?
        Assess your multiple intelligences with Pathways to Learning

4. F   Why Explore Who You Are as a Learner? *and* How Can You Use
        Your Self-Knowledge?

5. F   How Can You Use Your Self-Knowledge?

6. T   What Tools Can Help You Assess How You Learn and Interact
        with Others?
        Assess your multiple intelligences with Pathways to Learning

7. F   How Can You Develop Cultural Competence?
        Identify and evaluate personal perceptions and attitudes

8. F   How Can You Develop Cultural Competence?
        Identify and evaluate personal perceptions and attitudes

9. T   How Can You Communicate Effectively?
        Adjust to communication styles

10. T   How Can You Communicate Effectively?
        Adjust to communication styles

Fill in the Blank

Test Item Assesses This Learning Objective/Topic

1. *assessment*

   Why Explore Who You Are as a Learner?

2. *Adventurer*

   What Tools Can Help You Assess How You Learn and Interact with Others?

   Assess your multiple intelligences with Pathways to Learning

3. *experience-based presentation*

   How Can You Use Your Self-Knowledge?

4. *intelligences*

   Why Explore Who You Are as a Learner?

   Assessments can help you learn about yourself

5. *random presentation*

   How Can You Use Your Self-Knowledge?

6. *value diversity*

   How Can You Develop Cultural Competence?
   Value diversity

7. *hate crime*

   How Can You Develop Cultural Competence?

   Be aware of opportunities and challenges that occur when cultures interact

8. *discrimination*

   How Can You Develop Cultural Competence?

   Be aware of opportunities and challenges that occur when cultures interact

9. *knowledge* (or) *information*

   How Can You Develop Cultural Competence?
   Build cultural knowledge

10. *adjustment*

    How Can You Communicate Effectively?

    Adjust to communication styles

Critical, Creative, and Practical Thinking
Solving Problems and Making Decisions

BRIEF CHAPTER OVERVIEW

This chapter begins Part II: Developing Skills for School and for Life. The five chapters in this part of the text form the backbone for academic and life success. Almost every student needs to devote more attention to practical study skills (reading and studying, listening, note taking, memory, and test taking) as well as life skills (wellness, money management, and career planning).

Chapter 4 expands on the introduction of successful intelligence from chapter 1. It helps students build abilities in each of the three successful intelligence areas: analytical thinking, creating thinking and practical thinking. Furthermore, it integrates those skills into a comprehensive discussion of the essential processes of problem solving and decision making.

When finished with this chapter, students should have a strong grasp of the differences in the three intelligence areas and of their own competence in each area, as well as tools for improvement where they are lacking, and they should have strengthened their practical problem-solving and decision-making skills.

Note the successful intelligence skills your students will build in chapter 4:

Analytical	Creative	Practical
▪ Evaluating fact, opinion, assumptions, and perspectives	▪ Brainstorming	▪ How to identify problems and decisions
▪ Analyzing whether examples support ideas	▪ Taking risks and promoting a creative environment	▪ How to use a plan to work through problems and decisions
▪ Evaluating potential and actual solutions and choices	▪ Developing potential solutions and choices	▪ How to adapt to your environment and learn from experience

CHAPTER FOUR OUTLINE

What Does It Mean to Think With Successful Intelligence?

- Successfully Intelligent Thinking Means Asking and Answering Questions

- Successfully Intelligent Thinking Requires Purpose and Drive

How Can You Improve Your Analytical Thinking Skills?

- Gather Information

- Analyze and Clarify Information

- Evaluate Information

How Can You Improve Your Creative Thinking Skills?

- Brainstorm

- Take a New and Different Look

- Set the Stage for Creativity

- Take Risks

How Can You Improve Your Practical Thinking Skills?

- Why Practical Thinking Is Important

- Through Experience You Acquire Emotional and Social Intelligence

- Practical Thinking Means Action

How Can You Use Successful Intelligence to Solve Problems and Make Decisions?

- Solving a Problem

- Making a Decision

- Keeping Your Balance

COMMUNICATE CONTENT
TOPICS COVERED IN THE CHAPTER

[Chapter and part intro and chapter 3 review: PowerPoint slides 1, 2, 3, 4]

The *Real Questions, Practical Answers* Discussion Starter Question:
How can I succeed in college if I don't test well? [See PowerPoint slide 5.]

The questioner here is concerned with test taking abilities. Ask students if they have similar concerns. It often helps build community in a classroom when students see each others' struggles with similar areas of academic study. Possible questions to ask students:

- What specifically is Parisa struggling with? (multiple choice tests)
- What are Parisa's strengths? (essays and conversation)
- How do you think Parisa determined her strengths or weaknesses?
- Ask a student to read aloud or summarize in his/her own words what the professional answer is for Parisa. (take practice and sample tests to learn how to answer properly, read slowly and carefully)
- The professional answer to Parisa's question includes a great illustration of combing all three successful intelligence skills in a career. Ask students to volunteer a similar illustration from their own jobs. Begin by using your own job as an illustration. "As a teacher, I combine analytical work (figuring out what to teach), creative work (figuring out how to make it fun and easy to remember), and practical work (writing tests, quizzes, and the syllabus)." Encourage students to venture to fill in the same model sentence. If they are stuck, have students help each other. This is a great community builder and it shows that students are grasping the three elemental skills of successful intelligence.

To transition to lecture, note that Parisa is aware of her weaknesses and is seeking help, which is an active part of successful intelligence.

(For more discussion starters, see p. 155 of this IM chapter.)

Question 1: What Does It Mean to Think With Successful Intelligence?

[Section overview: PowerPoint slide 6]

One Skill at a Time versus Combined Skills: Help students understand that life requires different strategies at different times. Sometimes, we use one skill in a situation. When we are trying to solve problems, however, acting with successful intelligence – using all the skills we have – will give us the greatest chance of success. **[See PowerPoint slides 7, 8]**

Have students review the chart in Key 4.1 "Successful Intelligence helps us achieve goals in any discipline." After reviewing several columns in the chart, pose discussion questions, offering other disciplines such as Music, Art or Computer Science. It would be a good idea for each student to share his/her major and have the class collaboratively brainstorm the ways analytical, creative and practical thinking are used in each field.

Thinking: Thinking is asking questions and moving forward with answers. Point out that questions are used in all three skills: to analyze, to come up with creative ideas, and to apply practical solutions. It is good to practice these questions with small sample problems. For example:

My cell phone is not working.

- Analyze: Why is my cell phone not working?
- Create: How else can I contact my friends?
- Take practical action: Where can I go to get help with my cell phone?

Ask students to pose problems they are currently facing within their families, work or education and ask these questions together as a class.

(Consider using the "Develop Your Questioning Skills" exercise on pp. 155-156 and Practice Problem Solving and Decision Making handout p. 166 of this IM chapter.)

Drive: Discuss the noun **drive** – as in, having the drive to do or achieve something – with the class. Read this phrase aloud from the text and have the students comment: "…having the skills isn't enough – you also have to want to use them." Ask student if they struggle with drive sometimes and how they deal with it. Students with more positive outlooks may be able to encourage those students in the class who have less drive. Drive is infectious. Ask students to comment on that statement. Draw them out by helping them think aloud about the term *infectious* – and *infection*.

 # Question 2: How Can You Improve Your Analytical Thinking Skills?

[Section overview: PowerPoint slide 9]

Definition and Process of Analytical Thinking: Analytical thinking is the process of gathering information, analyzing it in different ways, and evaluating it for the purpose of gaining understanding, solving a problem, or making a decision. After a student reads the definition aloud in class, review that there is an end goal: stress the words: "for the purpose of…"

150

The example that runs through this section (writing a paper on young teen use of the Internet) illustrates all of the steps of analytical thinking clearly, and highlights information literacy to boot. You may find it useful to reference it during your discussion.

Review the steps in thinking analytically. **[See PowerPoint slide 10.]**

- Gather information: Examples include reviewing the assignment and gathering information from different sources such as books, magazines, and the Internet.

- Analyze and clarify information: Discuss the following actions: break the information into parts, separate the ideas, compare and contrast, examine cause and effect, and look for themes, patterns, and categories. Be sure to draw students' attention to the important caution about analyzing for true (as opposed to false) causes.

  Note: Many of the activities related to analyzing information focus on distinguishing fact from opinion. Many students struggle with this concept and assume that everything they read in the newspaper and on the Internet is fact. It is worth taking extra time, in the form of discussion and activities, to make sure these concepts are clearly communicated. **[See PowerPoint slide 11.]**

(Consider using the "Fact or Opinion?" exercise and handout on p. 161 of this IM chapter.)

(Consider using the "Test Your Assumptions" exercise on p. 156 of this IM chapter.)

- Evaluate information: At this step, students must determine the significance of information. It is good to review Key 4.3 *"Ask questions like these in order to analyze"* (these appear on a handout on p. 162 of this IM chapter). It may help to ask these questions together about a current topic in the news.

Question 3: How Can You Improve Your Creative Thinking Skills?

[Section overview: PowerPoint slide 12]
Discuss creativity: There are several answers listed in the text. Brainstorm as a class other definitions and ideas that students have about creativity. Ask them, "Do you know a creative person? Describe him or her to the class." Highlight the various aspects of the definitions given in the text, including the idea that "To think creatively is to generate new ideas that may bring change." **[See PowerPoint slide 13.]**

Stress with the class that there is a **result** from creative thinking. Discuss as a class those who may feel that they are not so good at creative thinking. Ask other students what they can suggest to encourage those students in their pursuit of enhanced creative thinking skills.

Actions that can improve creativity include

- Brainstorming: Point out to the class that brainstorming is also called *divergent thinking* or *deliberate creative thinking*. Practice a few spontaneous brainstorming minutes in the class. Have students turn to the student next to them and brainstorm a possible solution to a world or national problem: poverty, war, crime, etc.

(Consider using the "Brainstorming 30" exercise on p. 157 of this IM chapter.)

- Taking a new and different look by challenging assumptions and shifting perspective. Shifting perspective is often difficult for a late adolescent – or an older adult with long-held views. Encouraged students to read this part of the text carefully and discuss any questions they may have. Older students in the class may be able to assist in this discussion by offering examples of different perspectives they have had during changing life stages: singleness, married life, retirement, etc. **[See PowerPoint slide 15]**

- Setting the stage for creativity discusses several strategies such as choosing or creating environments that free your mind, encouraging curiosity, and giving yourself time to "sit" with a question. **[See PowerPoint slide 14]**

- Taking risks. Be sure to discuss with the class the definition of sensible risk-taking. Ask students to clarify some examples of sensible risk-taking or suggest several risky activities and ask the class whether or not they are sensible. For example, riding a motorcycle without a helmet (risky), trying out for a play (sensible risk-taking), driving drunk (risky), engaging in unprotected sex (risky), asking a classmate out for coffee (sensible risk-taking).

Questioning is paramount in all creative thinking. Review Key 4.5 *Ask questions like these in order to jump-start creative thinking* (these appear on a handout on p. 163 of this IM chapter). *(Consider using the "What If?" exercise on p. 157 of this IM chapter.)*

 Question 4: How Can You Improve Your Practical Thinking Skills?

[Section overview: PowerPoint slide 16]

Among the three processes of successfully intelligent thinking, practical thinking is the most unfamiliar to students and often the hardest for them to "get" – largely because, as mentioned in chapter 1 of this manual, it goes beyond just knowing how to put something together or follow a map. It is helpful to discuss aspects that they might recognize, such as common sense, street smarts, or "how-to's," to get them moving in the right direction. However, those concepts are just part of practical intelligence.

More comprehensively, practical thinking is how you adapt to your environment, or change your environment to adapt to you, in order to move ahead toward your goals. The beginning of this section in the text has some helpful examples to bring up with your students. **[See PowerPoint slide 17.]**

Experience is a key component – much of practical thinking comes from what you learn through experience.

The importance of practical thinking: Impress upon students that practical thinking is the "engine" of successful intelligence – it is what propels your analysis and creative ideas forward so that the goal is actually achieved. For example, you go to college and build analytical skills as you earn a degree in computer science. The more you learn, the more creative ideas you come up with for information technology solutions. What would happen if you stopped there? Not much…the payoff comes when you take an IT job and put your knowledge into practical action solving problems and innovating for your company. *That's practical intelligence.*

This section also references emotional and social intelligence, which are largely practical areas, being learned extensively (especially social intelligence) from experience. Remind students of the importance of these areas, particularly in their ability to use practical intelligence in group situations. **[See PowerPoint slide 18.]**

Keep the focus on questions in place by reviewing Key 4.7 *"Ask questions like these to activate practical thinking"* (these appear on a handout on p. 164 of this IM chapter).

(Consider using the "Using Resources to Solve Problems" exercise on pp. 156-157 of this IM chapter.)

The *Get Practical* exercise at the end of this section has students fill in a "Wheel of Successful Intelligence" using the scores from the three self-assessments they completed within the text of chapter 1. **[See PowerPoint slide 19.]** The wheel is a great way for students to get a visual representation of how they view their successful intelligence skills, and can motivate them to work in areas that look like they need improvement.

(Consider using the "Emotional Intelligence Worksheet" handout, accompanied by a showing of the ABC News segment on this topic from the PH Video Library, found on p. 160 of this IM chapter.)

Question 5: How Can You Use Successful Intelligence to Solve Problems and Make Decisions?

[Section overview: PowerPoint slide 20]
This section of the chapter opens with a key difference. Make sure students can clearly see the DIFFERENCE between Problem Solving and Decision Making. This difference is clearly highlighted in the text (see Key 4.9). Problem solving requires focus on possible solutions. Decision making, on the other hand, focuses on meeting a need (a positive thing) rather than managing or avoiding a situation (often a negative thing). See Key 4.9 for sample situations.

The following steps are useful in solving a problem **[see PowerPoint slide 21]**:
- Using probing questions to define problems
- Analyzing carefully
- Generating possible solutions based on causes, not effects
- Evaluating solutions and allowing future action

The text also highlights the following steps for making a decision:
- Looking at given options and then trying to think of more
- Thinking about how the decision may affect others
- Gathering perspectives
- Looking at long-term effects
- Considering all of the factors and recognizing those that may derail your thinking

Make sure students understand the importance of effective problem solving and decision making. This is where they synthesize their analytical, creative, and practical skills into what are arguably the most useful processes they have in their quest for goal achievement and success in any arena throughout their lives. Refer students to Keys 4.10 and 4.11 for helpful examples of a problem-solving process and a decision-making process.

(Consider setting aside class time for the "Teamwork: Create Solutions Together – Powerful Group Problem Solving" exercise from the end of the text chapter, described on p. 155 of this IM chapter.)

(Consider using the "Develop Your Questioning Skills" exercise on pp. 155-156 and "Practice Problem Solving and Decision Making" handout p. 166 of this IM chapter.)

This part of the chapter concludes with a discussion on balance. Balance is an important topic for college-age persons who may struggle with using all three successful intelligence skills at the same time. **[See PowerPoint slide 22.]**

[Successful Intelligence Wrap-Up: PowerPoint slide 23]
[End-of-chapter foreign word: PowerPoint slide 24]
[End-of-chapter thought-provoking quote: PowerPoint slide 25]

****

CREATE COMMUNITY

DISCUSSION STARTERS

1. Use the cues listed above to discuss creativity. In turn, ask students to each state a two-sentence description of a person in their life that they consider creative. Jot notes on the board as students describe creative people. As a class, review the list of notes and see if there are any common terms in all of the class descriptions.

2. Discussion of fact versus opinion can be very animated in the classroom. Begin by selecting an ad for a current product, perhaps the latest version of a gaming machine or cell phone service or product. You can copy an advertisement for the entire class or simply show it on an overhead projector or computer projector (most ads are available online). Begin to examine whether facts are supported ideas; distinguish fact from opinion (or fact from emotional appeal); analyze cause and effect versus correlation; find underlying assumptions; and talk about the overall ad evaluation. Remind them how important this thinking skill is in college (link it to reading, writing, and research assignments), and beyond (link it to work—what employers look for).

3. To begin a discussion about balance, ask students, "What parts of your life are difficult to balance?" (If they hesitate, mention work, relationships with peers, school work, relationships with family, class schedules, personal time.) Continue the discussion on balance by asking more questions like, "Does anyone have any practical ideas about balancing a schedule at this point in your life?" and "How about creative ideas – how many people have done something others would think was crazy just to achieve balance in their lives?"

GROUP EXERCISES

Teamwork: Create Solutions Together – *Powerful Group Problem Solving*

This exercise, found at the end of chapter 4 in the text, asks students to generate a list of problems and work through the same steps as the writing assignment for problem solving and decision making. It is useful to do this assignment in class before assigning the writing exercise that follows this one in the text.

Develop Your Questioning Skills

Because critical thinking involves research and generating questions that will give information and insight into a situation, have students spend time developing their questioning skills. Give them several examples of unresolved situations. Have them divide into pairs or small groups and ask them to generate lists of questions. Draw from the following list of unresolved scenarios or come up with your own. Alternatively, you could use any of the problems listed in the *"Practice Problem Solving and Decision Making"* handout on page 166.

1. <u>This morning when you were ready to leave for work you couldn't find your keys.</u>
   Sample Responses: When was the last time I saw them? When was the last time I drove? What was I carrying when I came into the house? What did I do when I came in the house? Where do I usually leave my keys? Did I unlock the door with my house key? Could I have left them in the car? Could they still be in the door?

2. <u>Your keys are locked in the car and you have an important meeting in half an hour.</u>
   Sample Responses: Can I afford to miss the meeting? Can the meeting be rescheduled? Who can I call to get my keys for me? How long will it take them to come and help? What if I call a taxi? How long will it take for the taxi to come? How will I pay them? Can a friend or family member come and pick me up?

3. <u>You don't get paid until Monday but your rent is due the Wednesday before.</u>
   Sample Responses: Will my landlord mind if my rent is late? Can I get my paycheck early? Will my parents float me the money until next week? What does my rental agreement say about late payments? Is there a three- to five-day grace period? What fee would the owner charge for a late payment? How is my previous payment record? Will my clean credit history have any bearing on my landlord's leniency?

Test Your Assumptions

Have students select a newspaper article to read. Read the headline of one article and ask if this is stating opinion or fact. Ask the students to give examples of facts and then decide what makes a fact (the information is verifiable, the information is objectively real, the information corresponds with reality). Remind them a good rule of thumb is to look at all information as opinion, then question the validity of what is being said. Next, have the students break into groups and find ways to challenge the following assumptions:

- Rich people are happier than poor people.
- Most men are stronger than women.
- Most women are nurturing.
- Eating three balanced meals a day is important for good health.
- Dogs require more attention and care than cats.
- Men are thinkers and women are feelers.
- 100 level classes are easier than 200 level classes.
- People who graduate from college make more money than people who don't

Using Resources to Solve Problems (Contributed by Prof. Karyn Schulz)

Have student groups use all three successful intelligence skills to come up with suggestions for one or more of the following scenarios. For each scenario, the question to ask is: "What resource(s) would be most beneficial for you? Why?"

1. You are a full-time student registered for 13 credits. You work 25 hours a week and are beginning to fall behind in your studies.
2. You were very active in high school. A member of various clubs, you participated on sports teams and made good grades. You want to become active at this school as well. You want to make sure your grades don't suffer.

3. You are registered for 9 credits and work full-time off campus. You want to decrease your off campus hours and begin working on campus.
4. You are having problems understanding the content in your courses. You read the textbook and do the assignments and homework, but it still is confusing.
5. You are experiencing a problem with one of your instructors. His evaluations do not seem fair. You cannot drop the course because it is required for your major.
6. You have a learning disability and need accommodations.

"What If?"

To illustrate how to use creative and practical skills, try this exercise: Divide the class into groups of 4-5 students. Write on the board: "What if you couldn't fail in college? What major and/or career would you aim for?" Give students 2 minutes to write a response on paper. Each group needs 1 student to volunteer, or be selected, as a "discussion subject." (More than one student can be discussed if time permits). The discussion subject reads his or her response. Working with what they know about creative thinking, the group offers ideas about how this person could achieve his or her goal despite obstacles. To sum up, the group devises a plan containing specific actions for the discussion subject to take.

Practice Problem Solving and Decision Making

For this exercise, use the *Practice Problem Solving and Decision Making* handout on p. 166 of this IM chapter. Photocopy the problem solving rubric (Key 4.12, or p. 165 of this IM chapter) for each student. Make sure you have reviewed the problem-solving and decision-making process. Make one copy of the handout and cut each problem into strips. Fold and place in a bowl or hat. Have student pairs or groups select a problem and together complete the rubric. Ask students to share the solution they chose with the class.

"Brainstorming 30" Writing Exercise

Give students 8 minutes to write down 30 questions that are important in their life. When the time is up, have them circle their top 3. Ask students to call out some of their circled questions. As students read, have students with similar questions gather. In other words, they are forming like-minded groups. Next, to engage their practical skills, have grouped students develop an action plan to work toward answering their common question.

POP CULTURE LINKS

Movies: There are quite a few films where the creative and practical "underdog" wins out over the more purely analytical "brainiac" person, group of people, or company. Referencing a film like this might help give students some examples of successful people who don't fit the stereotype of the high-powered, logical and verbal, focused student or worker. Consider Ferris Bueller's Day Off (1986), Ocean's 13 (2007), Erin Brockovich (2000).

Music: Almost any kind of music can provide an opportunity for you to discuss creativity – the creative process (how the music was written, revised, recorded), the creative product (the music, how it is used or sold), creative variety and individual creative vision (different kinds of music, or the musical evolution of an evolving artist like David Byrne or Paul Simon), and so on. In addition, the newly popular "beat-boxing" phenomenon grew out of creative music-making abilities. Generate discussion about music trends and how they are creatively fueled.

SUCCESSFUL INTELLIGENCE EXERCISES

Get Analytical! *Analyze a Statement*
Assign for in-class activity or homework. Requiring students to analyze the parts, fact/opinion, perspective, and assumptions within a statement, this is a quick exercise and a great warm-up for class. Remind students to take it seriously and put genuine effort into it.

Get Creative! *Activate Your Creative Powers*
Assign for in-class activity or homework. Here students are encouraged to evaluate their creative thinking in the past month. This is a fun, encouraging exercise. It is very positive and shows students who are not confident that they are indeed creative at times!

Get Practical! *Take a Practical Approach to Building Successful Intelligence*
Assign for in-class activity or homework. This exercise has students pull together all of their assessment scores from the three successful intelligence exercises from chapter 1, recording them on a "Wheel of Successful Intelligence" so that they can see a visual representation of them at a glance. It is a great tool for visual learners. Have students carefully follow the directions as some may not understand how to combine all three scores on the wheel diagram.

HOMEWORK

In-text exercises: All three successful intelligence exercises (*Get Analytical, Get Creative,* and *Get Practical*) can be assigned for homework.

Foreign word response: Ask students to write a responsive essay to the word "kunnskaping." Ask them to describe what their version of "kunnskaping" is and how they will aim to achieve it this term. This may be difficult for students. Encourage them to think of the word in terms of practical results in their school and relationships.

End-of-chapter exercises:
- **Successful Intelligence: Think, Create, Apply** – This is a very practical exercise. Encourage students to carefully follow each step in the text, defining the decision (they may need help with this step and it can be done as a class time activity), examining needs and concerns, generating options (this can also be done as a group exercise) and evaluating the options. The exercise concludes with a practical application. Students must list the specific steps they would take in order to implement the decision.
- **Writing: Journal and Put Skills to Work** – Students can complete the journal entry as homework. The real-life writing assignment – addressing a problem – is another great homework assignment and asks student to write a letter. This is also a good way to encourage students to write letters to the school newspaper in response to problems they see on campus. As an optional way to use this assignment, students may decide on a problem as a class and those students who complete the assignment and submit a letter to the school paper would receive credit.
- **Personal Portfolio:** This assignment can be completed as homework. It requires students to generate a list of ideas for potential internships in their intended career fields. You may want to encourage students to inquire at the school career office for potential internships on campus. Consider using the handout on p. 167 of this manual.

Quotes for Reflection

Use these quotes to generate discussion, start class, or offer as a short exercise. Have students reflect on what any or all of the following quotes mean to them in a short paper or presentation.

> The foolish and dead alone never change their opinions.
> *Lowell*

> Even a thought, even a possibility, can shatter us and transform us.
> *Nietzsche*

> We do not live to think, on the contrary, we think in order that we may succeed in surviving.
> *José Ortega y Gasset*

> To live a creative life, we must lose our fear of being wrong.
> *Joseph Chilton Pearce*

> Progress, not perfection, is what we should be asking of ourselves.
> *Julia Cameron*

> A rockpile ceases to be a rockpile the moment a single man contemplates it, bearing within him the image of a cathedral.
> *Antoine de Saint-Exupéry*

> The creative person, in all realms of life, is like a child who dares to inquire beyond the limits of conventional answers.
> *Paul Tillich*

Handouts

The following are exercises with handouts, or handouts that you can use on their own. Integrate them into your lesson plan as you see fit, or follow the suggestions in the "Communicate Content" section.

- Emotional Intelligence Worksheet (handout that can accompany ABC News segment on emotional intelligence)
- Fact or Opinion? (handout)
- Questions that Spark Analytical Thinking (handout)
- Questions that Spark Creative Thinking (handout)
- Questions that Spark Practical Thinking (handout)
- Problem-Solving Flowchart (handout)
- Practice Problems to Solve and Decisions to Make (handout)
- Personal Portfolio Handout to accompany chapter 4 Personal Portfolio exercise

Emotional Intelligence Worksheet

"IQ" is a measure of one type of intelligence. Standard IQ tests primarily measure verbal ability. Does this one measurement predict success of any kind? Quiet children may at first appear not to be good students. Overly verbal students with little ability to concentrate or focus may disrupt classroom learning all the time. No matter your IQ, you need to develop *emotional and social skills* to succeed and contribute to society.

Daniel Goleman's book <u>Emotional Intelligence</u> opened the door to understanding basic skills that are deemed necessary to succeed in life - no matter the setting. Children who do not develop social skills at the rate of their peers in playgroups or who never learn these skills often become adults shunned by others. Key areas to consider are

1) Do you know what to do with your anger?
2) Can you soothe yourself when anxious?
3) Can you read others' feelings through nonverbal communication?
4) Do you control impulses, and can you delay gratification?

Questions:

1) Take time to think about your own "emotional IQ." Rate yourself from 1 to 10 (with 10 being the best) on the following social and emotional skills:

_____ appropriate management of anger   _____ ability to soothe anxiety
_____ ability to control impulses   _____ ability to delay gratification
_____ ability to read others accurately from nonverbal communication

2. Social skills established early appear to remain consistent throughout adulthood. Think back to your elementary school days. What social behaviors were taught and expected by your teachers?

3. Think about your current skill levels. How would you rate your ability to get along with others? How resilient are you in overcoming obstacles and setbacks?

4. Based on questions 1 and 3, how will your emotional IQ affect your success in your chosen career? How well do you currently work in a team for group projects? In terms of emotional IQ areas, which of your strengths will be assets to you in your career?

5. How is *emotional intelligence* different from or similar to *successful intelligence* that we have discussed in class?

??? Fact or Opinion ???

Select an advertisement from your own media or from materials brought in by your instructor. Evaluate using the chart in Key 4.2. Find **examples** in the ad and list them in the table below.

Product advertised: _____

Look for examples of:	Opinions	Facts
Statements that show evaluation (**opinion**) *OR* Statements that deal with actual people, places, objects or events (**fact**)		
Statements that use abstract words (**opinion**) *OR* Statements that use concrete words or measurable statistics (**fact**)		
Statements that predict future events (**opinion**) *OR* Statements that describe current events in exact terms (**fact**)		
Statements that use emotional words (**opinion**) *OR* Statements that avoid emotional words and focus on the verifiable (**fact**)		
Statements that use absolutes (words like *all, none, never,* and *always*) (**opinions**) *OR* Statements that avoid absolutes (words like *some, may, a few*) (**fact**)		

Signatures of two people who worked on this activity:

_____   _____

QUESTIONS THAT SPARK ANALYTICAL THINKING

To gather information, ask:	∞ What kinds of information do I need to meet my goal?
	∞ What information is available? Where and when can I get to it?
	∞ Of the sources I found, which ones will best help me achieve my goal?
To analyze, ask:	▪ What are the parts of this information?
	▪ What is similar to this information? What is different?
	▪ What are the reasons for this? Why did this happen?
	▪ What ideas, themes, or conclusions emerge from this material?
	▪ How would you categorize this information?
To see if evidence or examples support an idea, ask:	▪ Does the evidence make sense?
	▪ How do the examples support the idea/claim?
	▪ Are there examples that might disprove the idea/claim?
To distinguish fact from opinion, ask:	▪ Do the words in this information signal fact or opinion?
	▪ What is the source of this information? Is the source reliable?
	▪ If this is an opinion, is it supported by facts?
To examine perspectives and assumptions, ask:	▪ What perspectives might the author have, and what may be emphasized or deemphasized as a result?
	▪ What assumptions might lie behind this statement or material?
	▪ How could I prove, or disprove, an assumption?
	▪ How might my perspective affect the way I see this material?
To evaluate, ask:	▪ What information will support what I'm trying to prove or accomplish?
	▪ Is this information true or false, and why?
	▪ How important is this information?

Adapted from http://www-ed.fnal.gov/trc/tutorial/taxonomy.html (Richard Paul, *Critical Thinking: How to Prepare Students for a Rapidly Changing World*, 1993) and from http://www.kcmetro.edu/longview/ctac/blooms.htm, Barbara Fowler, Longview Community College "Bloom's Taxonomy and Critical Thinking"

QUESTIONS THAT SPARK CREATIVE THINKING

To brainstorm, ask:	▪ What do I want to accomplish? ▪ What are the craziest ideas I can think of? ▪ What are ten ways that I can reach my goal? ▪ What ideas have worked before and how can I apply them?
To shift your perspective, ask:	▪ How has this always been done – and what would be a different way? ▪ How can I approach this task or situation from a new angle? ▪ How would someone else do this or view this? ▪ What if…?
To set the stage for creativity, ask:	▪ Where, and with whom, do I feel relaxed and inspired? ▪ What music helps me think out of the box? ▪ When in the day or night am I most likely to experience a flow of creative ideas? ▪ What do I think would be new and interesting to try, to see, to read?
To take risks, ask:	▪ What is the conventional way of doing this? What would be a totally different way? ▪ What would be a risky approach to this problem or question? ▪ What is the worst that can happen if I take this risk? What is the best? ▪ What have I learned from this mistake?

QUESTIONS THAT SPARK PRACTICAL THINKING

To learn from experience, ask:	▪ What worked well, or not so well, about my approach? My timing? My tone? My wording? ▪ What did others like or not like about what I did? ▪ What did I learn from that experience, conversation, event? ▪ How would I change things if I had to do it over again? ▪ What do I know I would do again?
To apply what you learn, ask:	▪ What have I learned that would work here? ▪ What have I seen others do, or heard about from them, that would be helpful here? ▪ What does this situation have in common with past situations I've been involved in? ▪ What has worked in similar situations in the past?
To boost your ability to take action, ask:	▪ How can I get motivated and remove limitations? ▪ How can I, in this situation, make the most of what I do well? ▪ If I fail, what can I learn from it? ▪ What steps will get me to my goal, and what trade-offs are involved? ▪ How can I manage my time more effectively?

PROBLEM-SOLVING FLOWCHART

Define Problem Here   Analyze the Problem

_____   _____

_____   _____

_____   _____

_____   _____

Use sections below to list and analyze possible solutions.

POTENTIAL POSITIVE EFFECTS   SOLUTION   POTENTIAL NEGATIVE EFFECTS

_____   1._____   _____

_____   _____   _____

_____   _____   _____

_____   _____   _____

_____   2._____   _____

_____   _____   _____

_____   _____   _____

_____   _____   _____

_____   3._____   _____

_____   _____   _____

_____   _____   _____

_____   _____   _____

Now choose the solution you think is best...

ACTUAL POSITIVE EFFECTS   ACTION TAKEN   ACTUAL NEGATIVE EFFECTS

_____   _____   _____

_____   _____   _____

_____   _____   _____

_____   _____   _____

Re-evaluate: Was it a good or bad solution?

_____

_____

_____

_____

_____

_____

Practice Problem Solving and Decision Making

- You (or your girlfriend) are pregnant! What are your choices? What is the practical action?

- You need to attend summer school BUT you have already accepted a new, exciting summer job that will help your career. What are your choices? What is the practical action?

- You parents are divorcing and they want you to decide where to live. Do you move to live with one parent or not move and live with another? What are your choices? What is the practical action?

- You are having a ton of trouble following your instructor's teaching style. What are your choices? What is the practical action?

- It is time to decide: should I transfer schools or NOT? What are your choices? What is the practical action?

- Your boyfriend/girlfriend decides to transfer to a far away school. What are your choices? What is the practical action?

- You have a car to sell. Your friend is borrowing it. She really needs it. She has no money to by it, but you could really use the money by selling it. What are your choices? What is the practical action?

- You're swamped. There is too much to do. Too much pressure. What are your choices? What is the practical action?

- You are in a car with some friends. They decide to commit a crime as part of a dare. What are your choices? What is the practical action?

- You really need to find a place to live with low rent. You are about to give up hope. What are your choices? What is the **practical** action?

PERSONAL PORTFOLIO ACTIVITY # 4
GENERATING IDEAS FOR INTERNSHIPS

Pursuing an internship is a practical way to ① get experience, ② learn what you like and don't like, and ③ make valuable connections.

Below, you will brainstorm career areas and potential internships (*see text for more information*).

Career areas that I'm considering:
1. _____ because _____

2. _____ because _____

3. _____ because _____

Potential people I could interview about their fields/professions:
1. _____ because _____

2. _____ because _____

3. _____ because _____

Creatively envision your internship experience!
➲ What would it look like? What would you do each day? Each week?

_____
_____
_____
_____
_____

➲ Where would you go?

_____
_____
_____

➲ With whom would you work?

_____
_____
_____

➲ What would you contribute with your gifts and talents?

CONSIDER COMPREHENSION

REVIEW WITH STUDENTS BEFORE YOU BEGIN THE NEXT CHAPTER:

- Name one way to improve your analytical thinking skills (compare and contrast, examine cause and effect, look for themes and patterns in gathered information).
- Name one way to improve your creative thinking skills (brainstorm, take risks, etc.)
- Name one way to improve your practical thinking skills (use emotional intelligence, take action).
- What is the difference between solving problems and making decisions? (Problem solving generates possibilities, decision making meets a need.)
- Give one example of how to compare facts versus opinions (refer to Key 4.2).

Chapter Four Vocabulary Quiz Answer Key
(Quiz appears on following page)

1. D
2. G
3. A
4. J
5. B
6. C
7. F
8. H
9. E
10. I

CHAPTER FOUR VOCABULARY QUIZ

1. _____ argument

2. _____ perspective

3. _____ assumption

4. _____ bias

5. _____ brainstorming

6. _____ emotional intelligence

7. _____ thinking

8. _____ statement of fact

9. _____ statement of opinion

10. _____ absolute qualifiers

B. Letting your mind free-associate to come up with different ideas or answers

C. The ability to perceive, assess, and manage one's own emotions

D. A set of ideas, supported by examples, made to prove or disprove a point

E. A belief, conclusion, or judgment that is inherently difficult to verify

F. What happens when you ask questions and move towards the answers

G. A characteristic way of thinking about people, situations, events and ideas

H. Information presented as objectively real and verifiable

I. Words such as *all*, *none*, and *always* which often are used to express opinion

J. A preference or inclination, especially one that prevents even-handed judgment

A. A judgment, generalization, or bias influenced by experience and values

Chapter Four Assessment

Multiple Choice
Circle or highlight the answer that seems to fit best.

1. What will give you the greatest chance to solve a problem successfully?
    a. Using your analytical skills
    b. Analyzing to separate fact from opinion
    c. Using your analytical, creative, and practical skills
    d. Evaluating each potential solution

2. Which is the most important question to ask when you are choosing a major?
    a. What majors are my friends choosing?
    b. What academic focus does my career choice require?
    c. What major has courses offered at times convenient to me, given my current commitments?
    d. What is the most popular major on campus?

3. Gathering information requires a careful analysis of all the following EXCEPT
    a. the amount of information you need.
    b. the amount of time to spend locating the information.
    c. the relevancy of the information.
    d. the ability to shift perspectives.

4. What strategy will best help you break down information to build your understanding?
    a. Separate the ideas and look for themes
    b. Compare and contrast
    c. Examine cause and effect
    d. All of the above

5. Facts include statements that
    a. include absolutes, abstract terms, emotional words, and evaluative statements.
    b. predict future events.
    c. use concrete words, measurable statistics, and references to actual people, places and events.
    d. include absolutes, qualifiers, and measurable statistics.

6. Opinions include statements that:
    a. include absolutes, abstract terms, emotional words, and evaluative statements.
    b. avoid predicting future events.
    c. use concrete words, measurable statistics, and references to actual people, places and events.
    d. include absolutes, qualifiers, and measurable statistics.

7. "Gas prices are going to increase because oil companies are hoarding profits." This statement is an example of
    a. fact.
    b. opinion.
    c. creative analysis.
    d. assumption.

8. "Studies show that higher education leads to better job prospects." This statement is an example of
    a. fact.
    b. opinion.
    c. creative analysis.
    d. assumption.

9. When thinking creatively, it's important to
    a. brainstorm.
    b. be willing to take risks.
    c. give yourself time to think.
    d. all of the above

10. A person who can devise clever new uses for common products, such as newspaper or duct tape, has very developed _____ thinking skills.
    a. analytical
    b. intrapersonal
    c. creative
    d. natural

11. Which sequence of events illustrates the most helpful problem-solving plan?
    a. Clearly state the problem, analyze its cause and effects, brainstorm possible solutions, evaluate the pros and cons of each potential choice, pick an option, try it out, and evaluate its success
    b. Think of a solution, execute it, and evaluate the positive and negative effects. If it doesn't work, try another solution.
    c. Clearly state the problem, get advice from a friend or teacher, and act on the best suggestion.
    d. Recall a time when someone you know had a similar problem, find out what they did, evaluate the pros and cons, and then evaluate your options.

12. To change the way you look at something, you should try to
    a. get advice from your instructor as soon as you encounter a new idea.
    b. ask yourself if it is consistent with your core beliefs.
    c. challenge assumptions, shift perspectives, and ask "what if" questions.
    d. give yourself as much time as you need to gather information.

13. Practical thinking is
    a. asking and answering "big picture" questions and then breaking those questions into manageable parts so you can reach your goals.
    b. finding ways to shape, change, or adapt to one's environment to implement important goals.
    c. thinking clearly and effectively under stress.
    d. all of the above

14. Practical thinking is important because it
    a. encourages you to take risks.
    b. helps you to understand your environment.
    c. helps you actively apply what you know in real-world situations.
    d. focuses on analytical thinking.

15. You have a choice between two summer jobs. Job #1 offers experience in your major but pays a lower wage. Job #2 pays more money but is not directly related to your field of study. What should be the *first* step to take as you make this decision?
    a. Discuss with a friend in your major the pros and cons of taking one job versus the other.
    b. Consider how much money you need to earn during the summer and the value job #1 would have in helping you make a career choice.
    c. Calculate the cost of any luxury purchases you plan to make over the summer to determine if you can afford to take job #1.
    d. Continue applying for other jobs so you'll have more options to choose from before you have to decide.

True/False
Determine whether each statement is true or false, and circle or highlight the answer.

1. Your education should give you the tools to work through problems and decisions.
   True
   False

2. Successfully intelligent thinking means you control the number of questions you ask yourself.
   True
   False

3. Analyzing information requires that you think about the "big picture" to examine the main points.
   True
   False

4. When analyzing information and reviewing the cause and effect of something, be careful because you may discover false causes along the way.
   True
   False

5. An effective way to separate fact from opinion is to look for underlying biases and assumptions.
    True
    False

6. Taking a break to do something fun while thinking about a problem is an effective way to enhance your creative thinking.
    True
    False

7. Brainstorming, also known as divergent thinking, is not creative thinking.
    True
    False

8. Social intelligence involves understanding people and how to maximize your relationships.
    True
    False

9. The key to using practical thinking successfully is to constantly shift your perspective, even if it means making mistakes.
    True
    False

10. The key to making effective decisions is to put your analytical, creative, and practical thinking skills together.
    True
    False

Fill in the Blank

Insert the word or phrase that BEST completes the sentence.

1. _____ is what happens when you ask questions and move toward the answers.

2. _____ is a Norwegian word that combines words meaning "knowledge" and "value creation."

3. _____ _____ is the process of gathering information and examining it in different ways.

4. A set of connected ideas, supported by examples, made by a writer to prove or disprove a point is a(n) _____.

5. _____ and _____ intelligence have a significant effect on your ability to communicate and maneuver among groups of people in way that helps you achieve your goals.

6. *Bias* is a preference or inclination, especially one that prevents even-handed _____.

7. To set your mind free and come up with different ideas or answers is to _____.

8. _____ _____ refers to how you adapt or change your environment to achieve your goals.

9. _____ is a characteristic way of thinking about people, situations, events and ideas.

10. Examining cause and effect means looking at the _____ why something happened as well as the _____.

Short Answer

1. Compare and contrast the steps in problem solving and decision making.

2. Define creative thinking and provide three examples of how you used it in the last month.

3. Define practical thinking and provide three examples of how you used it in the last month.

Essay

1. Assume you received a D on your first college paper. Go through the problem- solving steps to define your possible options and solutions to improve your work.

2. Describe the environment that would give you the best possible chance at generating creative ideas. Include setting, time, people involved (or not), materials, and any other important factors. If you don't currently have access to this environment, describe a plan for how you will create and/or access it.

3. Describe the thinking process you will follow to solve the problem of paying your college tuition. Give at least three possible solutions.

Word Exploration

Define this phrase: *emotional intelligence*

What does this word mean to you? How does it apply to your life?

Chapter Four Assessment Answer Key

Multiple Choice

Test Item Assesses This Learning Objective/Topic

1. c   What Does It Mean to Think With Successful Intelligence? *and* How Can You Use Successful Intelligence to Solve Problems and Make Decisions?

2. b   What Does It Mean to Think With Successful Intelligence?
Successfully intelligent thinking means asking and answering questions

3. d   How Can You Improve Your Analytical Thinking Skills?
Gather information

4. d   How Can You Improve Your Analytical Thinking Skills?
Analyze and clarify information

5. c   How Can You Improve Your Analytical Thinking Skills?
Analyze and clarify information

6. a   How Can You Improve Your Analytical Thinking Skills?
Analyze and clarify information

7. b   How Can You Improve Your Analytical Thinking Skills?
Analyze and clarify information

8. a   How Can You Improve Your Analytical Thinking Skills?
Analyze and clarify information

9. d   How Can You Improve Your Creative Thinking Skills?

10. c   How Can You Improve Your Creative Thinking Skills?

11. a   How Can You Use Successful Intelligence to Solve Problems and Make Decisions?

12. c   How Can You Improve Your Creative Thinking Skills?
Take a new and different look

13. b   How Can You Improve Your Practical Thinking Skills?

14. c   How Can You Improve Your Practical Thinking Skills?
Why practical thinking is important

15. b   How Can You Use Successful Intelligence to Solve Problems and Make Decisions?
Making a decision

True/False

Test item assesses this learning objective/topic

1. T   How Can You Use Successful Intelligence to Solve Problems and Make Decisions?

2. F   What Does It Mean to Think With Successful Intelligence?
Successfully intelligent thinking means asking and answering questions

3. F   How Can You Improve Your Analytical Thinking Skills?
Analyze and clarify information

4.	T	How Can You Improve Your Analytical Thinking Skills?
		Analyze and clarify information
5.	T	How Can You Improve Your Analytical Thinking Skills?
		Analyze and clarify information
6.	T	How Can You Improve Your Creative Thinking Skills?
7.	F	How Can You Improve Your Creative Thinking Skills? *Brainstorm*
8.	T	How Can You Improve Your Practical Thinking Skills?
		Through experience, you acquire emotional and social intelligence
9.	F	How Can You Improve Your Practical Thinking Skills? *and*
		How Can You Improve Your Creative Thinking Skills?
10.	T	How Can You Use Successful Intelligence to Solve
		Problems and Make Decisions? *Making a decision*

Fill in the Blank

Test item assesses this learning objective/topic

1.	*Thinking*	What Does It Mean to Think With Successful Intelligence?
2.	*Kunnskaping*	Successful Intelligence Wrap Up
3.	*Analytical thinking*	How Can You Improve Your Analytical Thinking Skills?
4.	*argument*	How Can You Improve Your Analytical Thinking Skills?
5.	*Emotional, social*	How Can You Improve Your Practical Thinking Skills?
(Note: either order is fine)		*Through experience you acquire emotional and social*
		intelligence
6.	*judgment*	How Can You Improve Your Analytical Thinking Skills?
		Analyze and clarify information
7.	*brainstorm*	How Can You Improve Your Creative Thinking Skills?
		Brainstorm
8.	*Practical thinking*	How Can You Improve Your Practical Thinking Skills?
9.	*Perspective*	How Can You Improve Your Analytical Thinking Skills?
10.	*reasons,*	What Does It Mean to Think With Successful Intelligence?
	consequences	

Reading and Studying
Focusing on Content

BRIEF CHAPTER OVERVIEW

Reading successfully involves coordinating analytical, creative, and practical thinking skills with a step-by-step approach to mastering the content of various reading materials. This chapter focuses on improving comprehension, using the SQ3R technique, and responding critically to materials. New at the end of the chapter is a practical discussion of how to mark up texts and other reading assignments in order to maximize retention and comprehension. The material on studying in groups, previously in this chapter, has moved to chapter 1 in order to bring this important skill to students' attention as early in the term as possible.

The challenge in this chapter is to convey the importance of committing the time and effort required to read effectively in college. Not only is the volume of reading high, but college readers must be self-sufficient enough to know what to do when a professor assigns a 400-page, dense text and informs students that the test is in five weeks. Commitment, comprehension, and strategy become crucial to student success.

We recommend that you give a lot of attention to the importance of strategies that will help students be as prepared as possible in their other coursework – completing reading assignments before class, working to comprehend the material, and asking clarifying questions. Many instructors tell us that the SQ3R method takes the bulk of the time they spend on this chapter, so you may want to plan accordingly.

Note the successful intelligence skills your students will build in chapter 5:

Analytical	Creative	Practical
▪ Identifying steps to improve comprehension	▪ Creating an environment that encourages concentration	▪ How to study word parts to build vocabulary
▪ Mastering SQ3R	▪ Adapting SQ3R to your unique studying needs	▪ How to make SQ3R.a personal tool
▪ Building vocabulary by mastering roots, prefixes, and suffixes	▪ Using colors and notations to highlight text and take text notes	▪ How to put highlighting and note-taking systems into action
▪ Critically evaluating reading passages		

CHAPTER FIVE OUTLINE

What Will Improve Your Reading Comprehension?

- Set Your Expectations
- Take an Active Approach to Difficult Texts
- Choose the Right Setting
- Learn to Concentrate
- Become Emotionally Involved
- Define Your Reading Purpose
- Spend Enough Time
- Use Special Strategies with Math and Science Texts
- Develop Strategies to Manage Learning Disabilities
- Expand Your Vocabulary

How Can SQ3R Help You Own What You Read?

- Survey
- Question
- Read
- Recite
- Review

How Can You Respond Critically to What You Read?

- Use Knowledge of Fact and Opinion to Evaluate Arguments

How Do You Customize Your Text with Highlighting and Notes?

- How to Highlight a Text
- How to Take Text Notes

COMMUNICATE CONTENT
TOPICS COVERED IN THE CHAPTER

[Chapter intro and chapter 4 review: PowerPoint slides 1, 2, 3]

The *Real Questions, Practical Answers* Discussion Starter Question:
How can I improve my reading and studying despite my learning disabilities?
[PowerPoint slide 4]

Many students will relate to the inquiry about reading struggles. In the spirit of creating community, ask if any students are willing to share similar difficulties with reading. It is hoped that students will be able to share openly this far into the term. If students are not willing to open up, share your own personal struggles with reading (if you have them) or those of a previous student or even your own children. If you sense this class has many students who have trouble reading, consider inviting a guest speaker from the campus tutoring center to discuss how and where to get individual help.

    The professional response to the questioner is very positive. Note that fact to the students. Write the phrase, "There is more than one way to succeed in college." Ask students to respond aloud with the ways that helped the responder succeed (attending every class, borrowing friends' notes, establishing personal relationships with teachers). It may be good at this point to ask students to write in their journal or on their own paper about a struggle they have with reading.

(For more discussion starters, see p. 186 of this IM chapter.)

Question 1: What Will Improve Your Reading Comprehension?

[Section overview: PowerPoint slide 5]
Reading is truly an analytical skill because readers must derive meaning from written words. Comprehension is the key to benefiting from reading. There are many factors that affect this skill and they are always different for each student. It is important to stress to the class that everyone can benefit from focusing on improving reading comprehension, regardless of their level of comfort with reading skills. Point out that part of why this is true is that college reading assignments will be longer and more complex than students have seen before.

    Review comprehension strategies in the text – here they are, some with additional notes:

- **Set expectations**. Be realistic about number and type of assignments and time frame.

- **Take an active approach to difficult texts**. Being active with a text requires thinking positively, having an open mind, looking for order and meaning in difficult passages, having reasonable expectations, approaching texts with a real sense of the extra work required, and a willingness to use a dictionary for difficult concepts and words. Encourage students to be honest with themselves, asking themselves questions about their level of understanding, such as "Do I understand what I just read?" **[See PowerPoint slide 6.]**

(Consider using the "More Than One Way to Succeed in College" exercise on p. 186 of this IM chapter.)

- **Choose the right setting**. Learning styles and preferences can often help students determine their best place to study. Ask the class to revisit the MI types or the Personality Spectrum categories and come up with examples of appropriate places to study. Review the in-text strategies regarding selecting right time, location, and company. If your class has some students who are also parents, talk about hints for managing children while studying (see Key 5.2).

- **Learn to concentrate. [See PowerPoint slide 7.]**

- **Become emotionally involved.**

- **Define reading purpose**. Defining reading purpose is a crucial skill. Point out that creating a goal for each study session and reading assignment will help students feel more in control. Four reading purposes are covered in the text: <u>Understanding</u>, <u>Critical Evaluation</u>, <u>Practical Application</u>, and <u>Pleasure</u>. Ensure that students can identify reading purpose by proposing several types of reading and asking them what the purpose may be for the reading assignment. **[See PowerPoint slide 8.]**

(Consider using the "Defining Reading Purpose" exercise and handout on pp. 189-191 of this IM chapter.)

- **Spend enough time**. Ask students: How much time do you spend reading and studying per week? **[See PowerPoint slide 9.]** Then try this quick calculation to bring home the point about how much time students need to set aside for reading and studying.

  Have students take out a piece of paper, list the number of credit hours they're taking, and multiply that number by 2 and by 3. The result from multiplying by 2 equals the minimum amount of time they need to read and study outside of class per week; the result from multiplying by 3 is the ideal number of hours spent reading and studying. So, students taking 12 credit hours should ideally read/study 36 hours per week. **[See PowerPoint slide 10.]**

- **Use special strategies with math and science texts**. Special strategies for math and science texts are also highlighted here. You may want to survey students to find out how many are struggling with math or science class required reading. Note that kinesthetic responses to math and science texts (the act of writing while you are reading) are often helpful to students. Encourage students to read ahead into chapter 6 if they are interested in using the mnemonic devices taught there to memorize specialized vocabulary. **[See PowerPoint slide 11.]**

- **Develop strategies to manage learning disabilities.**

- **Expand vocabulary**. Emphasize to students that the more words you understand, the less time you have to spend figuring out and/or looking up words. Students can build vocabulary through working on understanding word parts, using new words in context, and using the dictionaries and glossaries at the back of textbooks. For additional work, try crossword puzzles, hangman, and Scrabble to build vocabulary.

(Consider using the "Definitions Affect Reading for Meaning" exercise on p. 187 of this IM chapter.)

⟹ Question 2: How Can SQ3R Help You Own What You Read?

[Section overview: PowerPoint slide 12]
Students may be familiar with the SQ3R technique from their high school classes or from previous courses in college. Explain that a focused, attentive reading strategy improves comprehension and retention of the material required in many courses. For students new to this technique, encourage them to read the text carefully and learn the meaning of the letters in the acronym. Note the order of the three R's: *Read, Recite, Review.* Stress that this order is essential and important to memorize. Remind students that they can personalize the SQ3R strategy to fit their needs.
    Walk students through the parts of the technique **[see PowerPoint slide 13]**:

Survey (or Preview). Highlight the importance of looking through the entire text, from table of contents in the front to index in the back. Remind students how they naturally were inquisitive and surveyed their new books at the beginning of the semester, flipping through pages to get an idea of what topics the text covered.
(Consider using the "Class Textbook Pass" exercise on p. 186 of this IM chapter.)

    <u>Note</u>: It is important to review the *skimming* and *scanning* definitions BEFORE explaining surveying. Because skimming and scanning are introduced prior to surveying, the three S words are often confused by students. Skimming and scanning are methods used to perform the SQ3R technique and it is good to make this distinction for students before examining the specific letters of SQ3R.

Question. First review with students the questioning task as described in the text. You may want to discuss it from the perspective of Bloom's Taxonomy (see Key 5.6). To ask questions about a reading assignment, review the following with students:

1. Ask yourself what you know about the topic
2. Write questions linked to chapter headings. You may make an example of this textbook (since almost all students will have it with them in class) and do some practice questioning using upcoming chapters. See Key 5.5 for an example.

Read. For the 3R portion of SQ3R, reading is the first skill. The text stresses focusing on key points (from the survey part of SQ3R), then on the questions written, followed by an active approach of marking up the text and taking text notes. Finding the main idea of a sentence is an important skill that is often weak in students. There are many techniques for finding main ideas, with several highlighted in the text. **[See PowerPoint slide 14.]**

Recite. Recitation anchors ideas in memory. Reciting is probably one of the most neglected parts of the SQ3R technique. Remind students that it is important and should not be avoided. Reciting does not have to be aloud, so students do not need to be embarrassed about "talking to themselves" in public. Reciting can also be performed silently to yourself, or can be as simple as teaching the answers to another person.

Review. It is important that reviewing be done at different time intervals after reading a text. Reviewing can be done immediately after reading and also after an extended period of time. Reviewing over time will help students identify knowledge gaps. Make sure to have students read aloud the reviewing techniques listed in the text. Consider inviting them to comment on which ones work for them, which techniques they have used the most, and which ones they are curious to try the next time they face a difficult reading assignment.

Discuss reviewing alone and reviewing with others – ask students which they prefer and why. Discuss the value of reviewing their reading and lecture notes together to see how they fit and whether there are inconsistencies.

(Consider using "Teamwork: Create Solutions Together – Organize a Study Group" exercise from the text, described on p. 186 of this IM chapter.)

As a wrap-up to this topic: You may want to have students use SQ3R for one reading assignment for one of their content area courses. Have a class discussion or require a written response on the merits of SQ3R and a comparison/contrast of SQ3R with what they currently do.

(Consider using the "SQ3R" exercise and handout on pp.189 and 192 of this IM chapter.)

 # Question 3: How Can You Respond Critically to What You Read?

[Section overview: PowerPoint 15]
Critical reading, like critical thinking, applies analytical thinking skills to analyze and evaluate information. In research, for instance, many articles will have a perspective that readers will need to assess and evaluate. This short but pithy section of the text contains instruction on an essential element of effective reading: evaluating an *argument* and its supporting evidence for fact and opinion. Define the term "argument" with your students so that they understand it clearly and can distinguish materials based on an argument from informational materials without one.

Be sure to carefully review in class the questions in the text:
- What is the quality of the evidence?
- How well does the evidence support the idea?

 # Question 4: How Do You Customize Your Text with Highlighting and Notes?

[Section overview: PowerPoint slide 16]
The three concepts in this section require student application: developing a highlighting system, developing a system for taking notes in text margins, and creating complete text notes.

1. **Highlighting**: The text reviews some excellent highlighting techniques, including how to avoid overdoing color. Remind students that the key is to develop a system *beforehand* that complements their study/learning preferences and to use it consistently. Encourage students to read entire paragraphs before they begin highlighting, as it is easier to gain a sense of what is important when the passage is looked at as a whole.

2. **Taking Notes in Text Margins**: The text offers tips worth putting into practice. To help students master them, assign the *Get Practical "Mark Up a Page to Learn a Page"* exercise. That activity asks students to highlight and create notes in the margins of a business text excerpt.

3. **Taking Full-Text Notes**: This section, which focuses on summarizing text material, provides suggestions that force students to interact with the material in an active way. We recommend that you assign students 2 chapters' worth of text material from this course or another one of their courses (their choice, perhaps, depending on which class they feel they could use some extra work on) to summarize.

Be wary that some students do not like to write in textbooks because they are eager to sell them back at the end of the term. Reinforce that this text is a *workbook* with important exercises for practice and personal evaluation and assessment. Writing in a textbook helps students customize learning to their specific needs and abilities.

[Successful Intelligence Wrap-Up: PowerPoint slide 17]
[End-of-chapter foreign word: PowerPoint slide 18]
[End-of-chapter thought-provoking quote: PowerPoint slide 19]

****

CREATE COMMUNITY

DISCUSSION STARTERS

1. Ask students to share struggles with reading problems. Ask them to hold up textbooks that are difficult for them. Other students will usually begin to comment on the texts if they have also taken the course.
2. Ask students who already have a note-taking system to share with the class how they developed it, how it works for them, which specific subjects they use the system in, and so forth.
3. Present to students the SQ3R strategy. Ask students to share their experiences with the strategy. Some may have been using it for years. Ask students, "How has it helped you in specific classes?"

GROUP EXERCISES

Teamwork: Create Solutions Together – *Organize a Study Group*

This exercise, found at the end of chapter 5 in the text, asks students to organize a study group with three or four classmates. Make sure students look carefully at setting specific goals for the group and talking about the specific ways they will work together. The exercise also has a suggested initial group activity that you can have groups try.

More Than One Way to Succeed in College

This exercise promotes mutual encouragement. Distribute brightly colored half sheets of paper to the class. Ask students to write their initials on the back of the paper, discreetly in a corner. On the other side, ask them to write a struggle they are having with reading. Collect the papers, shuffle, and redistribute face up. Have students respond in writing, on the paper they receive, to their classmate's struggle with a positive encouragement or solution they have remembered from the text. After a few minutes have elapsed, have students shift papers to the right and write on another student's struggle.

After several shifts, each student should have at least three or four positive responses to their reading struggles. Collect the sheets, and redistribute to the owner of the struggle, using the initials on the back of the sheet. An interesting follow-up to this activity is to ask students a week or two later if they have implemented any of the suggestions given to them by their classmates.

Class Textbook Pass

Ask a student to lend you a textbook from another course for discovery purposes. Pass the book around the classroom, having each successive student name a feature, such as those listed in the portion of the text about the survey stage of SQ3R. Ask students for ideas about why these features help (show you main points, break text up into more "digestible" segments, tell you what will be discussed, show you what you will be responsible to know).

Definitions Affect Reading for Meaning

Break into small groups. Give students a difficult passage of reading. For instance, you may want to use a paragraph from a graduate text. Have students read individually, circle words they don't understand, and discuss what they think the meanings are (5 minutes). Give half the groups correct definitions and the other half false definitions. Have the groups try to reread and understand the passage with the new definitions. Each group should report back to the class their findings—especially whether they felt it was harder or easier to comprehend once they knew the unfamiliar words.

POP CULTURE LINKS

Movies: Ask students if they have seen any films that have been made from a book. Some possible ideas range from more classic material (Sense and Sensibility, Hamlet, All the President's Men, To Kill a Mockingbird) to modern novels (Even Cowgirls Get the Blues, Bonfire of the Vanities, Bridge to Terabithia, Pay it Forward, Bridget Jones' Diary, Forrest Gump, The Last King of Scotland, etc.). Although narrative material is different from most of the textbook material they are handling in school, you can talk about reading elements in terms of what they see in the film – questions that come up, what they remember most vividly and why, concepts that were difficult to understand. If you discuss difficult concepts and it helps some students understand them more clearly, you can use that as a springboard to a discussion of the value of study groups.

Music: Any kind of music that has words can help illustrate points about remembering what you read. Download and print a set of song lyrics from a current tune that some of your students will know – as long as it isn't objectionable – or go with something classic like the Beatles or Motown. Hand out lyrics, play the tune, and talk about why people are able to recall the material so well – make sure you include points like repetition, association with a tune, interest level, rhythm, etc. See if students can come up with some helpful study ideas from this discussion (i.e., ways in which they can rewrite important material to resemble a song).

SUCCESSFUL INTELLIGENCE EXERCISES

Get Analytical! *Assess Yourself as an Analytical Thinker*
Assign for in-class activity or homework. Here students are asked to survey a text. The assignment is not specific to any one text. Be specific with students if you are assigning their current text for this course. Otherwise, they are at liberty to choose another. This is a practical assignment and worksheet they can use for examining all textbooks, particularly at the beginning of a term, so they can gain a strong understanding of the course direction and philosophies.

Get Creative! *Assess Yourself as a Creative Thinker*

Assign for homework. Here students are challenged to read a book after they have seen a movie based on the book. They are asked to compare major differences and character details which enhance the plot. The exercise has an *optional* or *later* nature to it, so if you are going to require it as an assignment, be specific with students about due dates.

Get Practical! *Assess Yourself as a Practical Thinker*

Assign for in-class activity or homework. Here students are asked to mark up a sample reading assignment using highlighting and marginal notes. It is a good exercise for group work or pair work, as students can compare note taking systems and words highlighted with each other.

HOMEWORK

In-text exercises: All three successful intelligence exercises (*Get Analytical, Get Creative,* and *Get Practical*) can be assigned for homework.

Foreign word response: Ask students to write a responsive essay to the word "yokomeshi." Ask them to describe what their version of "yokomeshi" is and how they will aim to achieve it this term. *Yokomeshi* is a lighthearted word which encourages us to relax when approaching a difficult topic. This may also be a good classroom discussion, with students sharing humorous stories and anecdotes about taking on difficult courses and texts.

End-of-chapter exercises:
- **Successful Intelligence: Think, Create, Apply** – Ask students to read the typical college text excerpt. Then have them complete the exercise.
- **Writing: Journal and Put Skills to Work** – Students can choose the journal writing prompt or the real-life writing prompts and write in response.
- **Personal Portfolio:** This assignment involves a quick self-assessment on reading skills. Stress that rating oneself honestly is most important and that the ratings are not graded, only completion of the response to them! Consider using the accompanying handout on p. 195 of this manual.

QUOTES FOR REFLECTION

Use these quotes to generate discussion, start class, or offer as a short exercise. Have students reflect on what any or all of the following quotes mean to them in a short paper or presentation.

> In books, I could travel anywhere, be anybody, understand worlds long past and imaginary colonies in the future.
> *Rita Dove*

> Books must be read as deliberately and reservedly as they are written.
> *Henry David Thoreau*

> Literature is the one place in any society where, within the secrecy of our own heads, we can hear voices talking about everything in every possible way.
> *Salman Rushdie*

> 'Tis the good reader that makes the good book; in every book he finds passages which seem confidences or asides from all else meant for his ear; the profit of books is according to the sensibility of the reader; the profoundest

thought or passion sleeps within a mine, until it is discovered by an equal
mind and heart.
Ralph Waldo Emerson

HANDOUTS

The following are exercises with handouts, or handouts that you can use on their own.
Integrate them into your lesson plan as you see fit.

- Defining Reading Purpose (exercise with handout)
- SQ3R Activity (exercise with handout)
- Study Skills for How You Learn (handout)
- Multiple Intelligence Grid for Test Preparation Strategies (handout)
- Personal Portfolio Handout to accompany chapter 5 Personal Portfolio exercise

Defining Reading Purpose Group Activity

Count off the class in 4s so everyone has a number. Assign each number a reading purpose and
give everyone with that number a copy of the paragraph that corresponds to that purpose (Note:
You may use the paragraphs on the two-page handout that follows, or find ones of your own).

Have students take a few minutes to read individually. Then, students gather with others
who share the same number. Groups discuss their paragraphs. First, have them discuss the
paragraph itself. Second, ask them to share what they learned from the experience. Was their
assignment easy or difficult? How much concentration did it take?

Finally, each group reports briefly to the class on what was discussed. Ask, how do the
purposes compare to one another? Which reading purpose will help readers retain the most
information?

SQ3R

Students will be able to practice using the SQ3R strategy and become familiar with different
ways to review information. Hand out the SQ3R worksheet (p. 192 of this IM chapter) and a
preselected newspaper or magazine article (2 pages). After students read the article and use the
SQ3R worksheet along with it, call on volunteers to share their SQ3R forms and to share the
different strategies created to help someone study the information from the chosen article (bring
back the connection on different ways to get from one place to another).

READING PURPOSES

Critical Evaluation (1)

In his *Essay on Population*, Thomas Malthus wrote, "It may safely be pronounced, therefore, that [human] population, when unchecked, goes on doubling itself every 25 years, or increases in a geometrical ratio." Darwin and Wallace realized that a similar principle holds true for plant and animal populations. In fact, most organisms can reproduce much more rapidly than humans (consider rabbits, dandelions, and houseflies) and consequently could produce overwhelming populations in short order. Nonetheless, the world is not chest-deep in rabbits, dandelions, or horseflies: Natural populations do not grow "unchecked" but tend to remain approximately constant in size. Clearly, vast numbers of individuals must die in each generation, and most do not produce. In fact, population growth is checked by many environmental factors, including food supply, predators, disease, and weather.

(1) Audesirk, Gerald & Teresa. *Life On Earth*. Upper Saddle River, NJ: Prentice Hall, 1997. Page 295.

Understanding (2)

The symptoms of schizophrenia usually appear around age 20, although deficiencies in attention and emotional responses are frequently noted during childhood. Approximately 1.5 percent of the adult population has had the disorder. Although the rate of schizophrenia is about equal in men and women, it strikes men earlier. The symptoms frequently lead to significant social and occupational impairment. The overall death rate among victims of schizophrenia is twice the expected rate, in part because the suicide rate is ten times higher than it is among the general population.

(2) Davis, Stephen, & Joseph J. Paladin. *Psychology*, Second Edition. Upper Saddle River, NJ: Prentice Hall, 1997. Page 581.

Practical Application (3)

TALK is a visual communication program which copies lines typed on your screen to that of another user, and copies lines typed there back to your own screen. These programs allow you to contact another user directly, much the same way e-mail does, but in real time. If you wish to **TALK** to someone on your own system (the same host and domain that you are logged in to), then at the command prompt you type

talk name

where **name** is the user name of the person you are trying to reach. If the person is on a different system (different host or domain), then you would type

talk name@hostname.domainname

where **name** is the user name of the person you are trying to reach, and **hostname** and **domainname** make up the address of the system the person is on.

(3) Clark, Carol Lea. *A Student's Guide to the Internet.* Upper Saddle River, NJ: Prentice Hall. 1996. Pages 58-59.

Pleasure (4)

Friends cannot always be chosen. Fate and circumstance may lend you a friend, even decide who that friend will be. When Tasker followed me home, I did not feel I was in need of a friend – especially him. Short legs, a barrel chest, ears sticking out parallel with the ground, ridiculous rolls of fur crowning his forehead – he was a strange fellow who greeted everything with the queerest gurgling rasp in his throat and a quick cock of his head. But his oddness had a regality. And his loyalty had the sincerest integrity. Before I knew it, I had a comrade. There are friends you develop over time, and then there are friends who immediately plant the roots of their love firmly into your heart. Tasker was such a friend. Although my time with him was short – just eight, quick months before he lost his life to cancer – his friendship made my life so much richer. I did need a friend.

(4) Remien, Andrew, journalism student. *Tasker.* 1997. Reprinted by permission.

Name _____   Date _____

SQ3R

SURVEY – Name the elements that you noticed (title, headers, visuals, parts, etc.).

_____

_____

_____

QUESTION – What questions did you develop as you surveyed the article?

_____

_____

_____

READ – Describe your reading situation (setting, distractions if any, how long it took you to read, how successful you were at concentrating).

_____

_____

_____

RECITE – Write here the information you want to remember from the article. Choose a recitation technique (writing, speaking) and use it to review this information.

_____

_____

_____

REVIEW – Describe the review strategy that best helps you to recall information.

_____

_____

_____

STUDY SKILLS FOR HOW YOU LEARN

As you progress through the study skills chapters, use this grid to record the study strategies suited to your particular learning styles profile that you have found most effective.

Your dominant multiple intelligences: _____
_____

Your dominant Personality Spectrum dimensions: _____
_____

Study Skill	Key Strategies
Reading and studying	
Listening and memory	
Note taking	
Test taking	

MULTIPLE INTELLIGENCE STRATEGIES FOR READING

INTELLIGENCE	USE MI STRATEGIES TO BECOME A BETTER READER	WHAT WORKS FOR YOU? WRITE NEW IDEAS HERE
VERBAL-LINGUISTIC	∞ Use the steps in SQ3R, focusing especially on writing Q-stage questions, summaries, and so on. ∞ Make marginal text notes as you read.	
LOGICAL-MATHEMATICAL	∞ Logically connect what you are reading with what you already know. Consider similarities, differences, and cause-and-effect relationships. ∞ Draw charts showing relationships and analyze trends.	
BODILY-KINESTHETIC	∞ Use text highlighting to take a hands-on approach to reading. ∞ Take a hands-on approach to learning experiments by trying to recreate them yourself.	
VISUAL- SPATIAL	∞ Make charts, diagrams, or think links illustrating difficult ideas you encounter as you read. ∞ Take note of photos, tables, and other visual aids in the text.	
INTERPERSONAL	∞ Discuss reading material and clarify concepts in a study group. ∞ Talk to people who know about the topic you are studying.	
INTRAPERSONAL	∞ Apply concepts to your own life; think about how you would manage. ∞ Try to understand your personal strengths and weaknesses to lead a study group on the reading material.	
MUSICAL	∞ Recite text concepts to rhythms or write a song to depict them. ∞ Explore relevant musical links to the material.	
NATURALISTIC	∞ Tap into your ability to notice similarities and differences in objects and concepts by organizing reading materials into relevant groupings.	

PERSONAL PORTFOLIO ACTIVITY # 5

READING SKILLS ON THE JOB

Literacy is no longer defined as just the ability to read, but it involves more: the ability to read and <u>understand and use what you learn</u> from what you read!

    For each of the skill areas listed below, indicate ① how you would use that for the career you hope to have, then ② rate your ability. Finally, ③ mark the two skills from the list that you consider your strongest, and the two you think will be the most important for you to improve while in college.

Reading skill	Ways you will use it on the job	Current rating: 10 highest, 1 lowest	Check two that are your best.	Check two that need improvement.
Ability to define your reading purpose				
Reading speed				
Reading comprehension				
Vocabulary building				
Identification & use of surveying devices				
Using analytical thinking skills when reading				
Evaluating reading materials with others				
Ability to understand and use visual aids				

Apply Practical Thinking Skills:
Copy the two skills from above that need work and write down some ideas for improvement.

① _____

② _____

_____

CONSIDER COMPREHENSION

REVIEW WITH STUDENTS BEFORE YOU BEGIN THE NEXT CHAPTER:

- What are the aspects of SQ3R? (Survey, Question, Read, Recite, Review)
- Name two ways to improve reading comprehension. (take an active approach, choose the right setting, learn to concentrate, plan a reward, define your reading purpose, and so forth)
- Name at least one purpose for reading (read for understanding, read to evaluate analytically, read for practical application, read for pleasure).
- What does it mean to respond critically to what you read? (evaluate evidence)

Chapter Five Vocabulary Quiz Answer Key
(Quiz appears on following page)

1. F
2. C
3. A
4. H
5. G
6. B
7. I
8. J
9. D
10. E

CHAPTER FIVE VOCABULARY QUIZ

1. ____ concentration

2. ____ root

3. ____ skimming

4. ____ scanning

5. ____ surveying

6. ____ glossary

7. ____ question

8. ____ evidence

9. ____ highlighting

10. ____ argument

B. A section at the back of a book which defines terms found in the text

C. The central part or basis of a word around which prefixes and suffixes can be added to produce different words

D. The use of special markers or regular pens to flag important passages in a text

E. A persuasive case or a set of connected ideas supported by examples

F. The act of applying all of your mental energy and focus to your academic work

G. The process of previewing, or pre-reading, a book before you study it

H. Reading material in an investigative way to search for specific information

I. The process of asking questions, which leads to knowledge and is essential for critical thinking

J. Facts, statistics, and other materials that are presented in support of an argument

A. Rapid, superficial reading of material to determine central ideas and main elements

CHAPTER FIVE ASSESSMENT

Multiple Choice
Circle or highlight the answer that seems to fit best.

1. How does your level of familiarity with a subject affect your reading comprehension?
   a. It connects what you already know with the concepts being communicated.
   b. It alerts you to passages that you can skip.
   c. It helps you prioritize your reading assignments.
   d. It has no effect on overall comprehension.

2. Secondary sources are
   a. original documents.
   b. historical artifacts.
   c. the legitimate presentation of original documents for different purposes.
   d. scientific studies.

3. Determining your purpose for reading helps you complete assignments because you can
   a. improve your reading comprehension.
   b. use your study time more effectively.
   c. decide how much time and effort to expend.
   d. all of the above

4. What is NOT part of determining an effective setting for focused reading?
   a. Select the right location.
   b. Select the evening.
   c. Select a time of day when you are alert and focused.
   d. Select the right company.

5. Ways to increase your concentration when studying include
   a. avoiding social activities and fearing failure.
   b. taking breaks every hour and writing ideas on paper.
   c. organizing your books and analyzing your environment.
   d. structuring your study time and minimizing technology use.

6. People are more likely to remember something that generated a/an _____ _____ than any other material.
   a. creative response
   b. emotional response
   c. analytical response
   d. practical response

7. How can you determine the purpose of each assignment in class?
   a. Survey the textbook.
   b. Review the syllabus.
   c. Ask your classmates.
   d. Know the expectations.

8. When studying math you should
   a. understand the principle behind every formula.
   b. do some problems and then memorize the formula.
   c. move on even if you are unsure.
   d. skim over formulas to devote more time to concepts.

9. You're reading a report concerning the leading causes of climate change. Which of the following would suggest that the evidence supporting the author's position is faulty?
   a. The evidence comes from many primary sources, including several science experiments that have measurable, verifiable results.
   b. The evidence logically relates to the issues and reports unexpected results objectively.
   c. The evidence is mainly from two sources: large-scale studies sponsored by two different auto manufacturers.
   d. The report avoids emotional terms and the evidence is stated in clear, concrete terms that are easy to define.

10. Surveying before reading a chapter will help you to determine
    a. how many pages you need to read.
    b. what specific content is being covered in the chapter.
    c. how to review the material to prep for exams.
    d. the information to memorize.

11. What is the best way to build your vocabulary?
    a. Underline every new word you encounter as you read.
    b. Ask your instructor to define new terms related to the course.
    c. Define and use words in context.
    d. None of the above

12. When is the best time to recite information from your reading?
    a. After you have read the chapter
    b. After you have read one paragraph
    c. After you have read a text section
    d. After you have designed questions

13. The best critical readers
    a. choose a side if they are reading an argument.
    b. accept most of what they read as fact.
    c. offer constructive criticism about the reading.
    d. question every statement for accuracy, relevance, and logic.

14. Differentiating between reading for pleasure and reading for information involves a thinking process in which level of Bloom's Taxonomy?

a. Understanding
b. Evaluation
c. Analysis
d. Knowledge

15. Which of the following would be BEST to highlight as you read your textbook?
    a. Only the definitions
    b. Each sentence as you read it
    c. Key terms and concepts
    d. You shouldn't mark your textbook at all.

True/False
Determine whether each statement is true or false, and circle or highlight your answer.

1. If you can't understand the material in your introductory-level texts, you will not be prepared to understand the reading for more advanced courses.
    True
    False

2. Reading comprehension at the college level requires a lot of independent work.
    True
    False

3. A nursing textbook is an example of a primary source.
    True
    False

4. Writing is the least effective way to learn new material.
    True
    False

5. Reviewing immediately and periodically throughout the days and weeks after you read a chapter are the best ways to help you learn and remember what you read.
    True
    False

6. Using color to highlight while reading does not help the reader remember or recall the information better.
    True
    False

7. Rapid, superficial reading of a material is also known as scanning.
    True
    False

8. Effective questioning involves asking yourself what you already know and writing questions linked to chapter headers.
    True
    False

9. Waiting for the end of the chapter to recite information is too late.
    True
    False

10. Critical thinking is an integral part of understanding and evaluating what you read.
    True
    False

Fill in the Blank
Insert the word or phrase that BEST completes the sentence.

1. When reading at the college level, you need a _____ _____ that taps into your analytical and practical thinking skills.

2. Reading _____ refers to the ability to understand what you read.

3. _____ is an effective reading method that will enhance your studying, retention, and understanding of reading material.

4. _____ is a study technique in which you mark the most important points to read and review again.

5. _____ includes facts, statistics, and other materials that are presented in support of an argument.

6. The six levels of questions identified by Bloom are knowledge, understanding, application, analysis, _____, and evaluation.

7. To apply all of your mental energy and focus into something is called _____.

8. To choose the right setting for reading, you should select the right location and time and deal with internal _____.

9. _____ is the process of reading carefully to search for specific information.

10. The central part or basis of a word is called the_____.

Short Answer

1. What are some methods to learn content-specific vocabulary?

2. What elements should you look at to <u>survey</u> a chapter?

3. Describe the steps you should take to turn highlighting into a learning tool.

Essay

1. Describe three strategies from this chapter that you will use to improve your reading comprehension in the course you are currently taking that has the toughest reading assignments. (Be sure to identify the course and the reading material you find difficult.)

2. Describe this chapter's suggestions for taking *text* notes on assigned readings. How can these strategies help you as you prepare for your next set of exams?

3. Identify your learning preferences and then describe the study approach you plan to use to help you recall information effectively.

Word Exploration

```
Define this term:  yokomeshi [yo-ko-meh-shh]
```

What does this term mean to you? How does it apply to your life as a college student?

Chapter Five Assessment Answer Key

Multiple Choice

Test Item Assesses This Learning Objective/Topic

1. a   What Will Improve Your Reading Comprehension?

2. c   What Will Improve Your Reading Comprehension?
   Take an active approach to difficult texts

3. d   What Will Improve Your Reading Comprehension?
   Define your reading purpose

4. b   What Will Improve Your Reading Comprehension?
   Choose the right setting

5. d   What Will Improve Your Reading Comprehension?
   Choose the right setting

6. b   What Will Improve Your Reading Comprehension?
   Become emotionally involved

7. b   What Will Improve Your Reading Comprehension?
   Define your reading purpose

8. a   What Will Improve Your Reading Comprehension?
   Use special strategies with math and science texts

9. c   How Can You Respond Critically to What You Read?

10. b   How Can SQ3R Help You Own What You Read? *Survey*

11. c   What Will Improve Your Reading Comprehension?
    Expand your vocabulary

12. c   How Can SQ3R Help You Own What You Read? *Recite*

13. d   How Can You Respond Critically to What You Read?

14. c   How Can SQ3R Help You Own What You Read? *Question*

15. c   How Do You Customize Your Text with Highlighting and Notes?
    How to highlight a text

True/False

Test Item Assesses This Learning Objective/Topic

1. T   What Will Improve Your Reading Comprehension?
   Get Creative!   Assess yourself as a creative thinker

2. T   What Will Improve Your Reading Comprehension?
   Get Creative!   Assess yourself as a creative thinker

3. F   What Will Improve Your Reading Comprehension?
   Take an active approach to difficult texts

4. F   How Can SQ3R Help You Own What You Read? *Recite*

5. T   How Can SQ3R Help You Own What You Read? *Review*

6. F   Successful Intelligence Preview

7. F   How Can SQ3R Help You Own What You Read?

8. T   How Can SQ3R Help You Own What You Read? *Question*

9. T   How Can SQ3R Help You Own What You Read? *Recite*

10. T   How Can You Respond Critically to What You Read?

Fill in the Blank

Test item assesses this learning objective/topic

1. *systematic approach*   What Will Improve Your Reading Comprehension?

2. *comprehension*   What Will Improve Your Reading Comprehension?

3. *SQ3R*   How Can SQ3R Help You Own What You Read?

4. *Highlighting*   How Do You Customize Your Text with Highlighting and Notes? *How to highlight a text*

5. *Evidence*   How Can You Respond Critically to What You Read?

6. *synthesis*   How Can SQ3R Help You Own What You Read? *Question*

7. *concentration*   What Will Improve Your Reading Comprehension? *Learn to concentrate*

8. *distractions*   What Will Improve Your Reading Comprehension? *Choose the right setting*

9. *Scanning*   How Can SQ3R Help You Own What You Read?

10. *root*   What Will Improve Your Reading Comprehension? *Expand your vocabulary*

Listening, Note Taking, and Memory
Taking In, Recording, and Remembering Information

BRIEF CHAPTER OVERVIEW

This chapter covers three interrelated topics, *listening, note taking*, and *memory*—all of which can improve with practice and serve as a crucial foundation for test preparation. We recommend that you emphasize the relationships among these skills to aid student retention. For instance, you can show students how listening actively can improve memory and note-taking success and how effective note taking can provide better materials to remember.

Taking notes involves the student in the learning process. This chapter helps students make decisions during the note-taking process about what to write down. It also covers nuts-and-bolts information about how students can take notes efficiently, match their note-taking style to an instructor's teaching and delivery style, and study effectively from notes.

Many students have little knowledge of specific strategies that aid memory, so a common teaching challenge is helping students learn new methods and getting students to apply them. We offer numerous activities for you to choose from to help students practice new techniques.

The chapter covers theoretical and practical information on all the main topics. If time is short, we suggest that you spend more class time on application and quiz students on the theoretical information (such as the listening stages and the information encoding process).

Note the successful intelligence skills your students will build in chapter 6:

Analytical	Creative	Practical
■ Understanding the listening process and listening challenges	■ Constructing active-listening strategies that help you learn	■ How to overcome distractions to listen actively
■ Evaluating the importance of class notes and varied note-taking systems	■ Personalizing note-taking systems and strategies	■ How to use note-taking systems and shorthand and craft a master note set
■ Analyzing the nature of memory and why memory strategies work	■ Thinking of and using mnemonic devices to boost recall	■ How to use mnemonics to learn

CHAPTER SIX OUTLINE

How Can You Become a Better Listener?

- Know the Stages of Listening

- Manage Listening Challenges

- Become an Active Listener

How Can You Make the Most of Class Notes?

- Note-Taking Systems

- Note Taking is a Three-Step Process

- Combine Class and Reading Notes into a Master Set

How Can You Take Notes Faster?

How Can You Improve Your Memory?

- How Your Brain Remembers: Short-Term and Long-Term Memory

- Memory Strategies Improve Recall

- Use Mnemonic Devices

COMMUNICATE CONTENT
TOPICS COVERED IN THE CHAPTER

[Chapter intro and chapter 5 review: PowerPoint slides 1, 2, 3]

The *Real Questions, Practical Answers* Discussion Starter Question:
How can I improve my memory? **[PowerPoint slide 4]**

> The questioner here notes particular kinds of information and situations that give her memory trouble. Ask students to brainstorm one or both of the following:
> - Situations where they have trouble remembering (particular classes, settings, times of day, etc.)
> - Types of information they have trouble remembering (lists, technical terms, formulas, historical information, data, etc.)
>
> Make lists of students' ideas on the board. Have students volunteer personal stories about memory difficulties. Explain that everyone has some memory issues, and that this chapter's material will help them deal with these situations and types of information.

(For more discussion starters, see p. 212 of this IM chapter.)

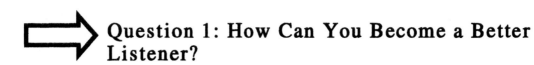 **Question 1: How Can You Become a Better Listener?**

[Section overview: PowerPoint slide 5]

Listening vs. Hearing: Remind students that listening and reading are two primary modes of taking in and making sense of information. In a lecture situation, listening is even more important than reading because the instructor will say far more than he or she will write. Ask students to describe the difference between listening and hearing. (Listening with energy and focus rewards the listener with retention of what was heard.)

> *Example*: At a noisy party you are introduced to a guest. You hear the name, say "nice to meet you," and approximately ten seconds later you have forgotten the name entirely. You heard it but didn't listen – didn't focus, concentrate.

The Four Listening Stages: Describe how listening is broken down into four stages or parts—sensation, interpretation, evaluation, and reaction (see Key 6.1) – and explain how difficulties occur in the listening process. For instance, in the sensation stage, hearing loss, preoccupation, and distractions can hinder listening. In the evaluation stage, different values due to age, ethnicity, or background can come into play. **[See PowerPoint slide 6.]**

Four Challenges to (and Solutions for) More Active Listening:

The text covers four listening challenges: divided attention, listening lapses, rushing to judgment, and hearing loss or disability. First, ask students for specific examples of each (or provide them yourself). Then ask students to create practical solutions – provide some yourself to jump-start the brainstorming. **[See PowerPoint slide 7.]**

(Consider using the "Listening Assessment" exercise and handout on p. 216 of this IM chapter.)

Strategies for Developing Active Listening Skills

Describe strategies for developing active, practical listening skills as described in the text **[see PowerPoint slide 8]**:

- Be there.
- Set purposes for listening.
- Ask questions.
- Pay attention to verbal signposts (see Key 6.2). **[See PowerPoint slide 9.]**
- Expect the unexpected.

 ## Question 2: How Can You Make the Most of Class Notes?

[Section overview: PowerPoint slide 10]

Overview of Note-Taking Importance: Begin by analyzing the importance of having good notes. (*Examples*: Note taking is probably our greatest memory aid and one of the best sources for studying class material.) The main connection between note taking and success is that *taking notes involves students in the learning process*. Note takers analyze what they hear, create a record of what happened in class, and develop a practical set of study materials. Students might share answers to questions like these:

- If you loaned your notes to others, could they be easily read?
- Can you read your own notes easily?
- Do you struggle keeping up with the instructor's lecture?
- Do you have difficulty taking notes when the instructor jumps from topic to topic?

(Consider assigning end-of-chapter group exercise "Create a Note-Taking Team," discussed on p. 212 of this IM chapter, and setting a time for discussing it at the end of the note-taking coverage.)

Note-Taking Systems. Let students know that for a few minutes you'll discuss, and they will practice, three different note-taking methods (Cornell, Think Link, Outline). **[See PowerPoint slide 11.]**

Outline. Begin with a review of formal and informal outlines (you can either show samples on the board, show **PowerPoint slide 12**, or have students review Keys 6.3 and 6.4 from the text). You may want to note the other visual note-taking strategies covered in the text.

Cornell. Then, ask students to take out a sheet of notebook paper. Have them write the date and the subject at the top of the page and draw an upside-down T below. Review what the right-hand, left-hand, and bottom sections are for. (For a sample, see Key 6.5 or **PowerPoint slide 13**. For a photocopy-ready blank Cornell template, see p. 219 of this IM chapter.)

Think Link. Conclude by giving the next part of your lecture in think link form. Draw a circle in the center of the board. In the middle, write the words "Think Link." Off to one side of the first circle, draw a line to another circle. In the center of this circle write "a visual note-taking system." Off that circle, draw two more lines. At the end of one of them write: "connects ideas using shapes and pictures." At the end of the other line write "links main points with supporting information." (For a sample, see Key 6.6 or **PowerPoint slide 14**).

Be sure to analyze with students *when and why* to use different systems. The main factors in the decision are 1) personal taste/comfort level, 2) course material, and 3) instructor style. For example, a student might generally take notes in outline form, but use a think link with an instructor who jumps around a lot within topics.

(Consider using group exercise "Comparing Note-Taking Systems" on p. 213 of this IM chapter.)

Prepare for Note Taking: Explain what practical actions constitute good preparation and its benefits (more details in the "Preparation" text section). Preparation includes coming to class with the reading completed and choosing the best note-taking system to match the course material, instructor's style, and how you learn; i.e., if you are a strong visual/spatial learner, the Cornell system may work because of the page layout.

Record Information Effectively During Class: Ask about current note-taking challenges, list them, and ask students to brainstorm solutions as an entire class or in small groups. Emphasize that the text provides several practical strategies that need to be tried to determine which ones work best. Consider demonstrating points such as dating and labeling each page, leaving space, and drawing diagrams or pictures.

Review and Revise Your Notes: First, get a read on how students use their notes for review purposes. The key point is that the most outstanding notes won't help unless they're USED – they should be read, analyzed, evaluated, rewritten, and condensed. Remind students that the review process helps solidify the information in memory so they can recall and use it to prepare for tests, complete assignments, or create new ideas.

Create a Master Set: Many students don't understand how or why to create a set of master notes (Key 6.8). Review the positive effects students will experience if they create a set (more comprehensive notes, more active studying, reinforced memory of key ideas, increased support for important concepts, critical thinking boost from making idea connections). Review the practical steps shown in the text for how to create, and study from, the master set.

(Consider using group exercise "Summarizing Notes" on p. 213 of this IM chapter.)

Question 3: How Can You Write Faster When Taking Notes?

[Section overview: PowerPoint slide 15]

Ask students (or remind them of the question if you asked it before) whether they ever feel their note taking isn't fast enough to keep pace with the lecture they are hearing. Ask them what they do to try to solve the problem (or whether they just give up).

Introduce the practical skill of using ***personal shorthand*** to enable faster writing. Because the writer is the only intended reader, individual students can abbreviate or shorten words and phrases in ways only they understand.

Many students already use a form of personal shorthand without knowing it – ask for examples. A great way to bring up this topic: ask students how many of them "text" one another and, if they do, whether they speed up their texting with abbreviations ("r u," "btw," etc.). Offer this experience as a base to work from when deciding how to use abbreviations in class, even though in school the language will be more sophisticated than what they use to text.

Important note: Remind students that although speed is important, their notes are useless unless they are accurate and legible!

Go through the list of types of shorthand that is found in the text, writing up examples for students to see. Then ask students for personal examples.

Question 4: How Can You Improve Your Memory?

[Section overview: PowerPoint slide 16]

Memory Overview

Remind students that learning is a physical process – the brain undergoes physical changes when hearing, interpreting, and remembering information. Explain that the more their brains work when remembering, the more able they will be to remember.

Because *learning depends on remembering,* no learning can take place without retaining knowledge. A powerful memory is a tool of *efficiency;* learning once and working to retain that memory takes far less time and energy than relearning over and over again. *Example:* Learning to drive a car. Your mind absorbs details about car operation, traffic rules, roads and intersections, etc. Then you use thinking skills to solve problems, make decisions, and evaluate situations on the road as you drive. But those actions cannot take place on a regular basis without long-term retention of the initial details. You can't forget what a flashing red light means or what the gearshift does and be a successful driver!

The Three Storage Banks of Memory

If time permits, review the three storage banks of memory: sensory memory, short-term memory, and long-term memory.

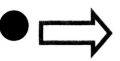

Next, have students analyze how the process of remembering relates to learning. For instance, ask them why cramming is so ineffective. Use questions like the following: "Have you ever crammed for a test? What did you remember after the test was over?" You might also ask about strategies they learned in school that they later had to remember and implement on the job – ask how that worked, and how they retained the information for later use.

Building Memory Skills: The text covers ten strategies in this section, including using critical thinking; recite, rehearse, and write; organizing items; studying during short and frequent sessions; and using flash cards (Key 6.9). **[See PowerPoint slide 17.]**

Ask students if they can recall commercials or theme songs from television shows. (If you're able, collect some and play them in a "name that tune" fashion or, if visual, show some ads.) After students have finished sharing, ask them to analyze why they think these ads and theme songs have stuck in their memory for so long. Let them know that simple songs, rhythm, catch phrases, and repetition all contribute to memory retention.

(Consider using group exercise "Recite, Rehearse, and Write" on p. 212 of this IM chapter.)

Ask students for their ideas about **mnemonic devices** – what are they, whether anyone can volunteer an example.

Then, reinforce the definition: *Memory techniques that involve associating new information with information you already know.* They depend on vivid, memorable associations, which give you a "hook" in your brain on which to "hang" a memory and retrieve it later.

Note that these devices take time and creativity to invent, and motivation to remember – so advise students to use them only when they really need them (for lists, difficult concepts, remembering objects in order).

Go through some key types of mnemonics (all covered in this section of the text): visual images and associations, mental walk strategy (Key 6.10 or **PowerPoint slide 18**), acronyms, and songs and rhymes. Advise students to use images, associations, and songs/rhymes that they already know and like, because those are often the ones most deeply anchored in memory.

(Consider using group exercise "Visual Images" on p. 213 of this IM chapter.)

Finally, remind students that if they put material into a form consistent with their multiple intelligence strengths, they can get the information into long-term memory more quickly. For example, a visual/spatial learner would convert lecture notes into a visual format such as a chart, graph, or think link.

(Consider using "Remembering Important Information" exercise and handout on pp. 217-218 of this IM chapter.)

[Successful Intelligence Wrap-Up: PowerPoint slide 19]
[End-of-chapter foreign word: PowerPoint slide 20]
[End-of-chapter thought-provoking quote: PowerPoint slide 21]

* *

CREATE COMMUNITY

DISCUSSION STARTERS

1. Have the students respond in writing to all of your verbal cues. Do not repeat any of the directions and keep the class quiet. Read these directions:

> Draw a two-inch circle in the middle of the paper.
> Draw a square around the circle.
> Draw an "X" in the middle of the circle.
> Draw two vertical lines from the bottom corners of the square to the end of the paper.
> Draw three horizontal lines across the center of the paper.

   Ask the students how they did during the listening activity and briefly explore why some didn't listen effectively (distractions, learning style, and so on).

2. Have students take 2-3 minutes to describe in writing their personal note-taking strategy as it currently exists – their structure, their goal, how successful they think they are, whether they end up with helpful materials. Then ask them to share their thoughts and what goals may have come up for them as a result of this exercise.

3. Write ten random words on the board. Give students one minute to read them. Then erase and have students write the words from memory. Afterwards, write the words up again so students can check their answers, and open up discussion about their experiences.

GROUP EXERCISES

Teamwork: Create Solutions Together – *Create a Note-Taking Team*

This exercise, found at the end of chapter 6 in the text, asks students to gather a weeks' worth of notes from class and meet in small groups to compare them. Make sure students look carefully at <u>legibility</u>, <u>completeness</u>, <u>organization</u>, and <u>value</u> of the notes as a study aid. You may want to have groups share significant ideas or findings with the class.

Recite, Rehearse, and Write

Have the students divide into three groups. Write the following set of numbers on the board: 1, 44, 17, 18, 29, 36, 33, 2, 55, 27, 28, 39, 49, and 43. Have one group recite the numbers aloud. (If you have the space, have this group of students step out into the hallway so the other students can't hear them recite.) Ask the second group to silently memorize the numbers. The third group should all write the numbers. Give each group two minutes to complete the project. When everyone is finished, erase the numbers from the board and have the students take out a clean piece of paper. At the top they should write which memorization technique they used. Have them write the list of numbers from memory. Let the students score their papers themselves. Discuss the results. Was one more effective than the other? Why?

Visual Images

Groups develop mnemonic devices involving visual images. They can work with any of the following: the four stages of the listening process, a set of key time management strategies from chapter 2, the stages of the problem-solving process from chapter 4, or the eight intelligences from chapter 3. Each group will present their device to the class. Note especially any variety among devices made for the same material.

Comparing Note-Taking Systems

Show a short, informative video segment in class. Tell students they will need to take notes as they watch the segment. Count off the students by 3s – then tell them that 1s will use outlines, 2s will use the Cornell or T-note system, and 3s will use think links or mind maps.

Show the segment and then group 1s, 2s, and 3s together. Have the groups compare notes and discuss their experiences with the system that they were assigned. Were some students more, or less, successful? Make sure students help each other evaluate why some students may have liked and benefited from a system more than others.

Summarizing Notes

You can use one of two types of materials for this exercise:

- Magazine or newspaper articles on topics relevant to your course
- Sets of notes taken by the students (in advance, collect notes from a particular day)

Divide students into groups of four. Each group should have copies of an individual article or set of notes. Give students ten minutes to read and summarize their material individually. Next, have students compare their summaries. Make sure they look at the differences, if they exist, in what each person thought was important enough to include in the summary. Also, have them compare summary length. Which length is most efficient?

POP CULTURE LINKS

Movies: <u>Eternal Sunshine of the Spotless Mind</u> (2004) is a fascinating look at a fictitious procedure to erase an experience from memory, and could inspire discussion of memory and its link to emotion and experience. Furthermore, any movie scene can support discussion of listening, of note taking, or of memory. Show a scene and then have a brief quiz on plot points, facts about the characters, details about the scene, etc. Discuss the role that listening and memory play in how successful students are on the quiz. Try having students take notes on a scene before a quiz, and see if that boosts quiz success.

Music: Almost any kind of music that has lyrics can serve you when discussing memory. Ask one or more students to sing, or speak the lyrics to, a song that they currently are into. If you get one or more students to easily recall these lyrics, talk about why this information comes so easily – desire to remember, repetition (listening to the song a lot), reciting (speaking or singing the words aloud). Discuss how to apply those factors to academic memory challenges.

SUCCESSFUL INTELLIGENCE EXERCISES

Get Analytical! *Discover Yourself as a Listener*
Assign for in-class activity or homework. Through some specific questions, students are asked to analyze and evaluate their listening process. You might have students discuss some answers in a classroom setting, or even expand on their answers by writing journal entries for a chosen question. Ask students about the strategies from the chapter that they listed as ones they want to choose, and see if certain strategies appear more useful than others (if so, you may want to focus on those in class).

Get Creative! *Assess Yourself as a Creative Thinker*
Assign as homework. Students create their own mnemonic device for information they have to remember for this or another course they are currently taking. Try offering a presentation time in class for students to share their mnemonics with another student or the class.

Get Practical! *Face a Note-Taking Challenge*
Assign for in-class activity or homework. This exercise has students develop a plan for note-taking success in one of their courses. Ask students to follow this course of action for a class period or two, and in the week following, have them write (or discuss in class) an evaluation of how well they followed their plan and what benefit it had for them, if any.

HOMEWORK

In-text exercises: All three successful intelligence exercises (*Get Analytical, Get Creative*, and *Get Practical*) can be assigned for homework.

Foreign word response: Ask students to write a responsive essay to the word "lagom." Ask them to describe what their version of "lagom" is and how they will aim to achieve it this term.

End-of-chapter exercises:
- **Successful Intelligence: Think, Create, Apply** – Ask students to read Victoria Gough's *Personal Triumph Case Study*. Then have them complete the exercise.
- **Writing: Journal and Put Skills to Work** – Students can complete the journal entry as homework. The real-life writing assignment – creating a master set of notes – is another great homework assignment.
- **Personal Portfolio:** This assignment can be completed as homework but will take some time, as it involves students' interviewing people. You may want to assign it over time with benchmarks for particular stages. Consider using the handout on p. 221 of this IM chapter.

QUOTES FOR REFLECTION

Use these quotes to generate discussion, start class, or offer as a short exercise. Have students reflect on what any or all of the following quotes mean to them in a short paper or presentation.

It's only through listening that you learn, and I never want to stop learning.
Drew Barrymore

Own only what you can carry with you; know language, know countries, know people. Let your memory be your travel bag.
Alexander Solzhenitsyn

No one cares to speak to an unwilling listener. An arrow never lodges in a stone.
St. Jerome

A good listener is not only popular everywhere, but after a while he knows something.
Wilson Mizner

None so deaf as those that will not hear.
Matthew Henry

The true art of memory is the art of attention.
Samuel Johnson

Discipline is remembering what you want.
David Campbell

We have two ears and only one tongue that we may hear more and speak less.
Diogenes

HANDOUTS

The following are exercises with handouts, or handouts that you can use on their own. Integrate them into your lesson plan as you see fit, or follow the suggestions in the "Communicate Content" section.

- Listening Assessment (exercise with handout)
- Remembering a Song (exercise with handout)
- Cornell Note-Taking Template (handout)
- Multiple Intelligence Grid for Note-Taking Strategies (handout)
- Personal Portfolio Handout to accompany chapter 6 Personal Portfolio exercise

Name _____ Date _____

<u>LISTENING ASSESSMENT</u>

Answer true or false to the following questions. When you are finished, rate your listening skills on a scale of 1–10, with 10 being excellent and 1 being poor. Discuss whether there is anything you can do to improve your listening skills.

T / F   In an argument, I usually am more interested in getting my point across than in hearing what the other person has to say.

T / F   Once the speaker says something I disagree with, I stop listening.

T / F   I am easily distracted by surrounding noises when someone is talking to me.

T / F   When I'm on the phone, I listen with one ear and take care of work, friends, or children with the other ear.

T / F   I only listen to things that interest me.

T / F   I frequently let the speaker know I am listening to him or her by nodding my head in response.

T / F   I keep my eyes focused on the speaker.

T / F   My friends think I am a great speaker.

T / F   My friends think I am a great listener.

T / F   I spend more time talking than I do listening.

T / F   When I have an idea I'm excited about, I will occasionally interrupt someone.

I would rate my listening skills as a: 1   2   3   4   5   6   7   8   9   10

I can improve my listening skills by:

_____

_____

_____

_____

Remembering Important Information

Materials: Handout on *"Study Strategies,"* selection of reading material

Activities/Assignments:
1. Ask the students what they think is included in good note-taking and memory skills (create a list on the board or on an overhead).
2. Have the students pair off. Assign each pair a number from 1 to 8. Give students the handout and tell them to note the study strategy that corresponds to their number.
3. Hand out a short selection of reading material that has important, and not too simplistic, material. This could be supplemental material on a course topic (workplace readiness, drinking on campus) or part of a newspaper or magazine article on an interesting topic (energy efficient cars, nutrition and fast food).
4. Have students read it, and also read it aloud to them, to bring in the listening angle. Tell the students to create study materials for the information, keeping their assigned study strategy in mind.
5. Give students 10 minutes to create a study strategy with their partner, corresponding with their number on the handout.

Closure: Have pairs share their study strategies with the class.

Benefits from this exercise:
  Students will
  1. Become more familiar with different study strategies.
  2. Practice their listening and note-taking skills.

Name _____Date _____

REMEMBERING IMPORTANT INFORMATION: STUDY STRATEGY

Directions: Using your assigned strategy, create study materials that teach the information.

1 Mnemonic Device	2 Visual Image
3 Flash Cards	4 Think Link
5 Acronyms	6 Notes
7 Repeat/Rehearse/Recite	8 Your Choice

CORNELL NOTE-TAKING TEMPLATE

MULTIPLE INTELLIGENCE STRATEGIES FOR NOTE TAKING

INTELLIGENCE	USE MI STRATEGIES TO BECOME A BETTER NOTE TAKER	WHAT WORKS FOR YOU? WRITE NEW IDEAS HERE
VERBAL-LINGUISTIC	∞ Rewrite your class notes in an alternate note-taking style to see connections more clearly. ∞ Combine class and text notes to get a complete picture.	
LOGICAL-MATHEMATICAL	∞ When combining notes into a master set, integrate the material into a logical sequence. ∞ Create tables that show relationships.	
BODILY-KINESTHETIC	∞ Think of your notes as a crafts project that enables you to see "knowledge layers." Use colored pens to add texture. ∞ Study with your notes spread in sequence around you so that you can see knowledge building from left to right.	
VISUAL- SPATIAL	∞ Take notes using colored markers or pens. ∞ Rewrite lecture notes in think link format, focusing on the most important points.	
INTERPERSONAL	∞ Schedule a study group after a lecture to discuss class notes. ∞ Review class notes with a study buddy. Compare notes to see what the other missed.	
INTRAPERSONAL	∞ Schedule some quiet time soon after a lecture to review and think about your notes. ∞ As you review your notes, decide whether you grasp the material or need help.	
MUSICAL	∞ Recite concepts in your notes to rhythms. ∞ Write a song that includes material from your class and text notes.	
NATURALISTIC	∞ As you create a master note set, compare concepts by organizing material into natural groupings.	

PERSONAL PORTFOLIO ACTIVITY # 6
MATCHING CAREER TO CURRICULUM

Put your listening and note-taking skills to the test. Interview two people in your chosen career area. Ask the following questions:

① What courses are required for this area? What courses are beneficial, but not required?
② How can I prepare myself for this career outside of class - extracurricular activities, internships, leadership roles, part-time work, anything else? What do you suggest?

Interview #1 - An instructor or academic advisor

Name: _____ Position: _____

① _____
_____
_____
_____

② _____
_____
_____
_____

Interview #2 - A person working in the career I hope to pursue

Name: _____ Position: _____

① _____
_____
_____
_____

② _____
_____
_____
_____

CONSIDER COMPREHENSION

REVIEW WITH STUDENTS BEFORE YOU BEGIN THE NEXT CHAPTER:

- What are the stages of listening and how can you be an active listener?
- How would you describe the three most common note-taking systems?
- What are some types of personal shorthand?
- How does your brain remember, and what strategies can aid memory?

Chapter Six Vocabulary Quiz Answer Key
(Quiz appears on following page)

1. G
2. D
3. F
4. A
5. E
6. B
7. H
8. C

CHAPTER SIX VOCABULARY QUIZ

1. _____ master note set

2. _____ mnemonic devices

3. _____ acronym

4. _____ long-term memory

5. _____ verbal signposts

6. _____ shorthand

7. _____ listening

8. _____ short-term memory

B. A system of rapid handwriting employing symbols and abbreviations

C. The brain's temporary information storehouse where information remains for a few seconds

D. Memory techniques that use vivid associations to link new information to information you already know

E. Spoken words or phrases that call attention to information that follows

F. A word formed from the first letters of a series of words

G. The complete, integrated set of notes that contains both class and text notes

H. A process that involves sensing, interpreting, evaluating, and reacting to spoken messages

A. The brain's permanent information storehouse from which information can be retrieved

CHAPTER SIX ASSESSMENT

Multiple Choice
Circle or highlight the answer that seems to fit best.

1. Listening consists of
    a. sensing, interpreting, evaluating, and hearing.
    b. interpreting, evaluating, listening, and sensing.
    c. sensing, interpreting, evaluating, and reacting.
    d. hearing, listening, evaluating, and interpreting.

2. An example of the sensing stage is
    a. attaching meaning to your message.
    b. your ears hearing sound waves.
    c. getting upset when you hear something you don't agree with.
    d. hearing only one side of a story.

3. Financial stress has been causing Eric to worry all of the time. This is affecting his attention in the classroom, which is an example of
    a. internal distraction.
    b. external distraction.
    c. evaluation stage.
    d. listening lapse.

4. The BEST ways to reduce distractions in the classroom are to
    a. put your worries aside in class and sit near the front of the room.
    b. get enough sleep and make sure you eat enough.
    c. move away from friends who talk during class.
    d. all of the above

5. Listening lapses can be caused by the following EXCEPT
    a. refocusing quickly.
    b. difficult information.
    c. boring information.
    d. focusing only on specific points.

6. How can a student become an active listener in the classroom?
    a. Sit back as someone else speaks.
    b. Read the assigned material before class.
    c. Show up a few minutes before class starts.
    d. b and c only

7. Which of the following is NOT an example of a verbal signpost?
   a. An instructor gets excited about a new concept.
   b. The instructor lectures in her regular format.
   c. The instructor repeats herself.
   d. The instructor says, "This is very important."

8. What are the two main purposes of taking notes?
   a. To help study for tests and record what was said in class
   b. To record what was said in class and use the Cornell method
   c. To help study for tests and use the think link method
   d. To use the Cornell and think link method

9. Students who take notes using colored pen are usually strong in what area of multiple intelligence?
   a. Logical-mathematical
   b. Verbal-linguistic
   c. Visual-spatial
   d. Interpersonal

10. Students who prefer to study in small groups or with a partner are usually strong in what area of multiple intelligence?
    a. Interpersonal
    b. Intrapersonal
    c. Kinesthetic
    d. Verbal-linguistic

11. The BEST way to organize your notes is to
    a. use time lines.
    b. use tables.
    c. use hierarchy charts.
    d. use any of the above, when appropriate.

12. Which of the following is NOT one of the three different areas where memories are stored?
    a. Sensory memory
    b. Short-term memory
    c. Long-term memory
    d. Random memory

13. Which of the following memory strategies will help improve your recall?
    a. Making an emotional connection with the material
    b. Understanding what you memorize
    c. Using critical thinking to associate new material with what you already know
    d. All of the above

14. When is the BEST time to review class lecture notes for the first time?
    a. Within a week of the class
    b. Within a day of the lecture
    c. Right before your test or quiz
    d. It's not necessary to review class notes

15. What are the three mnemonic devices that help to recall information?
    a. Visual images, associations, and acronyms
    b. Visual images, flash cards, and acronyms
    c. Acronyms, visual images, and repeating it out loud
    d. Associations, acronyms, and flash cards

True/False
Determine whether each statement is true or false and circle or highlight the correct answer.

1. Listening involves sensing the spoken message, but hearing is when the listener understands the speaker's intended message.
   True
   False

2. When listening to a statement that offends you or conflicts with your values, you need to be careful that you don't reject the message or statement.
   True
   False

3. Listening is a passive activity.
   True
   False

4. When taking notes, it's important to capture the main ideas of what the instructor says and not focus on writing down every word.
   True
   False

5. It's impossible to take notes on everything you hear in the classroom.
   True
   False

6. Good note-takers use their analytical intelligence to evaluate what is worth writing down and remembering.
   True
   False

7. Guided notes are very detailed notes given to the students by the instructor.
    True
    False

8. The Cornell note-taking system is also known as the L format.
    True
    False

9. The think link method is the most effective note-taking technique in the classroom.
    True
    False

10. Sleep can help your memory because it reduces interference from new information.
    True
    False

Fill in the Blank

Insert the word or phrase that BEST completes the sentence.

1. Keeping an eye on your cell phone during class to see who sends you text messages is an example of a/an _____ _____.

2. _____ _____are sometimes given to students by the instructor to help them take notes.

3. The listening stage that occurs when you attach meaning to a message is called the _____stage.

4. Retaining information in long-term memory follows the same four-stage process as____ ___.

5. Using_____ _____ helps you create vivid associations to link new information with information you already know.

6. When you combine your notes taken in the classroom with notes taken from your textbook and other readings, you are creating a _____ _____ _____.

7. That type of memory that is temporary and only remains in the brain for a few seconds is called _____ _____memory.

8. Three practical tools that promote active learning are recite, rehearse and ____.

9. The Swedish word that refers to the place between extremes is called_____.

10. When you hear something you don't like, you may rush to _____ and tune out the rest of the message.

Short Answer

1. What method will you use to take notes during class discussions in this course?

2. How can mnemonic devices help you to recall information?

Essay

1. Describe how you can improve how you take notes in each of your classes.

2. Describe five steps you will take to become an active listener in each of your courses.

3. Describe the most serious listening challenges you face in each of your classes and develop an action plan for overcoming them.

4. Explain why it is important for your academic success to create a master set of notes for each course that combines class and reading notes.

Word Exploration

Define this term: "listening lapses"

What does it mean to you? How does it apply to your life as a college student?

Chapter Six Assessment Answer Key

Multiple Choice

Test Item Assesses This Learning Objective/Topic

1. c   How Can You Become a Better Listener?
         Know the stages of listening

2. b   How Can You Become a Better Listener?
         Know the stages of listening

3. a   How Can You Become a Better Listener?
         Manage listening challenges

4. d   How Can You Become a Better Listener?
         Manage listening skills

5. a   How Can You Become a Better Listener?
         Listening lapses

6. d   How Can You Become a Better Listener?
         Become an active listener

7. b   How Can You Become a Better Listener?
         Become an active listener

8. a   How Can You Make the Most of Class Notes?

9. c   How Can You Make the Most of Class Notes?
         Multiple intelligence strategies for note taking

10. a   How Can You Make the Most of Class Notes?
         Multiple intelligence strategies for note taking

11. d   How Can You Make the Most of Class Notes?
         Use other visual strategies

12. d   How Can You Improve Your Memory?
         How your brain remembers: Short-term and long-term memory

13. d   How Can You Improve Your Memory?
         How your brain remembers: Short-term and long-term memory

14. b   How Can You Make the Most of Class Notes?
         Combine class and reading notes into a master set

15. a   How Can You Improve Your Memory?
         Use mnemonic devices

True/False

Test Item Assesses This Learning Objective/Topic

1. F   How Can You Become a Better Listener?
         Manage listening challenges

2. T   How Can You Become a Better Listener?

3. F   How Can You Become a Better Listener?
         Become an active listener

4.	T	How Can You Become a Better Listener?
		Become an active listener
5.	T	How Can You Make the Most of Class Notes?
6.	T	How Can You Make the Most of Class Notes?
7.	F	How Can You Make the Most of Class Notes?
8.	F	How Can You Make the Most of Class Notes?
		Use the Cornell system
9.	F	How Can You Make the Most of Class Notes?
		Create a think link
10.	T	How Can You Improve Your Memory?
		Memory strategies to improve recall

Fill in the Blank

Test item assesses this learning objective/topic

1. *external distraction* How Can You Become a Better Listener?
   Manage listening challenges
2. *guided notes* How Can You Make the Most of Class Notes?
3. *interpretation* How Can You Become a Better Listener?
   Know the stages of listening
4. *listening* How Can You Improve Your Memory?
5. *mnemonic devices* How Can You Improve Your Memory?
   Use mnemonic devices
6. *master note set* How Can You Make the Most of Class Notes?
   Combine class and reading notes into a
   master set
7. *short-term* How Can You Improve Your Memory?
8. *write* How Can You Improve Your Memory?
9. *lagom* Successful Intelligence Wrap-Up
10. *judgment* How Can You Become a Better Listener?
    Manage listening challenges

Test Taking
Showing What You Know

BRIEF CHAPTER OVERVIEW

Students who do poorly on tests usually do so from lack of planning and preparation. Still others prepare and plan, but suffer from test anxiety. Most students taking their first set of midterm exams are anxious, to say the least!

This chapter offers clear strategies to prepare and plan more effectively and provides guidance on overcoming test anxiety. The chapter continues with specific techniques to improve test performance on objective and subjective tests.

Many instructors tell us that students need the most help with essay questions. If that's the case in your class, spend the bulk of your time on that. For instance, many students haven't been asked to analyze or defend their ideas on tests and need coaching and practice to master those skills. For objective questions, you can poll the class for the question types students want the most help with and plan your class time accordingly. Or you can review past quizzes and tests and determine what they need help with.

Note the successful intelligence skills your students will build in chapter 7:

Analytical	Creative	Practical
▪ Matching test-preparation strategies with personal needs	▪ Constructing a new perspective of tests as helpful evaluative tools	▪ How to attack objective test questions
▪ Identifying the nature of test anxiety	▪ Developing a pretest to assess material mastery before an exam	▪ How to write a test essay
▪ Analyzing how to answer objective and subjective test questions	▪ Creating an effective study schedule and regimen	▪ How to evaluate and learn from test mistakes
▪ Identifying patterns that cause you to make test errors		

CHAPTER SEVEN OUTLINE

How Can Preparation Improve Test Performance?

- Identify Test Type and Material Covered
- Create a Study Schedule and Checklist
- Prepare Through Careful Review
- Take a Pretest
- Prepare Physically
- Make the Most of Last-Minute Cramming

How Can You Work Through Test Anxiety?

- Prepare and Have a Positive Attitude
- Test Anxiety and the Returning Student

What General Strategies Can Help You Succeed On Tests?

- Choose the Right Seat
- Write Down Key Facts
- Begin With an Overview
- Read Test Directions
- Mark Up the Questions
- Take Special Care on Machine-Scored Tests
- Work from Easy to Hard
- Watch the Clock
- Take a Strategic Approach to Questions You Cannot Answer
- Master the Art of Intelligent Guessing
- Be Prepared for Open-Book Exams
- Maintain Academic Integrity

How Can You Master Different Types of Test Questions?

- Multiple-Choice Questions
- True/False Questions
- Matching Questions
- Fill-in-the-Blank Questions
- Essay Questions

How Can You Learn From Test Mistakes?

COMMUNICATE CONTENT
TOPICS COVERED IN THE CHAPTER

[Chapter intro and chapter 6 review: PowerPoint slides 1, 2, 3]

The *Real Questions, Practical Answers* Discussion Starter Question:
How can I combat test anxiety? [PowerPoint slide 4]

Almost every student has *some* test anxiety. Ask students to volunteer the sorts of reactions that they have before or during a test – heart palpitations, shortness of breath, mind going blank, etc. Offer your own reactions/experiences – connect with them using personal information.

Then see if students can analyze the *why* – the reasons for their test stress. Guide them toward the idea that being, and feeling, prepared is the most effective way to calm test anxiety – and let them know that this entire chapter, full of test preparation and test-taking strategies, is a comprehensive anti-test-anxiety document. The more prepared they are, the more likely it is that their anxiety will decrease and their confidence will increase.

Finally, explore the idea – from the answer in this feature – that *some* level of anxiety is a good thing on test day! Reasonable stress levels can promote focus and drive in a testing situation. Everything in moderation.

(For more discussion starters, see p. 237 of this IM chapter.)

 ## Question 1: How Can Preparation Improve Test Performance?

[Section overview: PowerPoint slide 5]
The <u>best</u> preparation for tests is to be a responsible student and to keep on top of work during the term. [See PowerPoint slide 6.]

The activities that achieve the goal of test preparation enable students to learn and *retain* what they learn – the primary ingredient in successful test taking. Here are three:
- Attend class, listen actively, and participate.
- Take good notes and review them regularly.
- Keep up with reading and other assignments.

233

Preparing for a Test

Go through the list of preparation strategies found on in the first section of the chapter. Here, we've listed the top points.

Step 1: Find out what you can about the material tested. Study what has seemed important in lectures or readings. Talk to your instructor or TA about the test. Pay attention if your instructor discusses the test material. Study practice tests or sample tests, if available. **[See PowerPoint slide 7.]**

Step 2: Create a study schedule and checklist. Now that you know more about the test, estimate and plan how you will study, where, and with whom.

Step 3: Review carefully and regularly. Reviewing on a regular basis over time improves retention.

Step 4: Create and take a pretest.

Step 5: Prepare physically. Sleep well the night before and eat right.

Step 6: Make the most of last-minute cramming. Ask: "Have you ever crammed for a test? How did you do? What did you remember later?" Make the point that everyone crams from time to time, and that the most important goal is to make the most of the time you have – and to try to avoid having to cram, since it does not promote retention.

(Consider using group exercise "SQ3R Review" or pair exercise "Time Management and Test Prep" found on pp. 238 and 239 of this IM chapter.)

 # Question 2: How Can You Work Through Test Anxiety?

[Section overview: PowerPoint slide 8]
The two most effective ways to minimize test anxiety are *preparation* and a *positive attitude*. Invite a guest speaker from the counseling or tutoring center to discuss test anxiety in more detail, if time permits. Be sure they cover stress reduction techniques, such as deep breathing or meditation techniques, shoulder shrugs, and so on that students can use during a test. **[See PowerPoint slide 9.]**

Practice a relaxation or visualization activity in class. Here's one: Have students close their eyes. Ask them to think of a peaceful place and picture themselves there. Have them take a deep breath and then imagine themselves relaxing there. Another relaxation activity is to have students close their eyes and then tense and relax muscle groups starting with the face, then moving to the neck, shoulders, arms, stomach, hips, legs and ending with their feet. Both of these are simple practices that can be done prior to testing.

Note: To gauge how much time to spend on test anxiety, we suggest that you assign and collect the journal question at the end of this chapter, which should help you pinpoint how many students suffer from moderate-to-severe test anxiety.

(Consider using group exercise "Positive Attitude Brainstorm," on p. 238 of this IM chapter.)

Question 3: What General Strategies Can Help You Succeed On Tests?

[Section overview: PowerPoint slide 10]
Now, ask the class to imagine it is test time. Are they ready? Get students thinking with a brainstorming activity: Ask them for suggested ideas for test-taking strategies. Here are some key ideas from the text. Discuss them, and see if they can come up with others.

- Plan ahead. Know date, time, and location; arrive early; bring necessary materials.

- Read/listen to directions. Be careful with machine-scored exams.

- Look over the test before you start. Answer easiest questions first. It will boost your confidence and save time.

- Write down key facts, such as formulas, on scrap paper.

- When in doubt, stick with your first guess.

- Use critical-thinking skills to avoid errors.

- Maintain academic integrity.

 # Question 4: How Can You Master Different Types of Test Questions?

[Section overview: PowerPoint slide 11]
Discuss Objective versus Subjective (Essay) Tests

Open the floor to find out how your students respond to different types of test questions and which ones they do well or poorly on. "Do you find essay tests easier or harder than objective tests? Why?" If a majority has trouble with a particular kind, such as multiple choice or essay, we recommend that you prioritize your class time accordingly.

Make sure students know the essential difference between objective and subjective questions. Go through the definitions with them:

Objective tests examine your ability to recall and think about information. Ask students to name kinds of objective questions (multiple choice, matching, etc.). Go through tips for each of the following (tips are found in this section of the text). During the discussion, you may want to show sample questions on PowerPoint or point them out in Key 7.1.

- Multiple choice **[See PowerPoint slide 12.]**
- True/false **[See PowerPoint slide 13.]**
- Fill-in-the-blank **[See PowerPoint slide 14.]**

Subjective tests demand the same recall that objective tests do, but they also require the test taker to analyze information critically and draw conclusions. The wording in the question offers important clues as to what kinds of thought processes are needed to tackle the question. Get a read on their approach to essay questions by asking, "How do you normally approach an essay question on a test?" **[See PowerPoint slide 15.]**

Emphasize the importance of reading the questions carefully, since the action verbs give hints as to how to answer the question. Focus on the verbs from Key 7.2. You may want to use the board or **PowerPoint slide 15** to show these terms; ask students for definitions, discuss, and write in answers. Or, you can use the handout on p. 245 and have students write the answers in as the class examines them. Ask students to use critical thinking vocabulary, so that their thinking will be consistent with what they already know.

Other essay question tips to introduce (see last part of this chapter section):
- Budget time carefully.
- Answer easiest questions first.
- Plan before you write (point to outline in Key 7.3).
- Draft your answer.
- Revise.
- Edit.
- Be neat (consider telling of a time when you couldn't read an exam and what happened).

(Three alternatives – consider using group exercise "Cooperative Quiz," group exercise "Create a Test," or handout exercise "Create Test Questions," on pages 237, 242-243, and 244 of this IM chapter respectively.)

 Question 5: How Can You Learn From Test Mistakes?

[Section overview: PowerPoint slide 16]
Ask the students how many of them review their tests and rework the questions. Remind them how reworking these exams can help them increase and retain their learning. If the students have comprehensive exams, suggest that these tests become efficient study sheets. Ask students to pull out the exam you asked them to bring in, on which they didn't perform as well as they would have liked. If time permits, have them do the *Take Action: Learn From Your Mistakes* in class with the test in front of them and assign as homework the *"Analysis of How You Perform on Tests"* exercise that appears at the beginning of the end-of-chapter exercise set.

(Consider using group exercise "Study to Learn or to Pass a Test?" on p. 239 of this IM chapter.)

[Successful Intelligence Wrap-Up: PowerPoint slide 17]
[End-of-chapter foreign word: PowerPoint slide 18]
[End-of-chapter thought-provoking quote: PowerPoint slide 19]

****

CREATE COMMUNITY

DISCUSSION STARTERS

1. Ask students to volunteer ways in which they prepare for a test. Set up an environment in which they can be honest – i.e., saying "cramming the night before" if that applies.
2. Ask students to brainstorm situations that are "tests" in many senses of the word. Offer a personal example – overcoming a health issue, dealing with a big work project, facing a relationship challenge. Relate these to test taking in school
3. Inspire with a positive story – ask students to talk about their best test that they can remember – how they did, how they felt, what the test was in, why they think they did so well, what were the results.

GROUP EXERCISES

Teamwork: Create Solutions Together – *Test Study Group*

This exercise, found at the end of chapter 7 in the text, asks students to carefully examine their study habits in preparation for a test and to come together in a group to discuss the habits, evaluate their success, and compare notes. Schedule two meetings – one before study preparation will begin, and one following the test. You may want to challenge students, in their preparation before the test and group meeting, to focus on one particular study strategy that is comfortable for them and one that is unfamiliar.

Cooperative Quiz

Let the class choose a chapter of this text or some outside reading material (from course assignments) that they want to review. Divide into five groups, and assign to each group a category:

- Essay question
- True/false questions
- Fill-in-the-blank questions
- Multiple-choice questions
- Short-answer questions

Each group should meet and write ten questions, of the type assigned to them, based on material from the reading that was chosen (suggest that they note page numbers where the answers can be found). Groups submit their questions to you. Compile the best of each category into a quiz for the students to take. If you have time, do a post-mortem – how did it go? Was the quiz challenging? Were the students more motivated since they were involved in making the quiz? (If you don't have time, let students know that next term's class will be taking this quiz in the "pop quiz" opening assignment for the chapter.)

You may also choose to have groups share their answers with the class after the class completes the quiz, as an "interactive answer check."

SQ3R Review

Write the elements of SQ3R – Survey, Question, Read, Recite, Review – on the board. Divide students into five groups and assign an element to each. Ask each group to brainstorm ways in which the element helps them to review in preparation for a test.

Students should come up with variations on these basic themes:

- Surveying gives you an overview of topics.
- Questioning helps you focus through asking questions.
- Reading reminds you of the ideas and supporting information.
- Reciting anchors concepts in your head.
- Reviewing solidifies learning.

Each group should present its conclusions to the class. Instruct students to take notes during the presentations so that they know more about how to use each stage when they are reviewing for a test.

Positive Attitude Brainstorm

As a class, ask students to volunteer examples of negative attitudes that fuel test anxiety. You can use some of the following to show what you are looking for – or, alternatively, you can use this list instead of asking for student examples:

- "This teacher wants to torture me!"

- "If I fail this test, I'm a failure as a person."

- "I don't know anything on this test."

- "I'm so tense I can't think straight."

- "I always fail these things. Why should today be any different?"

- "If I get anything wrong on this test my life is over."

- "I will feel like such a loser if I don't do well on this test."

Break students up into groups of 3 or 4. Have them work on ways to turn these attitudes around and come up with motivational phrases that will help students feel positively about tests. After each group has addressed as many attitudes as possible, have them come together again to discuss their ideas. Come to a consensus on key ideas for each of the negative attitudes with which you began.

Time Management and Test Prep (Working in Pairs)

- Pair up students. Individually, each student takes five minutes to write up a generic week's plan for studying for an important exam, such as a midterm: when to study, how long to study, what materials to study.

- Students come together and compare plans. What is different? Why?

Study to Learn or to Pass a Test?

To emphasize why it's important to study for learning instead of just passing a test, have students try this exercise. Divide students into groups of four. Assign each group to one of the following professions:

- Emergency room surgeon
- Civil engineer
- Business manager
- President of the United States

Ask groups to discuss, and make notes on, the following in preparation for talking to the class about their discussion:

- What is the learning and the knowledge base behind being a success in each of these professions?

- What do these people create in our society? How does their job affect the student directly?

- If these people cut corners in their learning, what would the impact be?

- If these people develop competency in their learning, what is the impact?

- How does this analysis change the way you view your own learning and your future options?

POP CULTURE LINKS

Movies: Many films have some kind of test for the main protagonist as a central focus. Adventure-type films from Harry Potter to Spiderman usually contain a goal that must be achieved, and obstacles that must be overcome on the path toward that achievement. Something like Spellbound has a real-life documentary look at a test – the spelling bee. Choose a film that your class can relate to and discuss it in terms of preparation, hard work, and goal achievement. You may simply want to ask students for their ideas about film characters who have to pass a tough test and what they did to achieve that goal.

Music: As a test warm-up, play a current song for students (one with understandable lyrics) and have them take notes. Have a quiz prepared on the words and ideas in the song – you may even want to have quiz questions on the structure, musicality, or instruments used in the song (warn students ahead of time of the scope of the quiz). If you plan the song at the beginning of the class period, give the quiz toward the end, and leave time to talk about results.

SUCCESSFUL INTELLIGENCE EXERCISES

Get Analytical! *Write To the Verb*

Assign for in-class activity or homework. Students build their knowledge of essay question verbs by writing essay questions using different verbs and analyzing how each verb changes what the question asks. You can add on to this exercise in class by having students outline or write answers to one another's essay questions.

Get Creative! *Write Your Own Test*

Assign for homework. Students are challenged to write their own pretests in order to deepen their understanding of different test questions as well as solidify their understanding of the material – then they take their pretests to see how well they do. Consider having students take each other's pretests if the material is from your course, or collect all pretests and choose a well-made one to copy and hand out as a quiz.

Get Practical! *Learn From Your Mistakes*

Assign for homework. This exercise requires that students have on hand a test on which they didn't perform as well as they had hoped – or even a test where they got any questions wrong at all (anything wrong, or an essay receiving less than an A, can work for this exercise). Students will look for patterns in their errors or less-than-ideal performance, and identify practical steps to take to avoid the same problems next time.

HOMEWORK

In-text exercises: All three Successful Intelligence exercises (*Get Analytical, Get Creative,* and *Get Practical*) can be assigned for homework.

Foreign word response: Ask students to write a responsive essay to the word "hart ducha." Ask them to describe what they can think about that gives them "hart ducha" and how they can call it up when they need it at test time.

End-of-chapter exercises:
- **Successful Intelligence: Think, Create, Apply** – Students need to have a recent test handy, in any course, to complete this exercise. They are asked to evaluate specific elements of their performance on the test, and use creative and practical skills to make plans for what to do next time.
- **Writing: Journal and Put Skills to Work** – The test anxiety journal entry can be a homework assignment anytime. The real-life writing assignment is more situation-specific, because it requires that a student draft an e-mail to a professor regarding a grade on an essay exam (needs to be completed when the student has taken an essay exam and has questions).
- **Personal Portfolio:** This assignment involves compiling a résumé. If some of your students have a current résumé, have them reformat and update it for this assignment. Consider using the accompanying handout on p. 247 of this manual.

QUOTES FOR REFLECTION

Use these quotes to generate discussion, start class, or offer as a short exercise. Have students reflect on what any or all of the following quotes mean to them in a short paper or presentation.

Far better it is to dare mighty things, to win glorious triumphs even though checkered by failure, than to rank with those poor spirits who neither enjoy nor suffer much because they live in the gray twilight that knows neither victory nor defeat.
Theodore Roosevelt

As long as there are tests, there will be prayer in schools.
Unknown

Not everything that counts can be counted and not everything that can be counted counts.
Albert Einstein

There is no substitute for hard work.
Thomas Alva Edison

Nothing, I am sure, calls forth the faculties so much as the being obliged to struggle with the world.
Mary Wollstonecraft

Be curious always! For knowledge will not acquire you; you must acquire it.
Sudie Back

It is possible to store the mind with a million facts and still be uneducated.
Alec Bourne

No single test score can be considered a definitive measure of a student's knowledge.
National Research Council Report, High Stakes

HANDOUTS

The following are exercises with handouts, or handouts that you can use on their own. Integrate them into your lesson plan as you see fit, or follow the suggestions in the "Communicate Content" section.

- Create a Test (group exercise with handout)
- Create Test Questions (individual exercise with handout)
- Verbs That Help You Plan Answers to Essay Questions
- Multiple Intelligence Grid for Test Preparation Strategies (handout)
- Personal Portfolio Handout to accompany chapter 7 Personal Portfolio exercise

Create a Test

Class objective. Students will create examples of five types of test questions – multiple choice, true/false, matching, fill-in-the-blank, and essay.

Materials: Handout: Create a Test (see next page) plus textbook, chapter 7

Activities
1. Ask students if they have ever created questions that were used on an actual test. What types of questions did they ask? What kinds of answers did they expect to receive?
2. Ask students what they would include when creating a test for this chapter.
3. Have students count off from 1 to 5. After counting off students will get together with the other "1s", all the "2s" together, etc. The number they are will match the type of questions they will create.

Closure. Have students turn in the questions for the instructor to collate and hand out to do at the next class.

Benefits of this exercise. Students will
1. Create different types of questions.
2. Brainstorm ways to answer test questions.

CREATE A TEST

Guidelines for different types of test questions

Multiple Choice
- Have four choices – a., b., c., d., -- for each question.
- Consider having two choices that are similar.
- Make sure the correct choice isn't too obvious.
- Make sure your correct answer is accurate and grammatically agrees with the question (for example, the answer to "The _____ of mind are behaviors associated with successful problem solving" must be plural, not "habit").

True/False
- Pay attention to qualifiers that can change the meaning of a word or group of words – absolute qualifiers such as "all" or "never" often make a statement false, whereas qualifiers like "some" or "rarely" often make a statement true. Example: "All eggs are white" is false; "Some eggs are white" is true.
- Remember that if part of a statement is true and part is false, the entire statement is false.

Fill-In-The-Blank
- Match the number of blanks to your answer – for example, if you have a two-word answer, use two blanks.
- Use the blank to replace the most significant word/idea in your sentence.
- If you like, you may have more than one blank in separate positions in your sentence. Example: The United States flag has _____ stars and _____ stripes.

Matching
- Use the left-hand column for vocabulary words/phrases. Use the right-hand column for definitions/examples.
- Make sure you have the same number of entries in each column.
- Make sure that each word/phrase has one match.
- Mix up the right-hand column so that you have a variety of distances between the words/phrases and their matches.

Essay
- When crafting your question, consider what verb will best fit what you are asking (define, describe, list, summarize, compare, etc.).
- Keep your question narrow enough that it can be answered within a reasonable amount of time (10-15 minutes).

Name _____Date _____

CREATE TEST QUESTIONS

Part of preparing for a test is predicting what the instructor will test and studying thoroughly that information. To practice this skill I would like you to review assigned pages in our text and create test questions. Have another student review your questions and make suggestions before you give this to your instructor. Attach your questions to this sheet.

Please review pages _____.

Create two multiple choice questions. Mark the correct answer and page number for this answer.

       Answer _____ 1.
       Page   _____

       Answer _____ 2.
       Page   _____

Write two true/false questions. Include the answer and page number.

       Answer _____ 1.
       Page   _____

       Answer _____ 2.
       Page   _____

Write two fill-in-the-blank questions. Include the answer and page number.

       Answer _____ 1.
       Page   _____

       Answer _____ 2.
       Page   _____

Write one short answer or essay question. Include the answer and page number.

       Page: _____
       Answer (give brief guidelines as to what the essay should cover):

       _____
       _____

Deborah Maness, Pre-Curriculum Instructor, Wake Technical Community College, Raleigh, North Carolina.

VERBS THAT HELP YOU PLAN YOUR ANSWERS TO ESSAY QUESTIONS

Fill in a definition for each essay verb.

ANALYZE	
COMPARE	
CONTRAST	
CRITICIZE	
DEFINE	
DESCRIBE	
DISCUSS	
ENUMERATE/LIST	
EVALUATE	
EXPLAIN	
ILLUSTRATE	
INTERPRET	
OUTLINE	
PROVE	
REVIEW	
STATE	
SUMMARIZE	
TRACE	

MULTIPLE INTELLIGENCE STRATEGIES FOR TEST PREPARATION

INTELLIGENCE	USE MI STRATEGIES TO IMPROVE TEST PREPARATION	WHAT WORKS FOR YOU? WRITE NEW IDEAS HERE
VERBAL-LINGUISTIC	∞ Write test questions your instructor might ask. Answer them and then try rewriting them in a different format (essay, true/false, and so on.) ∞ Underline important words in review or practice questions.	
LOGICAL-MATHEMATICAL	∞ Logically connect what you are studying with what you know. Consider similarities, differences, and cause-and-effect relationships. ∞ Draw charts that show relationships and analyze trends.	
BODILY-KINESTHETIC	∞ Use text highlighting to take a hands-on approach to studying. ∞ Create a sculpture, model, or skit to depict a tough concept that will be on the test.	
VISUAL- SPATIAL	∞ Make charts, diagrams, or think links illustrating concepts. ∞ Make drawings related to possible test topics	
INTERPERSONAL	∞ Form a study group to prepare for your test. ∞ In your group, come up with possible test questions. Then use the questions to test each other's knowledge.	
INTRAPERSONAL	∞ Apply concepts to your own life; think about how you would manage. ∞ Brainstorm test questions and then take the sample "test" you developed.	
MUSICAL	∞ Recite text concepts to rhythms or write a song to depict them. ∞ Explore relevant musical links to reading material.	
NATURALISTIC	∞ Try to notice similarities and differences in objects and concepts by organizing your study materials into relevant	

PERSONAL PORTFOLIO ACTIVITY # 7

COMPILING A RÉSUMÉ

Be proud of your accomplishments at work and school. List your life experiences confidently on your résumé. Complete this brainstorming activity to collect ideas for your résumé (study the sample résumé in the text carefully first). Also, note: you must start each line of job activities with one of the verbs listed at the bottom – and use a different one for each line!

EDUCATION

• _____ to present: _____

• _____ to _____place: _____

• others: _____

PROFESSIONAL EMPLOYMENT

• _____ to present: Name of Company: _____
    Location: _____
    Job activities: 1) _____
        2) _____

• _____ to _____: Name of Company: _____
    Location: _____
    Job activities: 1) _____
        2) _____

• _____ to _____: Name of Company: _____
    Location: _____
    Job activities: 1) _____
        2) _____

SKILLS

• Languages: _____
• Computer: _____
• Personal: (talents, hobbies - things that show you have well-rounded experience)

_____
_____
_____

Action words to use for employment: (*Use one to start each line of "job activities"*)
researched, developed, worked, coordinated, advised, created, consulted, assisted, pursued, explored, examined, counseled, taught, organized, facilitated, provided, formed, performed, helped, supported, followed, tracked, discovered, searched, surveyed, inspected, studied, scanned, directed, trained

CONSIDER COMPREHENSION

REVIEW WITH STUDENTS BEFORE YOU BEGIN THE NEXT CHAPTER:

- What are some key test-preparation strategies?
- What are the two most important tools in the fight against test anxiety?
- Strategies for test success
- Techniques for handling different types of test questions

Chapter Seven Vocabulary Quiz Answer Key
(Quiz appears on following page)

1. D
2. C
3. F
4. G
5. B
6. H
7. A
8. E

Chapter Seven Vocabulary Quiz

1. ____test anxiety

2. ____objective questions

3. ____reading period

4. ____subjective questions

5. ____pretest

6. ____negatives

7. ____ qualifiers

8. ____cramming

B. A practice exam that is taken with the purpose of preparing for the exam

C. Short-answer questions that test your ability to recall, compare, and contrast information

D. A bad case of nerves that can make it hard to think or remember during an exam

E. Intensive, last-minute studying right before an exam

F. Particular days scheduled by a college for students to study for final exams

G. Essay questions that require written responses that tap your personal knowledge and perspective

H. Particular types of qualifiers such as *not* and *never*

A. Words and phrases that can alter the meaning of a test question

CHAPTER SEVEN ASSESSMENT

Multiple Choice
Circle or highlight the answer that seems to fit best.

1. The BEST way to prepare for a test is to
   a. participate and attend all classes.
   b. stay on top of assignments and complete all reading.
   c. delay all your studying until the night before the test.
   d. a and b only

2. Which of the following offers the BEST set of options to predict what will be on a test?
   a. Examine old tests, design your own study guide, and talk to people who completed the course and did well.
   b. Talk to people who took the course previously and practice intelligent guessing.
   c. Examine old tests and follow your instincts.
   d. Listen carefully to your instructor so you can think creatively about your instructor's perspective.

3. A good question to ask an instructor prior to a test would be:
   a. Do you follow the syllabus?
   b. How long will the test be and what are your office hours?
   c. What topics will be covered and what types of questions will be on the test?
   d. Who will grade the test, when can we expect the results, and how will we get the results?

4. Test anxiety can cause
   a. sweating.
   b. nausea.
   c. dizziness and headaches.
   d. all of the above

5. When preparing for a test, a study schedule helps you to
   a. ensure adequate time to prepare for the test.
   b. set goals for the term.
   c. choose what to study for the test.
   d. focus on information that is most likely to be on the exam.

6. Some test-taking strategies discussed in the chapter advise you to
   a. write down key facts, read test directions, and sit near friends.
   b. write down key facts, daydream, and read test directions.
   c. read test directions, write down key facts, and sit where you want.
   d. begin with an overview, write down key facts, and read directions.

7. When you pay attention to words such as *always, never,* or *every* in test questions, you are aware of
   a. how qualifiers modify the meaning of a question.
   b. how transitions help move readers to a new idea.
   c. how critical thinking helps avoid errors.

d. how ideas are linked to examples.

8. Essay questions ask for written responses and are an example of
    a. objective questions.
    b. subjective questions.
    c. creative questions.
    d. fill-in-the-blank questions.

9. On an essay test, if the question requires you to state and justify your opinion about the value or worth of something, you are being asked to
    a. evaluate.
    b. summarize.
    c. define.
    d. analyze.

10. When taking a test it is a bad idea to
    a. rush.
    b. watch the clock.
    c. make intelligent guesses.
    d. use critical thinking skills.

11. Answering an essay question is most like
    a. outlining a chapter.
    b. using the Cornell system.
    c. writing a research paper.
    d. answering fill-in-the blank questions.

12. The BEST strategies for answering essay questions are
    a. read the entire question, map out your time, and build a logical, evidence-based argument to support your thesis.
    b. read the entire question and begin writing your thoughts.
    c. map out your time, focus on action verbs, and list the points of your argument.
    d. be logical and read the entire question.

13. The BEST way to narrow down the correct answer on a multiple choice test is to ask yourself:
    a. Is the choice accurate?
    b. Is the choice relevant?
    c. Are there any qualifiers?
    d. All of the above

14. Spending a few minutes at the beginning of a test to get an overview is important because
    a. you're certain to have plenty of time to complete the exam.
    b. you can get a general sense of whether you will pass or fail.
    c. you can get an idea of the type of questions you face and how to approach them.
    d. you can decide which questions you have no hope of answering.

15. Of the following options, what would be the MOST effective test preparation technique(s) for a student who is dominant in the visual-spatial domain of multiple intelligence?
    a. Studying in a group setting
    b. Highlighting the text readings and class notes
    c. Making charts, diagrams, or think links
    d. Creating a detailed outline of key points and concepts

True/False
Determine whether each statement is true or false and circle or highlight the correct answer.

1. Before studying for a test, you should find out as much as you can about it.
   True
   False

2. Reading your notes is sufficient preparation for tests.
   True
   False

3. The BEST way to start answering questions on a test is to start with the hard questions first.
   True
   False

4. Even a small amount of stress is bad to experience before a test.
   True
   False

5. Objective test questions usually have one answer or a limited response.
   True
   False

6. The most important step in answering an essay test question is to start writing immediately.
   True
   False

7. On tests, a question may have a qualifier that changes the answer.
   True
   False

8. Students who write illegibly run the risk of losing points on a test.
   True
   False

9. When you must answer questions after reading a passage, you should read the questions first, and then the passage.
   True

False

10. If you fail an exam, it's best to throw it away and move on with your life.
    True
    False

Fill in the Blank
Insert the word or phrase that BEST completes the sentence.

1. Studying intensively primarily during the last 24 hours before an exam is called _____.

2. Words that change the meaning of a statement or test question are called _____.

3. Multiple choice, true/false, and sentence completion are _____ test questions.

4. _____ is a way to pass a test but it robs you of the opportunity to learn and is unethical.

5. One way to prepare for a test is to write your own ____ _____.

6. Check the course _____ to find out when your tests and quizzes are scheduled.

7. You should try to work from ____ to hard questions when taking a test.

8. According to the chapter, preparation is most basic defense against test _____.

9. A student taking a geometry course who is dominant in the _____-_____ type of multiple intelligence would benefit from using pencils, popsicle sticks, pipe cleaners, containers, or other materials to create the shapes on which he or she would be tested.

10. Reciting concepts to rhythms is one way a _____ learner would prefer to study for a test.

Short Answer

1. Describe three test-taking strategies for multiple-choice questions that you are likely to use on your next exam.

2. What are some of the most effective ways for you to deal with test anxiety?

3. What are the most effective strategies to use when you do not know the answer to an objective test question?

Essay

1. Develop and describe your own policy for students who cheat on exams, including the consequences if they are caught. Explain the reasons for your policy. For extra credit, outline the methods you would use to enforce your policy.

2. Consider the test-preparation strategies discussed in this chapter. List five strategies you think are most beneficial and describe how you plan to implement them this term.

3. When taking tests, what are your two biggest obstacles to performing well? How can you overcome these obstacles?

4. Consider the recommended steps for completing essay questions. Describe how you would modify the strategies suggested in the chapter to meet your personal style and needs.

Word Exploration

Define this term: *hart ducha* [hahrt doo-cha]

What does it mean to you? How does it apply to your life as a college student?

Chapter Seven Assessment Answer Key

Multiple Choice
Test Item Assesses This Learning Objective/Topic

1. d   How Can Preparation Improve Test Performance?
2. a   How Can Preparation Improve Test Performance?
   Identify test type and material covered
3. c   How Can Preparation Improve Test Performance?
   Identify test type and material covered
4. d   How Can You Work Through Test Anxiety?
5. a   How Can Preparation Improve Test Performance?
6. d   What General Strategies Can Help You Succeed on Tests?
7. a   How Can You Master Different Types of Test Questions?
8. b   How Can You Master Different Types of Test Questions?
   Get Analytical! Write to the verb
9. a   What General Strategies Can Help You Succeed on Tests?
10. a   What General Strategies Can Help You Succeed on Tests?
11. c   How Can You Master Different Types of Test Questions?
    Essay questions
12. a   How Can You Master Different Types of Test Questions?
    Essay questions
13. d   How Can You Master Different Types of Test Questions?
    Multiple-choice questions
14. c   What General Strategies Can Help You Succeed on Tests?
15. c   How Can You Master Different Types of Test Questions?
    Multiple intelligence strategies for test preparation

True/False
Test Item Assesses This Learning Objective/Topic

1. T   How Can Preparation Improve Test Performance?
   Identify test type and material covered
2. F   How Can Preparation Improve Test Performance?
3. F   What General Strategies Can Help You Succeed on Tests?
   Work from easy to hard
4. F   How Can You Work Through Test Anxiety?
5. T   How Can You Master Different Types of Test Questions?
6. F   How Can You Master Different Types of Test Questions?
   Essay questions
7. T   How Can You Learn from Test Mistakes?
8. T   How Can You Master Different Types of Test Questions?

Get analytical! Write to the verb

9. T   How Can You Master Different Types of Test Questions?
         Essay questions
10. F   How Can You Learn from Test Mistakes?

Fill in the Blank

Test Item Assesses This Learning Objective/Topic

1. *cramming*   How Can Preparation Improve Test Performance?
                  Make the most of last-minute cramming
2. *qualifiers*   What General Strategies Can Help You Succeed on Tests?
3. *objective*   How Can You Master Different Types of Test Questions?
4. *Cheating*   What General Strategies Can Help You Succeed on Tests?
                  Maintain academic integrity
5. *test questions*   How Can Preparation Improve Test Performance?
                  Write your own test: Get creative!
6. *syllabus*   How Can Preparation Improve Test Performance?
                  Identify test type and material covered
7. *easiest*   What General Strategies Can Help You Succeed on Tests?
                  Work from easy to hard
8. *anxiety*   How Can You Work Through Text Anxiety?
9. *bodily-kinesthetic*   How Can You Master Different Types of Test Questions?
                  Multiple intelligence strategies for test preparation
10. *musical*   How Can You Master Different Types of Test Questions?
                  Multiple intelligence strategies for test preparation

Wellness, Money, and Careers
Building a Successful Future

BRIEF CHAPTER OVERVIEW

This closing chapter covers skills that, if mastered, can greatly enhance students' success in college, work, and life. Usually, time is precious at this point in the course. If time has run out, you can assign the chapter as outside reading with some light homework as students prepare for finals. Our personal recommendation is that at the very least you have students reflect on how they've built their successful intelligence by completing the self-activators and analytical, creative, and practical thinking post-assessments.

First, the chapter explores wellness and stress management topics – eating, exercise, sleep, mental health, substances, and sexual decision making (if any of these topics cause discomfort for your students, you may wish to assign the reading and in-text exercises, giving students an opportunity to write about and examine these issues privately).

Next, the chapter explores money management and career exploration. The money section has been updated to include attitudes toward money, and the career section features information about how multiple intelligences and Personality Spectrum relate to career choice and shows how emotional and social intelligence link to career success.

Finally, the chapter revisits successful intelligence, giving students a chance to retake the self-assessment they completed at the end of chapter 1 on the twenty self-activators used by successfully intelligent thinkers. Bookending the text, the personal portfolio exercise has the students revisit the three self-assessments within chapter 1 on analytical, creative, and practical thinking.

Note the successful intelligence skills your students will build in chapter 8:

Analytical	Creative	Practical
■ Analyzing the effects of alcohol, tobacco, and drug use	■ Creating more beneficial eating, exercise, and sleeping habits	■ How to seek support for stress and health issues
■ Analyzing your money-related attitudes and goals	■ Creating new ways to connect how you learn to career areas	■ How to make effective decisions about substances and sex
■ Examining your development of the 20 self-activators	■ Brainstorming ways to look for a job on the Internet	■ How to use a monthly budget

CHAPTER EIGHT OUTLINE

How Can Focusing on Health Help You Manage Stress?

- Food and Eating Habits
- Exercise
- Sleep
- Recognize Mental Health Problems

How Can You Make Effective Decisions about Substances and Sex?

- Alcohol
- Tobacco
- Drugs
- Facing Addiction
- Sexual Decision Making

How Can You Manage Money Effectively?

- Analyze What Money Means in Your Life
- Learn to Manage Income and Expenses Through Budgeting
- Manage Credit Card Use

How Can You Prepare for Career Success?

- Investigate Career Paths
- Consider Your Personality and Strengths
- Know What Employers Want
- Searching for a Job – and a Career

How Can You Continue to Activate Your Successful Intelligence?

COMMUNICATE CONTENT
TOPICS COVERED IN THE CHAPTER

[Chapter intro and chapter 7 review: PowerPoint slides 1, 2, 3]

The *Real Questions, Practical Answers* Discussion Starter Question:
What knowledge will help me succeed in a changing world? **[PowerPoint slide 4]**

> Humans tend to assume that they can count on things happening in a predictable way. As much as it goes against human nature, students need to develop tools to deal with change – and build core skills that promote success in *any* situation.
>
> This questioner is pursing a specific area (acting), but wants to know what college skills will serve her outside of her training in that specific area. The responder focuses on teamwork, leadership, and values. Ask students: When have you planned to be ready for a situation, only to have it turned on its head? What abilities do you have that are useful no matter what course you take or work you do? Get them to focus on those broad-spectrum, transferable skills.

(For more discussion starters, see p. 268 of this IM chapter.)

 ## Question 1: How Can Focusing on Health Help You Manage Stress?

[Section overview: PowerPoint slide 5]
Open the discussion by making sure students have a clear idea of the definition of stress – as a reaction to pressure, not as something inherently bad or good. Use Keys 8.1 and 8.2 to show that stress can come from all kinds of situations, even ones people consider positive, and that moderate levels of stress can actually have a motivational effect. **[See PowerPoint slide 6.]**

Link to wellness topics: *physical and mental health allow you to manage stress as effectively as possible.* Emphasize the mind-body-stress connection. Offer stress management ideas in addition to those shown in the text.

(Consider using the "Teamwork: Create Solutions Together – Actively Dealing with Stress" exercise from the text, described on p. 268 of this IM chapter.)

Ways to Improve Physical Health
For the topic of physical wellness, we suggest that you begin by emphasizing to students that the body requires adequate maintenance to enable student success. Food, exercise, sleep and positive societal connections keep the body fueled and running smoothly and efficiently. If you put a plant in a dark closet at the start of the term and don't give it sunlight or water, the plant

will wither and die by the end of term. So too, if students don't take care of their health, they may end up in a sorry state when it's time for final exams.

The following points can lead to improved physical health:

- Eat right. Aim for balanced meals, use moderation, and watch for weight gain or loss. Know where to go for help. This is a hot topic, and the text chapter has the latest information on BMI and the challenge of making healthful choices in today's "toxic food environment" (especially for college students with their particular lifestyles).
- Exercise. Exercise helps improve the body's efficiency, and releases endorphins, which are natural mood elevators. Ask students to give examples of the kinds of exercise they like best and how they schedule exercise. Introduce the three important categories of exercise: cardiovascular, strength, and flexibility training.

(Consider using the "Exercise and Eating Log" exercise and handout on p. 276 of this IM chapter.)

- Get sleep. Sleep deprivation is common for college students. Ask for a show of hands of how many people get at least 7-8 hours a night – or ask the question about a variety of time frames (3-4 hours, 5-6 hours, 7-8 hours, 9-10 hours) and tally the results. Alternatively, you could ask how many students feel that they don't get enough sleep (you will probably see many). Review text suggestions for getting adequate sleep.

Recognizing Mental Health Problems

This is the follow-up to the general stress management material from early in the chapter. Because mental health topics are so personal, they might not be good candidates for in-depth class time. You can judge based on your group how much you want to cover – you may want to choose one or two of the most pertinent topics. Some basic points to cover:

- Definitions and symptoms of problems, such as depression or eating disorders
- Steps to take if there is significant concern (include specifics about who can help on your campus and where/how to find them – counseling, student health, etc.)

These topics also provide an ideal opportunity for a presentation by someone from your student health center or other on-campus organization focused on a health issue.

Unfortunately, depression and its problematic effects are on the rise on college campuses. Review causes and symptoms for depression. Note that it is crucial to seek help. A qualified professional can help students find solutions. Offer suggestions for places or people to contact on campus or in the community if seeking help.

Note: If you assign and collect journals on a regular basis, be alert for signs of distress in journal writing.

Eating disorders

The text chapter has information on weight control issues – *anorexia, bulimia,* and *binge eating disorder.* Bring in pictures from magazines showing the media's portrayal of women and men. Use the pictures as a springboard to discuss how our culture contributes to the prevalence of eating disorders.

(Consider using the "Advice Columns" exercise, or the "Did You Know That" exercise and handout, on p. 268 and pp. 274-275 of this IM chapter respectively.)

An idea for an extra-credit activity: At the start of the term, give students the opportunity to attend any lecture or special event having to do with health and wellness, or try a new form of exercise with an instructor (such as a Tai Chi class). Have students write a 1-page paper describing the event, lecture, or activity (date, place, description), what they learned, and what their reaction was.

 Question 2: How Can You Make Effective Decisions about Substances and Sex?

[Section overview: PowerPoint slide 7]
With topics such as these, lecturing may sound like preaching to students. Focus on delivering the *cause-and-effect facts*, pairing your message with a *continual emphasis on personal responsibility*. This will convey to students a sense that you respect them: They are responsible for thinking through their own decisions and living with the consequences. At some point in your coverage, make sure that students know – or look up – your schools' specific policies regarding substance use and abuse. This will further support your emphasis on students thinking through the potential consequences of particular decisions (i.e., "this could be fun, but is it really worth getting thrown out of school?")

When possible, get students talking about what they see or experience. Personal stories are always compelling (you can use your own as well if they are appropriate and topical). Cover the basic points found in the text:

- Alcohol. Mention the biggest problem on campus – binge drinking. Ask students if they know the legal standards for drunkenness while driving in your state. Then ask who knows how much alcohol it takes to reach the legal limit (note that body weight is a factor – the more a person weighs, the more alcohol it will take to get them to the legal limit). **[See PowerPoint slide 8.]**

- Tobacco. Emphasize that nicotine is an addictive drug. Mention that if a young smoker quits, his/her lungs can rejuvenate in a year's time. **[See PowerPoint slide 9.]**

- Drugs. If there is time and interest, discuss drug details from Key 8.3 (updated to reflect the latest in common drug use). Don't forget to bring up the legal consequences of possession and use, which can be devastating, especially in a "zero tolerance" legal climate. In addition, have students consider the effects of drug use on the family, friends, and employers surrounding the user. **[See PowerPoint slide 10.]**

- Addiction. Make the point to students that addiction occurs when a person loses control over one aspect of their lives. It doesn't mean the person is inherently bad or morally weak. It means that, for whatever reason, the person needs help. Personal stories are helpful here; if you know of someone who has been through a fight with addiction, tell the story, keeping names out of it. Discuss counseling, detox centers, and support groups as sources of aid.

(Consider using the "Case Scenario: Finding Resources" exercise on p. 269 of this IM chapter. To have students to evaluate their own use of alcohol, tobacco, or drugs, use the "Evaluate Your Substance Use" exercise on p. 277 of this IM chapter.)

- Sexual decision making. Emphasize that although sex is a private business, it also by nature involves other people. It's crucial that individuals think critically about their actions in terms of potential effects (pregnancy, sexually transmitted diseases [STDs], emotional consequences). Suggest that students think practically about how sex fits in with their emotional, social, academic, and other life goals.**[See PowerPoint slide 11.]**

<u>Note</u>: Students may already know a lot about AIDS and HIV, and/or may be reluctant to take on these topics in class. Keys 8.4 and 8.5 contain detailed information on birth control and STDs that you can point out and assess to ensure students have mastered the information. Abstinence/virginity is a valid choice to discuss – one that some college students are making or considering.

<u>Bottom line to express to students</u>: You are your own best champion. You will have to endure the consequences of any act. Make choices that you can live with and then communicate your limits clearly to others.

Question 3: How Can You Manage Money Effectively?

[Section overview: PowerPoint slide 12]
There are students out there who don't have money woes – but chances are you won't find many of them in your schools or courses. Money is high on the list of stressors for nearly every college student. Many students not only have to pay for expenses and contribute to tuition but also must support children or other family members.

Emphasize to students: Money does not have the same meaning for all people. People handle and view money in different ways, depending on values, goals, and self-image. These views and habits around money also influence career and lifestyle choices.

Give yourself or someone you know as an example of how a choice to pursue a particular career led to various decisions about economic situation and where to live.

Get students to use their analytical powers to examine:

<u>Their individual way of managing money</u> (spender or saver; planner or moment-by-moment purchaser; charge or cash; money equals self-worth, or money is separate from self-worth). Influential factors include:

- Values
- Personality
- Culture
- Family/peer group

<u>The time you spend earning money is an opportunity cost</u>. Ask students to examine whether their purchases are worth the time spent earning the money. Is the iPod worth a full week's work? Is the car worth two years' part-time salary (a total of 2080 hours of work)? Help students see what they spend in terms of the time they had to take to earn it, and this may lead to some more considered decision-making when it comes time to spend. Point out how making changes in day-to-day discretionary spending can lead to savings over the long term.

In this context, point out the value of a college education, despite its cost. Explain the concept of "opportunity cost" – what you give up in order to get something. Although college students give up time they could be spending earning money at work, the learning they gain will likely be worth far more to them in the future.

262

Learn to Manage Income and Expenses Through Budgeting

Start out by getting an idea of whether, and how, students budget their money.

Emphasize that *money is a crucial survival resource; budgeting involves planning activities and expenditures according to the amount of income available, thus maximizing that resource.* Emphasize that budgeting is, at its base, a simple *balancing act;* making sure that what you spend (needs) doesn't exceed what you take in (resources).

Budgeting needs to occur *in advance* and should include setting money aside for unexpected expenditures. Extreme stress can occur when no prior plans are made and the money doesn't make it to the end of the month. You may want to include a personal story or ask students for situations when that has happened.

Examples: An unexpected pregnancy increases health costs, a job layoff reduces income, a family event requires some expensive travel.

Go through <u>budgeting steps</u> as discussed in the text **[see PowerPoint slide 13]**; recommend a month as a unit of measure.

- Figure out how much you will earn (or are given).

- Figure out how much you will spend.

- Look at how much money will remain (or won't).

- Adjust as needed.

Many students, after going through this process of evaluation, find that they are spending more than they should. U.S. culture emphasizes "now" and "spend" much more than "future" and "save" – often to the detriment of the individual financial situation.

(Consider using the "Map Out Your Budget" exercise on pp. 279-280 of this IM chapter.)

Manage Credit Card Use

Credit is a two-sided coin; it can be a lifesaver or a debt-maker. College is a prime opportunity for credit-card companies to solicit new customers (consider having students bring in solicitations as examples – you can look at them in class, comparing annual fees, interest rates, etc.). Stress that credit is someone else's money and should be spent sparingly if at all possible. **[See PowerPoint slide 14.]**

The use of credit requires critical thinking. Go through the basics of credit use, found in Key 8.6. If time permits, explore the potential positive and negative effects of credit use:

- <u>Positive effects</u> – builds good credit history (if properly used—must use less than 50% of your credit maximum and have on-time payments of minimum), emergencies, record of purchases, bonuses (airline miles, cash back, etc.)

- <u>Negative effects</u> – bad credit rating (if poor payment history) resulting in trouble taking out loans; cost of high interest rates (anywhere from 5% to 23%) compared to bank loan rates, which are often far lower; unrealistic view of spending ability.

Suggested Guest Speaker. Have a speaker from a local consumer credit agency explain credit histories and how card companies exploit students.

AND/OR

If you have not covered financial aid previously, invite a guest speaker from your college's financial aid office. Have the speaker go through how to track down grant, loan, and scholarship funding for college. Make sure the speaker emphasizes financial aid opportunities offered specifically at or by your college that students may not know about.

(Consider using the "Brainstorm Day-to-Day Ways to Save Money" exercise on p. 270 of this IM chapter.)

 # Question 4: How Can You Prepare for Career Success?

[Section overview: PowerPoint slide 15]
Many traditional students rate "career" fairly low when thinking about their current values. Ask for a show of hands to find out. Begin by emphasizing that students are in all stages of thinking about careers at this point in their academic experience:
- Completely unsure of a career choice
- Thinking about a few different career areas that interest them
- Solidly focused on one particular area
- Already in a career area and looking to move up or switch gears

Pose the question to get a read on where your students fall on this continuum.

Stress that college is a time of discovery of personal talents and career desires. However, it is also a time-, energy-, and money-consuming endeavor. Students who take time to explore career options can begin making decisions (including which careers they don't want to pursue) that will help them reach their life goals more effectively. Emphasize that it's not simply coursework that helps you land your first job, it's also your strengths, life experience, and outside activities.

Encourage students to take the time to explore careers. Go through the career exploration strategies in the text.

- Investigate career paths (career areas, the wide variety of jobs within any career area, salaries, and building knowledge and experience through jobs, courses, internships, volunteering).

- Consider personality and strengths. (How you learn relates to what you do well at work: see Keys 8.8 and 8.9 for how multiple intelligences and Personality Spectrum strengths can inform career investigation. Have students reflect back to the results of their self-assessments in chapter 3.)

- Know what employers want. A skillset goes beyond specific technical skills, comprising critical thinking and problem solving, teamwork, and emotional and social intelligence. Key 8.10 has more specifics **[see PowerPoint slide 16]**.

(Consider using the "Qualities That Do and Don't Work" exercise on p. 269 of this IM chapter.)

Searching for a Job – and a Career. This is a nuts-and-bolts overview of job hunting. Again, how extensively you cover this may depend on how much your particular group of students is interacting with the job market. Go through the three basic categories of job-search strategies.

Use available resources. This means:

- Career planning and placement office
- Networking skills
- Classified ads and online services

Networking is a key point here. Start by asking whether anyone has any experience networking. Hear examples. Give an example from your own life (how you got your teaching job or other job). From those examples, define the idea: *networking is the exchange of information or services among individuals, groups, or institutions* (in this case, to further a career). The process of networking helps open and maintain lines of communication with people who have the potential to help with advice or direction. Ask students who they consider part of their network. Some may include:

- Friends
- Current/former employers
- Peers

- Instructors/advisors
- Career counselors
- Relatives

How have such people helped them? Ask for examples. They could seek the following in networking:

- How to get established in a field
- Challenges/benefits of a particular job
- A description of a typical day
- Salary, benefits, other important information
- Requirements of the job
- People to contact in the job search itself
- Regulations to follow in the search (when to call, what kind of résumé to send, etc.)

(Consider using the "Building a Network" exercise on p. 270 of this IM chapter.)

Ask students to discuss the benefits or drawbacks of other job-search strategies such as classified ads, employment agencies, or online services. If you have computer access, exhibit online job sites such as Monster.com.

Your résumé, cover letter, and interview. The text only has the basics on these, as extensive information is available in books and online. Your school's career center should also have a good selection of up-to-date letter and résumé examples. Help students find updated résumé models to use when crafting résumés. Consider bringing in someone from the professional world to talk about interviewing and offer stories that illustrate what, and what not, to do.

Point that connects college to the modern career world: Many employers reviewing the résumés of prospective employees now make it standard practice to look at Facebook and MySpace sites. Advise your students to clean up personal sites if they are actively searching for a job. *(Consider distributing and discussing the "Possible Interview Questions and Answers" handout on pp. 281-282 of this IM chapter.)*

Be strategic. This is where time management and goal setting skills come in. Talk about how those skills can help students stay in control of the process, maintain awareness of information and dates, and ultimately succeed in landing a job.

(Consider using the "Build Interview Skills" teamwork exercise on p. 269 of this IM chapter.)

Question 5: How Can You Continue to Activate Your Successful Intelligence?

[Overview of self-activators: PowerPoint slide 17]

Now is the time for students to reflect on the entire course, including what they learned and what skills they will need to keep building as they strive for success in college and beyond. Revisiting the self-activator self-assessment (in the *Get Analytical* exercise) offers a concrete benchmark of their progress in many key areas over the term. You might choose to

- Have students complete the self-assessment in class.
- Refer students back to their chapter 1 self-assessments for comparison.
- Give students 5 minutes to compare and freewrite a short reaction to what they observe from their comparison.
- Give students a chance to share how they grew, what surprised them, and so on.

Emphasize that the self-activators are great to keep handy and visible, as tangible actions that will help students grow in the area of successful intelligence.

(Consider using the "Useful Self-Activators" exercise on p. 270 of this IM chapter.)

To go further with your review of the value of successful intelligence, you can explore the ways in which the students built all three intelligence areas in the course. A straightforward way to do this is to refer to the Successful Intelligence Wrap-Ups that end each chapter – they detail what students learned and practiced in that chapter.

Here are some sample ideas from the text:

1. <u>Analytical</u>:

    I learned how to
    - examine values and assumptions.
    - evaluate strategies in skill areas such as listening, memory, decision making, problem solving, test taking, communication, and budgeting.
    - read and listen critically.
    - recognize that perspectives may differ but they are not necessarily wrong.

2. <u>Creative</u>:

    I learned how to
    - develop options when problems occur.
    - find new solutions or ways of working to match learning or communication styles.
    - create work products that have personal vision or style.
    - explore majors and career areas with open-mindedness.
    - experience other cultures or arts to gather new ideas.
    - brainstorm ideas for projects or papers.
    - shift perspective.
    - persist even when others don't offer support.

3. <u>Practical</u>:

    I learned how to
    - use experience to learn and instinct to read a situation clearly.
    - manage myself, stay motivated, and avoid procrastination.
    - adapt to various situations.
    - implement goals.

- translate knowledge about how I learn into useful strategies.
- manage money and career preparation with common sense.
- recognize when to stop and when to go on.

The key for students is to make the most of their abilities and strive for balance.

(Consider using the "Taking Successful Intelligence Into the Future" exercise on p. 270 of this IM chapter.)

As you wind up the course, remind students that an effective way to grow and move with the changes life brings is to continue to examine who you are and what you want out of life. Recap: Success requires a willingness to continue learning throughout a lifetime. Congratulate them on their progress and encourage them on their journey!

[For end-of-term thought-provoking questions, see PowerPoint slides 18 through 22.]

(As a final day activity, consider using the "Letter to a New Student" exercise on p. 283 of this IM chapter.)

[Successful Intelligence Wrap-Up: PowerPoint slide 23]
[End-of-chapter foreign word: PowerPoint slide 24]
[End-of-chapter thought-provoking quote: PowerPoint slide 25]

****

CREATE COMMUNITY

DISCUSSION STARTERS

1. Ask students how often they would say they are under a significant level of stress. Follow up by asking what they think are the most frequent causes.
2. Ask students: "If you couldn't have both, which would you choose: Loving what you do, or making good money at what you do?" Let discussion follow of the pros and cons of both setups.
3. Ask students to write on 3 by 5 cards the answer to this question: "What are your "keys to success" that will help you reach your goals during the rest of your college experience?"

GROUP EXERCISES

Teamwork: Create Solutions Together – *Actively Dealing with Stress*

This exercise, found at the end of chapter 8 in the text, has students first work individually, using the Holmes-Rahe scale near the beginning of the text chapter to tally their personal "stress score." Then the class identifies the four most commonly experienced stressors from the Holmes-Rahe list. Finally, the class divides into four groups, each brainstorming a list of coping strategies for one particular stressor.

You might want to have groups type up their lists of strategies and distribute them to the entire class, after making a short presentation about what they discussed.

Advice Columns

Divide the class into small groups. For each group, assign a health topic and hand out files with articles that relate to the topic. (The topics could all be different for each group, or the whole class could tackle the same issue.) Some suggested topics follow:

Depression	Suicide
Anorexia	Bulimia
Binge eating	Drug abuse
Bipolar disorder	Alcoholism

The files should contain sufficient information to allow each group to write an advice column to a person who is concerned about a friend with the specific problem. The column should include the definition of the problem, its symptoms and causes, and concrete suggestions for getting help. If time allows, groups read their advice columns to the class when finished, leaving time afterwards for response and discussion from the class. Alternatively, they could submit them to you for a grade.
Note: Your student health or advising center may keep articles and facts on file that will provide sufficient information for the topic files.

Case Scenario: Finding Resources

Write the following on a board, or print on sheets to pass out to all students:

Your friend is using some type of drug that's affecting her health. She's not sleeping or eating much. She's stopped going to class. The last time you spoke with her, she asked to borrow money and got really angry when you told her no. You're worried, especially now you've heard from her brother who's really concerned.

Have students gather in groups to discuss the scenario. Groups should compile a list of 5 resources the person could use to get answers to specific questions about the friend's drug use and what he or she can do to help the friend. Have groups list the name, contact person, phone numbers, address, Web sites, etc. of each resource and a one-liner summarizing the purpose of the resource and how it would best be used.

Build Interview Skills

Divide into pairs—students will take turns interviewing each other about themselves and their career aspirations. Be as interested – and as interesting – as you can. Follow these steps.

1. Independently, take three minutes to brainstorm questions you'll ask the other person. Focus on learning style, interests, and initial career ideas. You might ask questions like these:
   - ∞ If you could have any job in the world, what would it be?
   - ∞ What do you think would be the toughest part of achieving success in that profession?
   - ∞ Who are you as a learner and worker?
   - ∞ What sacrifices are you willing to make to realize your dreams?
   - ∞ What is your greatest failure, and what have you learned from it?
   - ∞ Who is a role model to you in terms of career success?
2. Person A interviews Person B for 5 to 10 minutes and takes notes.
3. Switch roles: Person B interviews Person A and takes notes. Remember that each person uses his or her own questions developed in step 1.
4. Share with each other what interesting ideas stand out to you from the interviews. If you have any, offer constructive criticism to your interviewee about his or her interview skills.
5. Finally, submit your notes to your instructor for feedback.

This exercise will build your ability to glean information from others and to answer questions during an interview. You will use this skill throughout your professional life.

Qualities That Do and Don't Work

Brainstorm as a class the qualities that employers value most in people they hire. Ask the students to put themselves in the role of general manager of a Fortune 500 company. Ask one student to record the qualities on the board or on a white sheet. What qualities do they seek in their most valued employees? What are the qualities that will tip the scales between the candidate who has the technical background and the others who are all competing for the same job? (Most qualities will mirror what the whole class has been about.)

Next, write out the qualities that can prevent people from getting hired. List the qualities. Ask the students to comment on the differences between these two lists. How does this clarify what they are willing to create in their lives?

Brainstorm Day-to-Day Ways to Save Money

Have students think about all the ways they spend money in a month's time. Ask them: Where can you trim a bit? What expense can you do without? Where can you look for savings or discounts? Can you barter a product or service for one that a friend can provide? Have pairs or groups brainstorm a list of ideas on a sheet of paper or computer and pick out their five most workable ideas to share with the class.

Consider having students choose a set of ideas to try for a month, putting cash into a jar daily or weekly in the amounts that these changes are saving them. Check in with them at the end of the month and have them report on the results.

Building a Network

Instruct students to take a few minutes to think about people they know – family, friends, business acquaintances – who have interesting jobs and who seem satisfied with their work and job situations. Each student should come up with at least three people and a description of their jobs. (Or assign the list as homework during the prior class meeting.)

Next, break students into groups of 4 or 5. (You may want to divide groups by majors or Personality Spectrum types.) Each group member reads his or her "interesting jobs" list. As each person speaks, other members take notes if they hear about a job or career area that sounds interesting. After everyone has shared, group members who are interested in further information ask specific questions. Finally, the group agrees on a short list of jobs/careers that sound most promising to the group as a whole.

If there is time, each group can share their "greatest hits" list with the class and encourage students to continue the networking conversation with one another outside of class.

Useful Self-Activators

Divide the class into small groups. Give each group a few of the 20 self-activators, so that all 20 are assigned. Have the group brainstorm, write down, and ultimately share with the class a list of situations in which each of their self-activators are important (situations can be work, school, or personal).

Taking Successful Intelligence Into the Future

This is a think-pair-share exercise. Individually, have students think and write on one or more of the following questions:

- Which of the three aspects of successful intelligence has been most instrumental in their growth during the term and why?
- Which of the three aspects will present the biggest challenge and why?
- Which of the three aspects will be most important to their future success and why?

Have students pair up and discuss their thoughts. Finally, have students share with the class.

POP CULTURE LINKS

Movies: Use movies to illustrate the tough consequences of substance abuse (Leaving Las Vegas [1995], Traffic [2000]). Ask students if they have ever seen a movie and become interested in a profession because of a character who worked in that profession. Encourage them to do research following any interest of this kind. Although Robin Williams in Dead Poets Society (1989) and Hillary Swank in Freedom Writers (2007) may not be completely realistic as teachers, for example, their work can lead to students reading books about teaching, watching documentaries, and talking to teachers about what they do. For inspiration at the end of the term, many films provide moving stories of people overcoming adversity to succeed.

Gandhi (1982), <u>Mr. Holland's Opus</u> (1996), and <u>A Beautiful Mind</u> (2002) are some ideas. Ask students about movies that have inspired them.

Music: Discuss the positive effect that listening to or playing music can have on stress levels, and the way that music can be a more healthful choice for blowing off steam. Ask students how they use music to cope. Remind students of your discussion, at the beginning of the term, about music that inspires, motivates, and/or focuses them. If you were able to make it happen, hand out the class CD with everyone's favorite motivational tunes.

SUCCESSFUL INTELLIGENCE EXERCISES

Get Analytical! *Evaluate Your Self-Activators*
Assign for in-class activity or homework. This exercise has students revisit the self-assessment they completed at the end of chapter 1. Make sure they don't look at their old results first – you may prefer to have them complete this in class so they won't be tempted to look back. When it is complete and they have tallied their results, then have them turn to chapter 1 and see what difference they perceive, noting five changes that they think are important as well as one area where they still want to grow.

Get Creative! *Find More Fun*
Assign for homework. Here students use creativity to come up with ways to have fun at school (i.e., alternatives to more destructive social activities involving substance abuse). You can also have students meet in pairs or groups in class to help one another come up with ideas. Provide student handbooks, pamphlets, directories, and any other helpful resources that students may find useful for this exercise.

Get Practical! *Take Steps Toward Better Health*
Assign for homework. Students can use Internet, written sources, or in-person visits and conversations to identify particular health resources at your school, including counseling, student health center, and exercise facilities.

HOMEWORK

In-text exercises: All three successful intelligence exercises (*Get Analytical, Get Creative,* and *Get Practical*) can be assigned for homework.

Foreign word response: Ask students to write a responsive essay to the word "hozh'q." Ask them to describe how "hozh'q" looks to them, and how their experience this term has helped them move closer to it.

End-of-chapter exercises:
- **Successful Intelligence: Think, Create, Apply** – Ask students to read Joe Martin's *Personal Triumph Case Study*. Then have them complete the case questions and exercise.
- **Writing: Journal and Put Skills to Work** – Students can complete the journal entry, describing their behaviors and attitudes toward money, as homework. The real-

life writing assignment has students fill out and send two applications for scholarships: you could assign this in conjunction with an in-class visit from a financial aid officer.

- **Personal Portfolio:** This assignment involves revisiting the successful intelligence self-assessments, creating a new Wheel of Successful Intelligence, and comparing the results to those from chapter 1 to assess growth and change. Consider using the accompanying handout on p. 284 of this manual.

QUOTES FOR REFLECTION

Use these quotes to generate discussion, start class, or offer as a short exercise. Have students reflect on what any or all of the following quotes mean to them in a short paper or presentation.

The greatest weapon against stress is our ability to choose one thought over another.
William James

A lot of what passes for depression these days is nothing more than a body saying it needs work.
Geoffrey Norman

He who has health has hope, and he who has hope has everything.
Arabian Proverb

The definition of insanity is doing the same thing over and over again while expecting different results.
Unknown

Debt is a bottomless sea.
Carlyle

Money can't buy happiness. It just helps you look for it in more places.
Milton Berle

Eighty percent of success is showing up.
Woody Allen

When you leave college, there are thousands of people out there with the same degree you have; when you get a job, there will be thousands of people doing what you want to do for a living. But you are the only person alive who has sole custody of your life.
Anna Quindlen

You are not here merely to make a living. You are here in order to enable the world to live more amply, with greater vision, with a finer spirit of hope and achievement. You are here to enrich the world, and you impoverish yourself if you forget the errand.
Woodrow Wilson

And life is what we make it, always has been, always will be.
Grandma Moses

My life was a risk – and I took it!
Robert Frost

The word impossible is not in my dictionary.
Napoleon

HANDOUTS

The following are exercises with handouts, or handouts that you can use on their own. Integrate them into your lesson plan as you see fit, or follow the suggestions in the "Communicate Content" section.

- Did You Know That...? (exercise with handout)
- Exercise and Eating Log (handout)
- Evaluate Your Substance Use (handout)
- Multiple Intelligence Strategies for Stress Management (handout)
- Map Out Your Budget (handout)
- Possible Interview Questions and Answers (handout)
- Letter to a New Student (handout)
- Personal Portfolio Handout to accompany chapter 8 Personal Portfolio exercise

Did You Know That . . . ?

Purpose: Students will learn about topics related to health and nutrition, sex, drugs, alcohol, etc. through research and sharing information.

Materials:
- Handout: *Did You Know That . . . ?* (To be distributed during the class meeting prior to this one.)
- A container with 10-20 different topics written on pieces of paper (depending on your class size and if you want any of them to be duplicates).
- Previously written statistics on topics from teacher's choice.

Process:
- At the previous class meeting, students should select topics at random from the container. Assign students to find a research article on their specific topic and bring it to the next class meeting.
- Open the class period by reading selected statistics on health topics and discuss students' reactions.
- Have students meet in groups of three. They should share the information they learned from their articles and record the topics and statistics on the handout.

Closure: Have one person from each group share the statistics.

Name _____ Date _____

DID YOU KNOW THAT . . . ?

Directions. Find a research article that relates to your topic and fill in the information in the first column only. Bring this paper to our next class.

TOPIC			
SOURCE			
NAME OF ARTICLE			
BRIEF SUMMARY			
STATISTIC			
REACTION			

Name _____Date _____

EXERCISE AND EATING LOG

Instructions: Keep a log of what you eat and the duration of your exercise for one week. Be sure to note the items you eat—fruits, vegetables, protein, type of carbohydrate; milk/dairy; fats/sweets--and how much water and other beverages you drink per day.

	Saturday	Sunday	Monday	Tuesday	Wednesday	Thursday	Friday
Breakfast							
Lunch							
Dinner							
Snack(s)							
Amount of Water							
Other Beverages							
Exercise Type							
Exercise Duration							

At the end of the week, ask yourself: Where were you off balance? What surprised you? What habits do you want to change as a result of keeping this log?

EVALUATE YOUR SUBSTANCE USE

Even one "yes" answer may indicate a need to evaluate your substance use. Answering "yes" to three or more questions indicates that you may benefit from speaking with a counselor.

Within the Last Year:

Y N 1. Have you tried to stop drinking or taking drugs but couldn't do so for long?

Y N 2. Do you get tired of people saying they're concerned about your drinking or drug use?

Y N 3. Have you felt guilty about your drinking or drug use?

Y N 4. Have you felt that you needed a drink or drugs in the morning—as an "eye-opener"—in order to improve a hangover?

Y N 5. Do you drink or use drugs alone?

Y N 6. Do you drink or use drugs every day?

Y N 7. Do you regularly think or say "I need" a drink or any type of drug?

Y N 8. Have you lied about or concealed your drinking or drug use?

Y N 9. Do you drink or use drugs to escape worries, problems, mistakes, or shyness?

Y N 10. Do you find you need increasingly larger amounts of drugs or alcohol in order to achieve a desired effect?

Y N 11. Have you forgotten what happened while drinking or using drugs (had a blackout)?

Y N 12. Have you been surprised by how much you were using alcohol or drugs?

Y N 13. Have you spent a lot of time, energy, or money getting alcohol or drugs?

Y N 14. Has your drinking or drug use caused you to neglect friends, your partner, your children, or other family members, or caused other problems at home?

Y N 15. Have you gotten into an argument or a fight that was alcohol- or drug-related?

Y N 16. Has your drinking or drug use caused you to miss class, fail a test, or ignore schoolwork?

Y N 17. Have you rejected planned social events in favor of drinking or using drugs?

Y N 18. Have you been choosing to drink or use drugs instead of performing other activities or hobbies you used to enjoy?

Y N 19. Has your drinking or drug use affected your efficiency on the job or caused you to fail to show up at work?

Y N 20. Have you continued to drink or use drugs despite any physical problems or health risks that your use has caused or made worse?

Y N 21. Have you driven a car or performed any other potentially dangerous tasks while under the influence of alcohol or drugs?

Y N 22. Have you had a drug- or alcohol-related legal problem or arrest (possession, use, disorderly conduct, driving while intoxicated, etc.)?

Source: Compiled and adapted from the Criteria for Substance Dependence and Criteria for Substance Abuse in the *Diagnostic and Statistical Manual of Mental Disorders*, fourth edition, published by the American Psychiatric Association, Washington, D.C., and from materials titled "Are You An Alcoholic?" developed by Johns Hopkins University.

MULTIPLE INTELLIGENCE STRATEGIES FOR STRESS MANAGEMENT

INTELLIGENCE	USE MI STRATEGIES TO MANAGE STRESS	WHAT WORKS FOR YOU? WRITE NEW IDEAS HERE
VERBAL-LINGUISTIC	∞ Keep a journal of situations or people that cause stress. ∞ Write letters or e-mail friends about your problems.	
LOGICAL-MATHEMATICAL	∞ Think through problems using a problem-solving process, and devise a detailed plan. ∞ Analyze the negative and positive effects that may result from a stressful situation.	
BODILY-KINESTHETIC	∞ Choose a relaxing physical activity and do it regularly. ∞ Plan physical activities during free time – go for a hike, take a bike ride, go dancing.	
VISUAL- SPATIAL	∞ Enjoy things that appeal to you visually – visit an exhibit, see an art film, shoot photos. ∞ Use a visual organizer to plan out a solution to a problem.	
INTERPERSONAL	∞ Talk with people who care about you and are supportive. ∞ Shift your focus by being a good listener to others who need to talk about their stresses.	
INTRAPERSONAL	∞ Schedule down time when you can think through what is causing stress. ∞ Allow yourself five minutes a day of meditation where you visualize a positive way to resolve a stressful situation.	
MUSICAL	∞ Listen to music that relaxes, inspires, and/or energizes you. ∞ Write a song about what is bothering you.	
NATURALISTIC	∞ See if the things that cause you stress fall into categories that can give you helpful ideas about how to handle situations. ∞ If nature is calming for you, interact with it– spend time outdoors, watch nature-focused TV, read books or articles on nature or science.	

MAP OUT YOUR BUDGET

Step 1: Estimate your current expenses in dollars per month, using the following table. This may require tracking expenses for a month, if you don't already keep a record of your spending. The grand total is your total monthly expenses.

Expense	Amount Spent
Rent/mortgage or room and board payment	$
Utilities (electric, heat, gas, water, cable, online services)	$
Food (shopping, eating out, meal plan)	$
Telephone (land line, fax line, mobile phone)	$
Books, lab fees, other educational expenses	$
Loan payments (educational or bank loans)	$
Car (repairs, insurance, payments, gas)	$
Public transportation	$
Clothing/personal items	$
Entertainment	$
Child care (caregivers, clothing/supplies)	$
Medical care/insurance	$
Other	$
TOTAL	**$**

Step 2: Calculate your average monthly income. If it's easiest to come up with a yearly figure, divide by 12 to derive the monthly figure. For example, if you have a $6,000 scholarship for the year, your monthly income would be $500 ($6,000 divided by 12).

Income Source	Amount Received
Regular work salary/wages (full-time or part-time)	$
Grants or work-study programs	$
Scholarships	$
Assistance from family members	$
Other	$
TOTAL	**$**

Step 3: Subtract the grand total of your monthly expenses from the grand total of your monthly income:

Income per month	$
Expenses per month	-$
CASH FLOW	**$**

Step 4: If you have a negative cash flow, you can increase income, decrease spending, or both. List here four workable ideas about how you can get your cash flow back in the black – two that increase income, and two that decrease spending.

To increase income, I can:

1. _____

2. _____

To decrease spending, I can:

1. _____

2. _____

POSSIBLE INTERVIEW QUESTIONS AND ANSWERS

Possible Questions	Interviewer's Goal with the Question	What You Could Say
"Why did you leave your last job?"	Trying to determine if there were any problems and understand your motivations in your career path.	Wanted more challenge; moved; downsizing; no room for advancement.
"What are your strengths?"	This actually can be the interviewer's way of trying to give you a chance to shine.	Seize the moment. Answer this with a skill that can be used in the job you're seeking, including a "transferable" skill like problem-solving, etc.
"What are your weaknesses?"	Trying to get an idea of what you think of yourself: who better will know your weaknesses than you? Trying to determine if you have a realistic sense of who you are.	Try to turn this into a positive like "I sometimes get so involved I lose track of time." Or bring up a skill that does not involve this job, like "I type with two fingers only." Or identify a weakness which you are correcting: "I don't consider myself to be the world's greatest speaker, but I recently joined Toastmasters and the six speeches I've made have increased my confidence."
"What are your strengths and weaknesses?"	Again, do you have self-knowledge? Can you maximize your strengths and minimize your weaknesses?	Often our strengths are also our weaknesses, and we can phrase them that way. For instance, "My strength of perseverance is also my weakness because I can sometimes get too single-minded." (For "and" questions, be sure you answer both parts of the question.)
"Tell me about a time when your boss was dissatisfied with the job you did."	Trying to learn more about weaknesses and how you deal with pressure and criticism. This question allows for storytelling without value judgments.	Describe a time when you had a bad experience but learned from it. Try to use an incident that you turned around.
"What is your ideal job?"	Trying to get an idea of where and how you want to grow in your career; your answer should also reflect your strengths and weaknesses.	Discuss jobs that use talents and skills related to the job you're interviewing for. Make your answer task-oriented rather than benefit-oriented. Be honest – what is your ideal job, anyway?
"Why should I hire you?"	This sounds like a no-win, set up question. Actually, it can just be an honest inquiry: what makes you different? What makes you *you*?	Discuss what makes you special. Talk about positive qualities like tireless energy, self-starter, team player, etc. Give believable examples.

Possible Questions	Interviewer's Goal with the Question	What You Could Say
"How do you feel about detail?"	Exploring a skill that is necessary in virtually every job – important but not the glorious part of work.	Talk about the detail you have used in setting up a project or job that you have been assigned. Avoid saying whether you hate or love detail.
"What if you have to work overtime or another shift on occasion?"	They are questioning your flexibility and reliability; your team player mentality.	Talk about being a team player and wanting to do what you can to get the job done. If you can work overtime, tell them. Indicate shift preference.
"What is special about you?"	Do you have a unique vision for yourself?	Think of what makes you special and say something straightforward: "I am creative, dedicated, and determined to make a difference for your company." Give believable examples.
"How is your attendance – any problems?"	Anticipating where trouble may lie with a new employee who otherwise appears to be responsible.	If you have had a problem, try to present a solution to that problem or a good reason (like surgery or illness). Let them know that it's behind you.
"How would a former boss or coworkers describe you?"	Identifying skills again, as well as personality traits. Are you easy or difficult to get along with?	If you are widely known for a positive work trait, use that trait; otherwise say something about good work ethics, hard-working team player, etc. Ask your coworkers how they would describe you for some good insights.
"Tell me a difficult problem you've had at work."	Looking for how you identify problems as well as how you solve them.	Think of a work-related problem and how you solved it. If possible, stay away from problems with a boss or coworker that might indicate personality problems.
"What contribution or accomplishment are you most proud of? Why?"	Again, trying to identify skills and abilities to complete projects. In many ways, trying to let you shine. What is the magnitude of your contribution?	Think through one or two answers to this question. Why did your accomplishment make you proud? What did you learn?
"What do you do in your spare time?"	Trying to get to know you personally. Are you an interesting/inspiring person? Do you have a sense of balance in your life?	Think of your hobbies. Did you record any on your résumé? Be honest – don't start talking about bookkeeping if you've never done it (your interviewer will probably be an expert on it).

Letter to a New Student

A good friend or yours, or maybe your younger sibling, will be starting college next term and has asked you for advice on how to make it in school. He got through high school with above average grades, but didn't have to work very hard. He really doesn't think that he knows how to study for college courses. He hopes to get a degree at a community college, then transfer to a university and is wondering if he can do it. You know that he is intelligent and capable. Write him a letter with suggestions about how to develop skills and attitudes to become a successful, responsible student based on what you have read from the textbook and learned in class.

Consider including points on the following topics:
- What analytical, creative, and practical thinking skills can mean for success in college
- How personal responsibility and self-management skills affect the college experience
- Self-examination strategies that can help create a successful and satisfying experience in college
- The role of study skills, such as listening, note taking, reading, thinking, problem solving, and writing, in success

Brainstorm your list of important points to make here:

1. _____

2. _____

3. _____

4. _____

5. _____

6. _____

7. _____

8. _____

Make an outline on a separate sheet of paper that organizes and prioritizes this list. Finally, type and print your letter double-spaced on plain white paper – two pages maximum.

(Contributed by Prof. Karyn Shulz)

PERSONAL PORTFOLIO ACTIVITY # 8
REVISIT YOUR SUCCESSFUL INTELLIGENCE

Successful intelligence is an essential ingredient for success on the job as well as in school and in life. The analytical, creative, and practical skills you've built throughout the term will help you make a difference in any career as well as impress any employer.

Use the table below to enter your scores from the chapter 1 assessments (the beginning of the term) and the chapter 8 assessments (the end of the term). Consider how you've progressed.

Continuing to Develop Successful Intelligence		
	Chapter 1 score	Chapter 8 score
- Analytical skills		
- Creative skills		
- Practical skills		

For each area, note two instances where you grew as a successfully intelligent thinker.

Analytical Skills You Employed

One:

Two:

Creative Ideas You Developed

One:

Two:

Practical Actions You Took

One:

Two:

CONSIDER COMPREHENSION

REVIEW WITH STUDENTS TO CLOSE THE COURSE:

- What is stress and how does it function in your life?
- Aspects of physical and mental health
- How to manage money effectively
- What considerations are important as you prepare for career success?
- What are the three parts of successful intelligence and the twenty related "self-activators?"

Chapter Eight Vocabulary Quiz Answer Key
(Quiz appears on following page)

1. I
2. J
3. C
4. D
5. B
6. G
7. A
8. E
9. F
10. H

CHAPTER EIGHT VOCABULARY QUIZ

1. ____ bulimia

2. ____ creditor

3. ____ addiction

4. ____ self-activators

5. ____ networking

6. ____ human papillomavirus (HPV)

7. ____ secondhand smoke

8. ____ grace period

9. ____ Body Mass Index (BMI)

10. ____ binge drinking

B. The exchange of information or services among individuals or groups

C. The compulsive need for a habit-forming substance

D. Actions that successfully intelligent people take to keep moving toward their goals

E. A number of days after a payment due date during which no penalty will occur for a late payment

F. The ratio of your weight to your height

G. A sexually transmitted virus linked to cervical cancer in women

H. Having five or more drinks at one sitting

I. An eating disorder characterized by binging and purging

J. A person or company to whom a debt is owed

A. Smoke in the air exhaled by smokers or given off by cigarettes, cigars, or pipes

CHAPTER EIGHT ASSESSMENT

Multiple Choice
Circle or highlight the answer that seems to fit best.

1. All of the following are effective stress-management tools EXCEPT
   a. being physically and mentally healthy.
   b. eating right and exercising.
   c. finding time each day to meditate.
   d. getting all your work done as quickly as possible.

2. What is the main reason students struggle when trying to eat healthfully?
   a. Healthful foods are more expensive than unhealthful foods.
   b. Students don't have time to make healthful meals.
   c. Students are faced with fast food and busy schedules, which cause difficulty in preparing healthful foods.
   d. Students don't have fully functional kitchens.

3. Obesity refers to
   a. being 25% overweight.
   b. having a BMI of 25 to 29.
   c. being 30% overweight.
   d. having a BMI of 22 to 25.

4. According to the American Psychological Association, what percentage of college students is affected by varying degrees of depression?
   a. 10 percent
   b. 15 percent
   c. 40 percent
   d. Nearly half of all students

5. What is the most common eating disorder among men and women?
   a. Anorexia nervosa
   b. Bulimia nervosa
   c. Binge eating disorder
   d. Overexercising disorder

6. What is the most serious substance-related health problem among college students today?
   a. Binge drinking
   b. Eating disorders
   c. Depression
   d. Drug addiction

7. What is an effective way a *verbal-linguistic* learner can work towards reducing stress in his or her life?
   a. Think about and analyze what is causing the stress and how to reduce it.
   b. Choose physical activities to help release tension.

c. Journal about the situations that are causing stress and possible solutions.
d. Use a planner to determine ways to reduce stress.

8. How can your values affect the monetary choices you make?
a. What is most important to you is reflected in how you spend your money.
b. You tend to purchase what your parents view as important.
c. Values are not connected to monetary choices because they are more important than money.
d. You tend to spend money in ways opposite to your personal values.

9. One way to identify the value of every purchase is to
a. cut back on your expenses.
b. work.
c. consider how many hours you must work to purchase an item.
d. charge the items you buy on your credit card.

10. How can you identify the income you have available to spend each year?
a. Record your take-home pay from all full-time and part-time jobs.
b. Record money you received from family, friends, and grants or scholarships.
c. A and B only.
d. Record what you spend throughout the year.

11. What is the MOST serious risk of charging your daily expenses on a credit card?
a. Forgetting to pay your credit card bill on time and paying late fees.
b. Maximizing the credit card to its limit and not having the funds to meet monthly payments, including high interest.
c. Purchasing items that you don't really need.
d. Not having cash on hand to make small purchases.

12. A temporary work program, often unpaid, in which a student can gain experience in a particular field is called
a. an apprenticeship.
b. a grant.
c. an internship.
d. a work-study program.

13. How does knowing how you learn help with your career search?
    a. Self-knowledge helps you identify your interests and talents.
    b. Knowing your personality type helps you understand how you work with others.
    c. Both of the above.
    d. None of the above.

14. Sources of career information include which of the following?
    a. networking
    b. school career planning and placement offices
    c. online employment information services
    d. all of the above

15. One of the self-activators that successfully intelligent people use to accomplish important goals is *delaying gratification*, which refers to
    a. aiming for immediate satisfaction.
    b. focusing effort on significant rewards that take time and patience to achieve.
    c. looking to others for help with working toward a goal.
    d. avoiding the trap of feeling sorry for yourself.

True/False
Determine whether each statement is true or false and circle or highlight the correct answer.

1. Stress is always related to negative events.
   True
   False

2. To eat healthfully, you should diet and eliminate all junk food.
   True
   False

3. Using a cross-training approach to exercise will diminish your ability to maintain an effective physical fitness routine.
   True
   False

4. Not knowing how to avoid sexually transmitted diseases can have lifelong consequences.
   True
   False

5. Making a budget can help you manage your money.
   True
   False

6. The more credit cards you have, the better your credit rating.
   True
   False

7. The better you know yourself, the more likely you will select a career that fits with your interests and personality.
   True
   False

8. The primary focus for students is to choose a major and stick with it. Gaining work experience along the way will delay graduation and keep you from getting a job.
   True
   False

9. Information on different careers can come from the library and Internet, instructors, and certain college courses.
   True
   False

10. Successfully intelligent people examine their mistakes and learn from them.
    True
    False

Fill in the Blank
Insert the word or phrase that BEST completes the sentence.

1. _____ is defined as a compulsive need for a habit-forming substance.

2. The highly addictive substance in all tobacco products is _____.

3. The physical or mental strain that occurs when your body reacts to pressure is called _____.

4. You are responsible for analyzing the potential _____ of what you introduce into your body.

5. Although going to college is the key to finding better jobs and having more job opportunities, employers are looking for you to have a particular _____ in addition to having a degree.

6. A great way to get connected to great job opportunities is to talk to others and share your job interests. This is known as _____.

7. When reviewing a credit card statement, your statement may have a(an) _____ _____ , which is the total amount you owe on your card.

8. Because success depends on your ability to work with people from different backgrounds and with different personalities and abilities, _____ _____ is especially important to your career.

9. One key characteristic of successfully intelligent thinkers is that they have a
_____ orientation – they focus on results.

10. Successfully intelligent thinkers finish what they start – they know how to
_____ _____ on their plans.

Short Answer

1. Why is secondhand smoke a health concern?

2. Discuss three risks and three benefits of using credit cards to make day-to-day
purchases.

3. Define social intelligence and provide examples that demonstrate its relevance to career
success.

Essay

1. Describe and discuss an aspect of your physical or mental health you would like to
improve. What goals will you set for yourself? How will you achieve them?

2. Based on the assessments you have completed in this text and the discussions on majors
and careers in this course, what major (or course emphasis) are you considering? Why?
Describe any connection this major might have with a career area that interests you.

3. Describe how you have grown as an analytical, creative, and practical thinker. Then
discuss how you can apply your successful intelligence skills in your coursework next
term.

Word Exploration

Define the word *hozh'q* [hoe-shk].

What does it mean to you? How does it apply to your life as a college student?

Chapter Eight Assessment Answer Key

Multiple Choice

Test Item Assesses This Learning Objective/Topic

1. d   How Can Focusing on Health Help You Manage Stress?

2. c   How Can Focusing on Health Help You Manage Stress?
   Food and eating habits

3. b   How Can Focusing on Health Help You Manage Stress?
   Food and eating habits

4. d   How Can Focusing on Health Help You Manage Stress?
   Recognize mental health problems

5. c   How Can Focusing on Health Help You Manage Stress?
   Recognize mental health problems

6. a   How Can You Make Effective Decisions about Alcohol,
   Tobacco, and Drugs? *Alcohol*

7. c   How Can You Make Effective Decisions about Substances and Sex?
   Multiple intelligence strategies

8. a   How Can You Manage Money Effectively?
   Analyze what money means in your life

9. c   How Can You Manage Money Effectively?
   Analyze what money means in your life

10. c   How Can You Manage Money Effectively?
    Learn to manage income and expenses through budgeting

11. b   How Can You Manage Money Effectively?
    Manage credit card use

12. c   How Can You Prepare For Career Success?
    Build knowledge and experience

13. c   How Can You Prepare For Career Success?
    Consider your personality and strengths

14. d   How Can You Prepare for Career Success?
    Search for a job – and a career

15. b   How Can You Continue to Activate Your Successful Intelligence?

True/False

Test Item Assesses This Learning Objective/Topic

1.   F   How Can Focusing on Health Help You Manage Stress?

2.   F   How Can Focusing on Health Help You Manage Stress?
   Food and eating habits

3.   F   How Can Focusing on Health Help You Manage Stress?
   Exercise

4. T   How Can You Make Effective Decisions about Substances and Sex?
   Sexual decision making

5. T How Can You Manage Money Effectively?
Learn to manage income and expenses through budgeting
6. F How Can You Manage Money Effectively?
Manage credit card use
7. T How Can You Prepare for Career Success?
Consider your personality and strengths
8. F How Can You Prepare for Career Success?
Build knowledge and experience
9. T How Can You Prepare for Career Success?
Build knowledge and experience
10. T How Can You Continue to Activate Your Successful Intelligence?

Fill in the Blank

Test Item Assesses This Learning Objective/Topic

1. *Addiction* How Can You Make Effective Decisions about Substances and Sex? *Facing addiction*

2. *nicotine* How Can You Make Effective Decisions about Substances and Sex? *Tobacco*

3. *stress* How Can Focusing on Health Help You Manage Stress?

4. *consequences* How Can You Make Effective Decisions about Substances and Sex? *Drugs*

5. *skillset* How Can You Prepare for Career Success?
Know what employers want

6. *networking* How Can You Prepare for Career Success?
Searching for a job – and a career

7. *outstanding balance* Key 8.6

8. *social intelligence* How Can You Prepare For Career Success?
Know what employers want

9. *product* How Can You Continue to Activate Your Successful Intelligence?

10. *follow through* How Can You Continue to Activate Your Successful Intelligence?